The Linux Development Platform

Configuring, Using, and Maintaining a Complete Programming Environment

D1608706

ISBN 013009115-4

9 780130 091154

94999

Bruce Perens' Open Source Series

- *Implementing CIFS: The Common Internet File System*
  Christopher R. Hertel

- *Embedded Software Development with eCos*
  Anthony J. Massa

- *The Linux Development Platform: Configuring, Using, and Maintaining a Complete Programming Environment*
  Rafeeq Ur Rehman, Christopher Paul

The Linux Development Platform

Configuring, Using, and Maintaining a Complete Programming Environment

Rafeeq Ur Rehman
Christopher Paul

PRENTICE
HALL
PTR
Prentice Hall PTR
Upper Saddle River, New Jersey 07458
www.phptr.com

Library of Congress Cataloging-in-Publication Data

A CIP catalog record for this book can be obtained from the Library of Congress.

Editorial/production supervision: *Mary Sudul*
Cover design director: *Jerry Votta*
Cover design: *DesignSource*
Manufacturing manager: *Alexis Heydt-Long*
Acquisitions editor: *Jill Harry*
Editorial assistant: *Kate Wolf*
Marketing manager: *Dan DePasquale*

 © 2003 Pearson Education, Inc.
Publishing as Prentice Hall PTR
Upper Saddle River, New Jersey 07458

Prentice Hall books are widely used by corporations and government agencies for training, marketing,
and resale.
The publisher offers discounts on this book when ordered in bulk quantities. For more information,
contact Corporate Sales Department, Phone: 800-382-3419; FAX: 201-236-7141;
E-mail: corpsales@prenhall.com
Or write: Prentice Hall PTR, Corporate Sales Dept., One Lake Street, Upper Saddle River, NJ 07458.

Printed in the United States of America
10   9   8   7   6   5   4   3   2   1

ISBN 0-13-009115-4

Pearson Education LTD.
Pearson Education Australia PTY, Limited
Pearson Education Singapore, Pte. Ltd.
Pearson Education North Asia Ltd.
Pearson Education Canada, Ltd.
Pearson Educación de Mexico, S.A. de C.V.
Pearson Education — Japan
Pearson Education Malaysia, Pte. Ltd.

To Asia, Afnan, and Faris for their love and support.
—Rafeeq Ur Rehman

To Cheryl, Rachel, and Sarah for the moral support and unending encouragement to complete this project. I'd be lost without you.
—Christopher Paul

CONTENTS

PREFACE

Setting up a complete development environment using open source tools has always been a challenging task. Although all of the development tools are available in the open source, no comprehensive development environment exists as of today. This book is an effort to enable the reader to set up and use open source to create such an environment. Each chapter of the book is dedicated to a particular component of the development environment.

Chapter 1 provides an introduction to the practical software development life cycle and stages. The chapter also provides information about the documentation required for all serious software development projects. Guidelines are provided about criteria for selecting hardware and software platforms.

Chapter 2 is about using editors. Editors are essential components of any software development system. Selection of a good editor saves time and money in the development life cycle. This chapter provides information about commonly used editors like Emacs, Jed and vim (vi Improved).

Chapter 3 is about the GNU set of compilers commonly known as GCC. The procedure for installation and use of gcc with different languages is presented here.

Larger software projects contain hundreds or thousands of files. Compiling these files in an orderly fashion and then building the final executable product is a challenging task. GNU make is a tool used to build a project by compiling and linking source code files. Chapter 4 provides information on how to install and use this important tool.

Chapter 5 discusses debuggers. An introduction to commonly used debuggers is provided in this chapter with an emphasis on the GNU debugger gdb.

Chapter 6 introduces CVS, which is the open source revision control system and is most widely used in open source development. Setting up a CVS server is detailed in this chapter. You will learn how to use remote the CVS server in a secure way.

There are tools other than compilers, debuggers and editors. These tools are discussed in Chapter 7. These tools help in building good products.

Open source tools are also widely used in embedded and cross-platform development. Chapter 8 provides information using open source tools in such environments. Remote debugging is an important concept and it is explained in this chapter.

Chapter 9 is the last chapter of the book and it provides a basic introduction to open source Java development.

There is one important thing that you must keep in mind while reading this book. It is not a tutorial on any language or programming techniques. It is about development tools and how to use these. You need other books to learn programming languages and techniques.

The book explains the installation procedures of different tools. By the time you read this book, new versions of these tools may be available. The installation procedures will not vary drastically in these versions and you can use the steps explained in this book. In fact, most of the open source tools employ the same compiling and installation procedure that you will note in this book. This process has been consistent and is expected to remain the same in future as well.

After reading this book, we are very much hopeful that the reader will be able to understand different components of a development system. You will also be able to create such a system from scratch using open source tools.

Rafeeq Ur Rehman
Christopher Paul

ABOUT THE CD

This book comes with a CD-ROM. The CD-ROM contains source code of all software and utilities used in this book. You can compile and install these tools as explained in this book. If you need latest versions of these tools, you can download these from the links provided in the book.

ACKNOWLEDGMENTS

This is my third book and I have been very fortunate to get help from many people around me in all of these projects. Professor Shahid Bokhari at the University of Engineering and Technology Lahore, Pakistan, provided valuable suggestions while I was creating table of contents for this book. In fact he proposed a mini table of contents about what should be included in the book to make it useful both for the developers and students of computer science and engineering. I am grateful for his continued support.

Mike Schoenborn, Amgad Fahmy, and Greg Ratcliff at Peco II Inc. continuously encouraged me during the time I was writing the manuscript and I am thankful to all of them. I am also thankful to Victor Kean for providing his life experiences both in real social life and software development.

I am also thankful to Jill Harry and Mary Sudul at Prentice Hall PTR for bearing with me and pushing me to meet deadlines which really helped bring this book to the market in time.

Drew Streib did a great job in reviewing the manuscript and giving very useful suggestions to improve it. Thanks Drew.

Jim Shappell at Arcom Control Systems provided x86 based board for testing embedded development examples and remote debugging. Cole Creighton at Artesyn Communication Products provided PowerPC based board for cross-platform development testing purpose. I am thankful to both of them for their help in developing the manuscript of this book.

Bruce Parens gave valuable suggestions about what to include in the book. He also agreed to print the book under his Open Source Series. I was excited to get his approval and I am thankful to him.

And I am thankful to the open source community all over the world for putting such a huge effort to build these open source tools. This book exists only because of the open source products and tools.

Above all, I am thankful to my father, who taught me how to read and write and work hard.

Rafeeq Ur Rehman
September 25, 2002

## CHAPTER 1

Introduction to Software Development

Software development is a complicated process. It requires careful planning and execution to meet the goals. Sometimes a developer must react quickly and aggressively to meet everchanging market demands. Maintaining software quality hinders fast-paced software development, as many testing cycles are necessary to ensure quality products.

This chapter provides an introduction to the software development process. As you will learn, there are many stages of any software development project. A commercial software product is usually derived from market demands. Sales and marketing people have first-hand knowledge of their customers' requirements. Based upon these market requirements, senior software developers create an architecture for the products along with functional and design specifications. Then the development process starts. After the initial development phase, software testing begins, and many times it is done in parallel with the development process. Documentation is also part of the development process because a product cannot be brought to market without manuals. Once development and testing are done, the software is released and the support cycle begins. This phase may include bug fixes and new releases.

After reading this chapter, you should understand how software development is done and the components of a software development system. At the end of the chapter, you will find an introduction to Linux Standard Base. This chapter is not specific to a particular hardware platform or tools. You will start learning about components of an actual software development platform in the next chapter.

1.1   Life Cycle of a Software Development Project

Software development is a complicated process comprising many stages. Each stage requires a lot of paperwork and documentation in addition to the development and planning process. This is in contrast to the common thinking of newcomers to the software industry who believe that software development is just "writing code." Each software development project has to go through at least the following stages:

- Requirement gathering
- Writing functional specifications
- Creating architecture and design documents
- Implementation and coding
- Testing and quality assurance
- Software release
- Documentation
- Support and new features

Figure 1-1 shows a typical development process for a new product.

There may be many additional steps and stages depending upon the nature of the software product. You may have to go through multiple cycles during the testing phase as software testers find problems and bugs and developers fix them before a software product is officially released. Let us go into some detail of these stages.

1.1.1   Requirement Gathering

Requirement gathering is usually the first part of any software product. This stage starts when you are thinking about developing software. In this phase, you meet customers or prospective customers, analyzing market requirements and features that are in demand. You also find out if there is a real need in the market for the software product you are trying to develop.

In this stage, marketing and sales people or people who have direct contact with the customers do most of the work. These people talk to these customers and try to understand what they need. A comprehensive understanding of the customers' needs and writing down features of the proposed software product are the keys to success in this phase. This phase is actually a base for the whole development effort. If the base is not laid correctly, the product will not find a place in the market. If you develop a very good software product which is not required in the market, it does not matter how well you build it. You can find many stories about software products that failed in the market because the customers did not require them. The marketing people

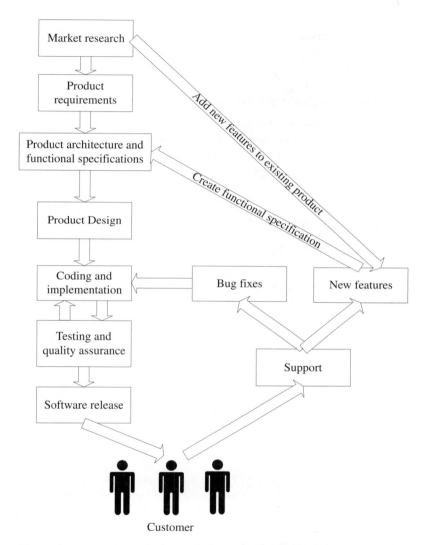

Figure 1-1 Typical processes for software development projects.

usually create a *Marketing Requirement Document* or MRD that contains formal data representation of market data gathered.

Spend some time doing market research and analysis. Consider your competitors' products (if any), a process called competitive analysis. List the features required by the product. You should also think about the economics of software creation at this point. Is there a market? Can I make money? Will the revenue justify the cost of development?

1.1.2   Writing Functional Specifications

Functional specifications may consist of one or more documents. Functional specification documents show the behavior or functionality of a software product on an abstract level. Assuming the product is a black box, the functional specifications define its input/output behavior. Functional specifications are based upon the product requirements documentation put forward by people who have contact with the enduser of the product or the customers.

In larger products, functional specifications may consist of separate documents for each feature of the product. For example, in a router product, you may have a functional specification document for RIP (Routing Information Protocol), another for security features, and so on.

Functional specifications are important because developers use them to create design documents. The documentation people also use them when they create manuals for end users. If different groups are working in different physical places, functional specifications and architecture documents (discussed next) are also a means to communicate among them. Keep in mind that sometimes during the product development phase you may need to amend functional specifications keeping in view new marketing requirements.

1.1.3   Creating Architecture and Design Documents

When you have all of the requirements collected and arranged, it is the turn of the technical architecture team, consisting of highly qualified technical specialists, to create the architecture of the product. The architecture defines different components of the product and how they interact with each other. In many cases the architecture also defines the technologies used to build the product. While creating the architecture documents of the project, the team also needs to consider the timelines of the project. This refers to the target date when the product is required to be on the market. Many excellent products fail because they are either too early or late to market. The marketing and sales people usually decide a suitable time frame to bring the product to market. Based on the timeline, the architecture team may drop some features of the product if it is not possible to bring the full-featured product to market within the required time limits.

Once components of the product have been decided and their functionality defined, interfaces are designed for these components to work together. In most cases, no component works in isolation; each one has to coordinate with other components of the product. Interfaces are the rules and regulations that define how these components will interact with each other. There may be major problems down the road if these interfaces are not designed properly and in a detailed way. Different people will work on different components of any large software development project and if they don't fully understand how a particular component will communicate with others, integration becomes a major problem.

For some products, new hardware is also required to make use of technology advancements. The architects of the product also need to consider this aspect of the product.

After defining architecture, software components and their interfaces, the next phase of development is the creation of design documents. At the architecture level, a component is defined as a black box that provides certain functionality. At the design documents stage, you have to define what is in that black box. Senior software developers usually create design documents and these documents define individual software components to the level of functions and procedures. The design document is the last document completed before development of the software begins. These design documents are passed on to software developers and they start coding. Architecture documents and MRDs typically need to stay in sync, as sales and marketing will work from MRDs while engineering works from engineering documents.

1.1.4   Implementation and Coding

The software developers take the design documents and development tools (editors, compilers, debuggers etc.) and start writing software. This is usually the longest phase in the product life cycle. Each developer has to write his/her own code and collaborate with other developers to make sure that different components can interoperate with each other. A revision control system such as CVS (Concurrent Versions System) is needed in this phase. There are a few other open source revision control systems as well as commercial options. The version control system provides a central repository to store individual files. A typical software project may contain anywhere from hundreds to thousands of files. In large and complex projects, someone also needs to decide directory hierarchy so that files are stored in appropriate locations. During the development cycle, multiple persons may modify files. If everyone is not following the rules, this may easily break the whole compilation and building process. For example, duplicate definitions of the same variables may cause problems. Similarly, if included files are not written properly, you can easily cause the creation of loops. Other problems pop up when multiple files are included in a single file with conflicting definitions of variables and functions.

Coding guidelines should also be defined by architects or senior software developers. For example, if software is intended to be ported to some other platform as well, it should be written on a standard like ANSI.

During the implementation process, developers must write enough comments inside the code so that if anybody starts working on the code later on, he/she is able to understand what has already been written. Writing good comments is very important as all other documents, no matter how good they are, will be lost eventually. Ten years after the initial work, you may find only that information which is present inside the code in the form of comments.

Development tools also play an important role in this phase of the project. Good development tools save a lot of time for the developers, as well as saving money in terms of improved productivity. The most important development tools for time saving are editors and debuggers. A good editor helps a developer to write code quickly. A good debugger helps make the written code operational in a short period of time. Before starting the coding process, you should spend some time choosing good development tools.

Review meetings during the development phase also prove helpful. Potential problems are caught earlier in the development. These meeting are also helpful to keep track of whether the product is on time or if more effort is needed complete it in the required time frame. Sometimes you may also need to make some changes in the design of some components because of new requirements from the marketing and sales people. Review meetings are a great tool to convey these new requirements. Again, architecture documents and MRDs are kept in sync with any changes/problems encountered during development.

1.1.5   Testing

Testing is probably the most important phase for long-term support as well as for the reputation of the company. If you don't control the quality of the software, it will not be able to compete with other products on the market. If software crashes at the customer site, your customer loses productivity as well money and you lose credibility. Sometimes these losses are huge. Unhappy customers will not buy your other products and will not refer other customers to you. You can avoid this situation by doing extensive testing. This testing is referred to as Quality Assurance, or QA, in most of the software world.

Usually testing starts as soon as the initial parts of the software are available. There are multiple types of testing and these are explained in this section. Each of these has its own importance.

1.1.5.1   Unit Testing

Unit testing is testing one part or one component of the product. The developer usually does this when he/she has completed writing code for that part of the product. This makes sure that the component is doing what it is intended to do. This also saves a lot of time for software testers as well as developers by eliminating many cycles of software being passed back and forth between the developer and the tester.

When a developer is confident that a particular part of the software is ready, he/she can write test cases to test functionality of this part of the software. The component is then forwarded to the software testing people who run test cases to make sure that the unit is working properly.

1.1.5.2   Sanity Testing

Sanity testing is a very basic check to see if all software components compile with each other without a problem. This is just to make sure that developers have not defined conflicting or multiple functions or global variable definitions.

1.1.5.3   Regression or Stress Testing

Regression or stress testing is a process done in some projects to carry out a test for a longer period of time. This type of testing is used to determine behavior of a product when used continuously over a period of time. It can reveal some bugs in software related to memory leakage. In some cases developers allocate memory but forget to release it. This problem is known as memory leakage. When a test is conducted for many days or weeks, this problem results in allocation of all of the available memory until no memory is left. This is the point where your software starts showing abnormal behavior.

Another potential problem in long-term operation is counter overflow. This occurs when you increment a counter but forget to decrement, it resulting in an overflow when the product is used for longer periods.

The regression testing may be started as soon as some components are ready. This testing process requires a very long period of time by its very nature. The process should be continued as more components of the product are integrated. The integration process and communication through interfaces may create new bugs in the code.

1.1.5.4   Functional Testing

Functional testing is carried out to make sure that the software is doing exactly what it is supposed to do. This type of testing is a must before any software is released to customers. Functional testing is done by people whose primary job is software testing, not the developers themselves. In small software projects where a company can't afford dedicated testers, other developers may do functional testing also. The key point to keep in mind is that the person who wrote a software component should not be the person who tested it. A developer will tend to test the software the way he/she has written it. He/she may easily miss any problems in the software.

The software testers need to prepare a testing plan for each component of the software. A testing plan consists of test cases that are run on the software. The software tester can prepare these test cases using functional specifications documents. The tester may also get help from the developer to create test cases. Each test case should include methodology used for testing and expected results.

In addition to test cases, the tester may also need to create a certain infrastructure or environment to test the functionality of a piece of code. For example, you may simulate a network to test routing algorithms that may be part of a routing product.

The next important job of the tester is to create a service request if an anomaly is found. The tester should include as much information in the service request as possible. Typical information included in reporting bugs includes:

- Test case description
- How the test was carried out
- Expected results
- Results obtained
- If a particular environment was created for testing, a description of that environment

The service request should be forwarded to the developer so that the developer may correct the problem. Many software packages are available in the market to track bugs and fix problems in software. There are many web-based tools as well. For a list of freely available open source projects, go to http://www.osdn.org or http://www.sourceforge.net and search for "bug track". OSDN (Open Source Developers Network) hosts many open source software development projects. You can find software packages that work with CVS also. CVS is explained in Chapter 6 of this book.

1.1.6   Software Releases

Before you start selling any software product, it is officially released. This means that you create a state of the software in your repository, make sure that it has been tested for functionality and freeze the code. A version number is assigned to released software. After releasing the software, development may continue but it will not make any change in the released software. The development is usually carried on in a new branch and it may contain new features of the product. The released software is updated only if a bug fixed version is released.

Usually companies assign incremental version numbers following some scheme when the next release of the software is sent to market. The change in version number depends on whether the new software contains a major change to the previous version or it contains bug fixes and enhancement to existing functionality. Releases are also important because they are typically compiled versions of a particular version of the code, and thus provide a stable set of binaries for testing.

1.1.6.1   Branches

In almost all serious software development projects, a revision or version control system is used. This version control system keeps a record of changes in source code files and is usually built in a tree-like structure. When software is released, the state of each file that is part of the release should be recorded. Future developments are made by creating branches to this state. Sometimes special branches may also be created that are solely used for bug fixing. CVS is discussed in detail in Chapter 6.

1.1.6.2   Release Notes

Every software version contains release notes. These release notes are prepared by people releasing the software version with the help of developers. Release notes show what happened in this software version. Typically the information includes:

- Bug fixes
- New functionality
- Detail of new features added to the software
- Any bugs that are not yet fixed
- Future enhancements
- If a user needs a change in the configuration process, it is also mentioned in the release notes

Typically a user should be given enough information to understand the new release enhancements and decide whether an upgrade is required or not.

1.1.7   Documentation

There are three broad categories of documentation related to software development processes.

1. Technical documentation developed during the development process. This includes architecture, functional and design documents.
2. Technical documentation prepared for technical support staff. This includes technical manuals that support staff use to provide customer support.
3. End-user manuals and guides. This is the documentation for the end user to assist the user getting started with the product and using it.

All three types of documents are necessary for different aspects of product support. Technical documents are necessary for future development, bug fixes, and adding new features. Technical documentation for technical support staff contains information that is too complicated for the end user to understand and use. The support staff needs this information in addition to user manuals to better support customers. Finally each product must contain user manuals.

Technical writers usually develop user manuals which are based on functional specifications. In the timelines of most software development projects, functional specifications are prepared before code development starts. So the technical writers can start writing user manuals while developers are writing code. By the time the product is ready, most of the work on user manuals has already been completed.

1.1.8   Support and New Features

Your customers need support when you start selling a product. This is true regardless of the size of the product, and even for products that are not software related. Most common support requests from customers are related to one of the following:

- The customer needs help in installation and getting started.
- The customer finds a bug and you need to release a patch or update to the whole product.
- The product does not fulfill customer requirements and a new feature is required by the customer.

In addition to that, you may also want to add new features to the product for the next release because competitor products have other features. Better support will increase your customer loyalty and will create referral business for you.

You may adopt two strategies to add new features. You may provide an upgrade to the current release as a patch, or wait until you have compiled and developed a list of new features and make a new version. Both of these strategies are useful depending how urgent the requirement for new features is.

1.2   Components of a Development System

Like any other system, a development system is composed of many components that work together to provide services to the developer for the software development task. Depending upon the requirements of a project, different types of components can be chosen. Many commercial companies also sell comprehensive development tools. On Linux systems, all of the development tools are available and you can choose some of these depending upon your level of expertise with these tools and your requirements. Typically each development platform consists of the following components:

- Hardware platform
- Operating system
- Editors
- Compilers and assemblers
- Debuggers
- Version control system
- Collaboration and bug tracking

Let us take a closer look on these components and what role they play in the development cycle.

1.2.1   Hardware Platform

This is the tangible part of the development system. A hardware platform is the choice of your hardware, PC or workstation, for the development system. You can choose a particular hardware platform depending upon different factors as listed below:

Cost	Depending upon budget, you may chose different types of hardware. Usually UNIX workstations are costly to buy and maintain. On the other hand, PC-based workstations are cheap and the maintenance cost is also low.
Performance	Usually UNIX workstations have high performance and stability as compared to PC-based solutions.
Tools	You also need to keep in mind availability of development tools on a particular platform.
Development Type	If the target system is the same as the host system on which development is done, the development is relatively easy and native tools are cheap as well, compared to cross-platform development tools.

Depending upon these factors, you may make a choice from the available hardware platforms for development.

If hardware is part of the final product, selection of hardware platform also depends upon customer/market requirement.

1.2.2   Operating System

Choice of a particular operating system may be made depending upon:

- Cost
- Availability of development tools
- Hardware platform
- Native or cross compiling

Some operating systems are cheaper than others. Linux is an excellent choice, as far as cost is concerned. Linux is also a very good operating system as it has all of the development tools available. Now you can install Linux on high-end workstations from Sun Microsystems, HP, and IBM as well as commodity PC hardware available everywhere. It provides stability and most of the people are familiar with development tools. You can also use the operating system for cross-platform development using GNU tools.

1.2.3   Editors

Editors play an important role in the development work. Easy-to-use and feature rich editors, like Emacs, increase developers' productivity. You should look at a few things while selecting editors. These features include:

- Understanding syntax of language
- Collapsing of context
- Support of tags
- Opening multiple files
- Easy editing for generally used editing functions like cut, copy, paste, search, replace and so on
- Multiple windows
- Support of user defined functions and macros

If you look at the open source community, you can find a lot of good editors available to developers. The most commonly used editors are Jed, Emacs and Xemacs. However, many other variants of these editors are also available. You can also use X-Windows-based editors available on Linux platform. A lot of people also edit in vi or vim, both of these have been very popular historically.

1.2.4   Compilers and Assemblers

Compilers and assemblers are the core development tools because they convert source code to executable form. Quality of compilers does affect the output code. For example, some compilers can do much better code optimization compared to others. If you are doing some cross-platform development, then your compiler should support code generation for the target machine as well.

GNU compilers collection, more commonly called GCC, is a comprehensive set of compilers for commonly used languages including the following:

- C
- C++
- Java
- Fortran

In addition to GCC, you can find a lot of other open source compilers available for Linux. Some of these are introduced in Chapter 3.

GNU utilities set, also known as binutils, includes GNU assembler and other utilities that can be used for many tasks. GNU assembler is used whenever you compile a program using GNU compiler.

1.2.5   Debuggers

Debuggers are the also an important part of all development systems. You can't write a program that is free of bugs. Debugging is a continuous part of software development and you need good tools for this purpose. GNU debugger, more commonly known as GDB, is a common debugger. Many other debuggers are also built on this debugger. The GNU debugger and some other debuggers will be introduced later in this book.

1.2.6   Version Control Systems

The revision control system is a must for any serious development effort where multiple developers work on a software product. The most popular version control system on Linux is known as Concurrent Versions System or CVS. CVS allows many people to work on files at the same time and provides a central repository to store files. Developers can check out files from this repository, make changes and check the files back into the repository. CVS also works with editors like GNU Emacs.

When multiple developers are modifying the same file at the same time, conflict may occur between different changes made by multiple developers. When a conflict is detected in the files being checked in, CVS provides a mechanism to merge the files appropriately.

CVS can be used over secure links as well. This is required when developers are not physically located at the same place. A server on the Internet can be used to provide secure access to the central software repository.

There are other version control systems as well which are popular in the software development community. Examples are Aegis, PRCS, RCS and SCCS.

1.2.7   E-mail and Collaboration

In any software development project, collaboration among developers, designers and architects as well as marketing people is a must. The objective can be achieved in many ways. Probably e-mail is the most efficient and cheapest way. Some collaboration tools provide more functionality than just e-mailing.

1.2.8   X-Windows

X-Windows is much more than just a GUI interface on Linux, but for development purposes, it provides a very good user interface. This is especially useful for editors like Emacs.

1.2.9 Miscellaneous Tools

Many miscellaneous tools are also important during the development process. Some of these tools are listed below:

- The `make` utility
- The `ar` program
- The `ranlib` utility
- The `hexdump` utility

Information about these tools is provided later in this book.

1.3   Selection Criteria for Hardware Platform

The development process needs computers, networks, storage, printing and other hardware components. However the important hardware decision is the selection of PCs and workstations for developers. There is no hard and fast rule about how to select a particular hardware platform. It depends upon the requirements of a development project. Some factors that you may keep in mind are as follows:

- Cost of the hardware.
- Availability of desired operating system on the hardware. For example, you can't run HP-UX on PCs.
- Availability of development tools.
- Maintenance cost.

There may be other factors as well and you are the best person to judge what you need. However, keep in mind that reliability of hardware is one major factor that people usually overlook. If you buy cheap systems that decrease productivity of developers, you lose a lot of money.

1.4   Selection Criteria for Software Development Tools

After selecting the hardware, software development tools are the next major initial expense in terms of money and time to set these up. Selection of software development tools depends upon the choice of hardware and operating system. In many cases GNU tools are very well suited. Selection of development tools also has a major effect on the productivity of the whole development team.

1.5   Managing Development Process

In large software development projects, management of the development process is a big task and a dedicated person may be needed to take care of this aspect of the project. A development manager usually acts as a binding and coordinating force among different parties with conflicting interests. These parties include:

- Marketing and sales people who put forward requirements, change requirements and come up with new requirements, usually when much of the work is already done!
- Architecture and design people.
- Software developers who always think that they always have less amount of time.
- Release management people.
- Software testers.
- Documentation writers.
- Senior managers who often push to complete the project earlier than the deadline.

Coordinating all of these parties is not an easy task. The manager has to convince senior management that a new feature needs that much time for development. At the same time he has to push developers to meet the deadlines. Some of the important tasks of software management in a real-life project are as follows.

1.5.1   Creating Deadlines

The manager usually coordinates with the software developers to set reasonable deadlines for certain features. These deadlines must conform to the product delivery time lines. The manager may have to arrange additional resources to complete feature development in the allotted time.

Project management software can help a manager to set and meet deadlines and track completion of different components.

1.5.2   Managing the Development Team

The manager has to keep track of how development among different parts of the software is going on. If part of the product is behind schedule, she has to re-arrange resources to get it back on track.. She may also need to hire new people to finish the development of a particular component on schedule.

1.5.3   Resolving Dependencies

Usually software components are dependent on one another. If the development of one component is lagging behind, it may affect development of other components. The development manager needs to keep an eye on these dependencies and how these may affect the overall progress of the project. Well-known project management methods are usually helpful for this task.

1.6   Linux Development Platform Specifications (LDPS) and Linux Standard Base (LSB)

Linux Development Platform Specifications or LDPS was an effort to design a common specification so that programs developed on one Linux distribution could be easily ported to other distributions. The specifications define components and packages that must be present on Linux development workstations. The latest version of the specifications at the time of writing this book is available at http://www.freestandards.org/ldps/1.1/ldps-1.1.html web site.

Linux Standard Base or LSB (http://www.linuxbase.org) is the new forum to standardize Linux distributions. LSB specifications 1.1.0 is available at the time of writing this book. LSB compliant applications can run on any LSB compliant distribution without any modification or recompilation process. Specifications are detailed and the latest version can be found at http://www.linuxbase.org/spec/.

1.6.1   Libraries

The following libraries will be available on LSB compliant systems. While developing applications for Linux, the developer can assume presence of these libraries on target machines, provided the target is LSB compliant.

- libX11
- libXt
- libGL
- libXext
- libICE
- libSM
- libdl
- libcrypt

- libz
- libncurses

1.6.2   Current Contributors to LSB

Major Linux vendors include:

- Caldera Inc.
- MandrakeSoft
- Red Hat Software
- The Debian Project
- TurboLinux Inc.
- SuSE
- VA Linux

References

1. LDPS web site at http://www.freestandards.org/ldps/
2. CVS web site at http://www.gnu.org/software/cvs/
3. Aegis at web site http://aegis.sourceforge.net/index.html
4. PRCS at its web site http://prcs.sourceforge.net/
5. GNU Software at http://www.gnu.org
6. Linux Standard Base at http://www.linuxbase.org
7. Open Source Developers Network at http://www.osdn.org

## CHAPTER 2

Working With Editors

One of the most fundamental tools required for application development on any platform is a text editor; and the Linux operating system offers programmers a wide variety to choose from. These editors offer a wide variety of functionality from simple editing features to syntax highlighting and reading e-mail.

In this chapter, we will focus on a couple of editors that offer features that will be of interest to developers, *Jed, vim,* and *Emacs.* All of these editors offer extended features beyond simple text editing.

2.1   What to Look for in an Editor

While editors like *pico* or even *ed* may be useful for editing system files or writing quick notes, programming editors have certain functions that permit the programmer to focus on the act of creating code and helps to manage the process and keep an eye on syntax.

2.1.1   Extensibility

One useful feature of programming editors is the ability to extend the out-of-the-box functionality with custom programming.

Emacs utilizes a full-featured Lisp language called Elisp to provide users with the ability to add just about any functionality they might require to the editor. The original Lisp language was written in the late 1950s as part of MIT's research into artificial intelligence. Elisp is derived from the original Lisp and provides surprising flexibility in extending Emacs for those who take the time to learn it.

Jed extensibility is based on the s-lang libraries (www.s-lang.org) that were developed by John E. Davis as a generic macro language that would become the basis for a number of different programs. S-lang programs resemble C in syntax and layout.

2.1.2   Understanding Syntax

By understanding the syntax of the programming, the editor can perform a number of functions that make it easier for the programmer to move through the code, locate bugs more quickly and perform other common functions.

Such functions include jumping to the beginning of a stanza in the code, highlighting that stanza, automatic indenting, highlighting syntax, and quickly inserting comments and commenting on entire sections of code.

2.1.3   Tag Support

The *ctags* and *etags* utilities that come with Linux are able to build a list of the various functions, classes, fragments, data blocks and other information within the various files that make up the application. Not all information is available for all languages. For example, while only subroutines are supported for the Perl language, support for the C/C++ languages includes:

- macros (names defined/undefined by #define / #undef)
- enumerators (enumerated values)
- function definitions, prototypes, and declarations
- class, enum, struct, and union names
- namespaces
- typedefs
- variables (definitions and declarations)
- class, struct, and union members

Both Emacs and vim provide the ability for the editor to understand standard tag files and help the programmer quickly locate and edit the portion of code that he/she is working on. Emacs uses the output from *etags*, while vi uses *ctags*.

2.1.4   Folding Code

Folding code refers to the ability of the editor to hide portions of code while they are not needed. For example, all of the functions or subroutines in the code can be folded so that only the names of the functions are seen until the programmer unfolds that routine to work on it.

2.2   Emacs

Emacs is a lisp-based editor that has been around in one form or another since the late 1970s; despite its long history, it remains one of the most up-to-date and widely used editing environments today. From within the editor a user can read and send mail, perform research on the Internet, and even send out for coffee to RFC2324 compliant coffee makers.

Configuration of Emacs is accomplished via the *.emacs* file that can be created in each user's $HOME directory. If the configuration does not exist, Emacs will use its built-in defaults. This file consists of a series of elisp expressions that the editor evaluates when the application runs.

2.2.1   Using Emacs

Navigating and using Emacs may appear confusing and counter-intuitive for those just learning how to use the editor, however the time taken to master this editor can prove well-spent when one considers the time savings that such an integrated and flexible development environment can provide.

If Emacs is started from within X-Windows, it will automatically open a new window in the desktop. To prevent this behavior, you can use the –nw option from the command line. Alternately, you can tell Emacs how large to make the window by specifying the size of the window, in characters, that you wish to create. Examples are:

```
$ emacs -nw main.c
$ emacs -geometry 80x24 main.c &
```

Figure 2-1 shows the initial Emacs screen if it is invoked without an initial file name.

```
Buffers Files Tools Edit Search Mule Help
Welcome to GNU Emacs, one component of a Linux-based GNU system.
The menu bar and scroll bar are sufficient for basic editing with the mouse.

Useful Files menu items:
Exit Emacs                 (or type Control-x followed by Control-c)
Recover Session            recover files you were editing before a crash

Important Help menu items:
Emacs Tutorial             Learn-by-doing tutorial for using Emacs efficiently.
(Non)Warranty              GNU Emacs comes with ABSOLUTELY NO WARRANTY
Copying Conditions         Conditions for redistributing and changing Emacs.
Getting New Versions       How to obtain the latest version of Emacs.


GNU Emacs 20.7.1 (i386-redhat-linux-gnu, X toolkit)
 of Fri Mar 16 2001 on porky.devel.redhat.com
Copyright (C) 1999 Free Software Foundation, Inc.




-1:--   *scratch*       (Lisp Interaction)--L1--All---------------------------
For information about the GNU Project and its goals, type C-h C-p.
```

Figure 2-1 The initial Emacs screen.

For a complete tutorial in using Emacs, from within the application itself, type ^H-t[1]. This tutorial covers many of the functions that are available within Emacs and takes you step-by-step through them.

2.2.2   Basic Emacs Concepts

Emacs uses several keyboard keys to enter commands into the application. The primary one is the Meta key. The Meta key is signified by M-. The Meta key is generally the ALT key on the keyboard, although it may be the ESC key in certain circumstances. If the ALT key does not work, try the ESC key. What works will depend on if you are logged in locally, accessing the console directly or using X-Windows. The ALT key is used in the same manner as the CTRL key. When using the ESC key, press and release the ESC key and then press the next indicated key. In all cases, typing ^U may be used in place of the Meta key. Just type and release ^U and then type the rest of the key sequence as you would for the ESC key.

Entering text into the buffer is accomplished in the default mode simply by typing on the keyboard. To abort a command that's currently running or asking for input, type ^G. This will return you to the current buffer.

Simple commands can be repeated by prefacing them with the key sequence **ESC #**. By pressing the escape key and typing any number, the next command that is issued will be repeated that number of times. For example, typing **ESC 75=** is the same as pressing the equal key 75 times.

To exit Emacs, use the command sequence **^X^C**.

Moving around

In additional to the basic functionality provided by the arrow keys on the keyboard, the key combinations shown in Table 2-1 may be used to move the pointer one character at a time in a given direction.

Table 2-1 Simple Movement Commands.

Arrow Key	Alternate Combination
Left Arrow	^F
Right Arrow	^B
Up Arrow	^P
Down Arrow	^N

---

1.   The caret symbol denotes a control character. To enter the key combination ^H-t, press and hold the CTRL key, and then press the 'H' key. Release both keys and then press the 't' key.

Movement can also be accomplished a word or a page at a time. This is accomplished by referring to Table 2-2.

Table 2-2 Movement Commands

Action	Command
M-b	Word Left
M-f	Word Right
^A	Beginning of Line
^E	End of Line
M-c or *Page-Up*	Page Up
^V or *Page-Down*	Page Down
M-<	Beginning of Buffer
M->	End of Buffer

Deleting

Just as there are several ways to move around in the buffer, there are several ways to quickly delete unwanted information. The <BACKSPACE> key or ^H can be used to delete the character before the pointer. By using ^D you can delete the character at the pointer.

In addition, there are ways to delete words, lines and portions of lines. There are also methods for blocking text and deleting entire sections of the buffer. For more information on working with blocks of text, see *Cutting and Pasting* below.

Table 2-3 shows the various commands used to perform these functions.

Table 2-3 Movement Commands

Action	Command
<BACKSPACE> or ^H	Delete character to the left
^D	Delete character to the right
M-DEL	Delete word to the left
M-d	Delete from pointer to end of current word
^A^K	Delete current line excluding the EOL character
^K	Delete from pointer to end of line
^X u	Undo previous command – may be used multiple times

File Operations

Editing within Emacs is done through a series of buffers. Each buffer may be edited separately and the changes saved back to the disk. Files may also be opened into new or existing buffers as shown in Table 2-4.

Table 2-4 File Commands

Action	Command
^X ^F	Open File
^X k	Close File
^X i	Insert File
^X ^S	Save File
^X w	Save File As
^X b	Change Buffer

Search and Replace

There are two search and replace functions within Emacs. The first one simply does a simple search (case insensitive by default) for the character string provided by the user. The second, more complex search function does a search and replace on regular expressions. See Table 2-5 for a list of these commands.

Table 2-5 Search and Replace Commands

Action	Command
^S ENTER	Search
^S	Continue Forward Search
^R ENTER	Search Backwards
^R	Continue Backwards Search
M-%	Search & Replace
M-X query-replace-regexp	Regular Expression (regex) Search & Replace
M-X occur	Find occurrences of a string in the current buffer

By typing `^S <ENTER>` you will be prompted to enter the string to search for. With the search string still active, typing `^S` again to search for the next occurrence of that string in the current buffer.

Typing `M-%` (usually accomplished by `ESC-%` rather than `ALT-%` under Linux) will bring up the same search function, but when you press RETURN after entering the search key, you will be prompted for a replacement string. Type in the string that you wish to replace the search key with and press RETURN. If the search string is found in the current buffer, you will be presented with the options shown in Table 2-6.

Table 2-6 Search and Replace Options

Action	Command
y or SPACE	Replace the string at the pointer with the replacement string and search for the next occurrence.
n or DEL	Leave the string at the pointer as is and search for the next occurrence.
!	Replace globally from the pointer forward in the buffer.
.	Replace the string at the pointer and then exit search and replace mode.
^	Move point back to previous match.
u	Undo the previous replacement.
q or ENTER	Exit search and replace mode.
?	Display help.

The more complex search and replace feature is available by default, only from the prompt and is not bound to a particular key combination. To access this feature, you need to type in the name of the mode, which in this case is "`query-match-regex`". The complete key sequence for this is:

```
M-X query-replace-regex <RETURN>
```

This command brings up a similar series of prompts that allows you to search for regular expressions in the current buffer and, using the same options shown in Table 2-5, replace them.

Emacs has an auto-completion option that you can use instead of typing the entire command shown above. By typing:

```
M-X que<ESC>
```

Emacs will search through its listing of modes and complete as much of the request as it can. If there is a conflict and there are one or more modes that begin with the phrase that you have typed in, pressing the <SPACEBAR> will cycle through the names. You can press <RETURN> to select the one currently displayed.

Emacs supports the use of parenthetical statements in regex search and replace commands. A portion of the search string may be used as part of the replacement string. The contents of the first set of parenthesis in the search string may be referenced as \1 in the replacement string. The second set would be referred to by \2.

For example:

```
Original string:The Dodo and the Griffin
Search string:\([Tt]h\)e \([a-zA-Z]*\)
Replacement string:\1ose \2s
New string:Those Dodos and those Griffins
```

Cutting and Pasting

Sections of the buffer may be marked and certain commands may be applied to those regions. These commands include copying, cutting and pasting text. To select a region of text, move the pointer to the beginning of the sections that you wish to select and press ^<SPACE-BAR>. When the pointer is moved, the text from the marked point to the current pointer position will be highlighted. Once the region is selected, issue the cut or copy command. To deselect the text without issuing the copy or paste command, simply press ^<SPACEBAR> again.

Table 2-7 shows a list of the various selection commands.

Table 2-7 Cut and Paste Commands

Action	Command
^<SPACEBAR>	Begin selection
^W	Cut
M-W	Copy
^Y	Paste

2.2.3   Using Buffers and Windows

As mentioned, Emacs has multiple buffers that can be opened and edited simultaneously. To navigate between buffers, press **^Xb** and type the name of the buffer that you wish to switch to. Buffers may be opened and closed by using the File Commands listed earlier in this chapter. To see a list of buffers, use **^X^B**.

As shown in Figure 2-2, each window may be split into two windows by using the **^X2** command. This will create a horizontal divide in the middle of the current window. The same file will be present in each pane, but they may be scrolled separately. To move between windows, press **^Xo**. Windows may be split multiple times. To close all other buffer, use **^X1**. The current buffer may be closed with **^X0**.

See Table 2-8 for a complete list of window commands and Figure 2-2 for an example of using multiple buffers. These buffers are 'main.c' and 'temp.c'.

Table 2-8 Window Commands

Action	Command
^Xb	Switch to buffer
^X^B	List buffers
^X2	Split current window
^Xo	Move to other window
^X0	Delete current window
^X1	Delete all over windows

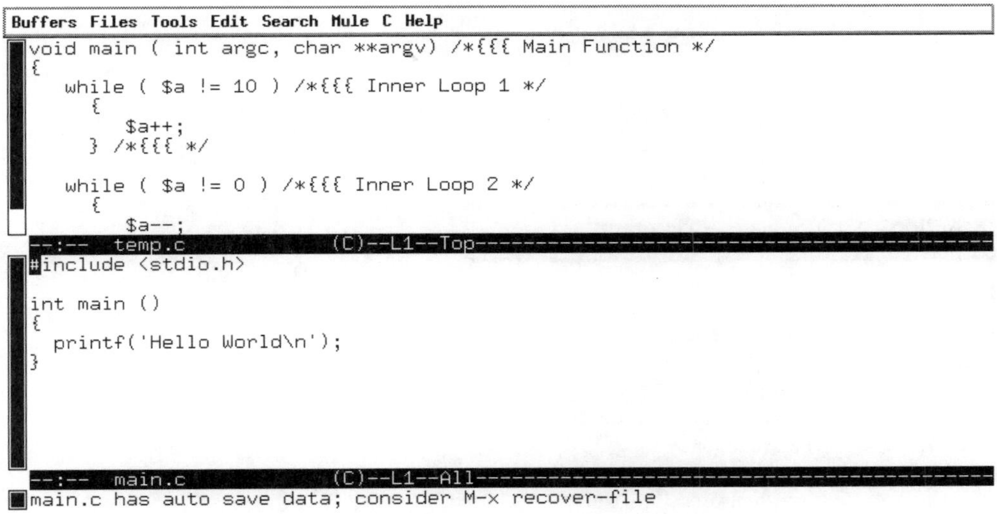

```
Buffers Files Tools Edit Search Mule C Help
void main ( int argc, char **argv) /*{{{ Main Function */
{
   while ( $a != 10 ) /*{{{ Inner Loop 1 */
      {
         $a++;
      } /*{{{ */

   while ( $a != 0 ) /*{{{ Inner Loop 2 */
      {
         $a--;
--:--   temp.c               (C)--L1--Top-----------------------------------
#include <stdio.h>

int main ()
{
  printf('Hello World\n');
}




--:--   main.c               (C)--L1--All-----------------------------------
main.c has auto save data; consider M-x recover-file
```

Figure 2-2 Using multiple buffers in Emacs.

2.2.4   Language Modes

Emacs recognizes a number of different programming language files based on their extensions. When you load a recognized source code file, Emacs will assume certain defaults and enter the appropriate mode for editing that file.

For example, when you load a file with a .c extension for editing, Emacs sets the appropriate mode and enables commands used to automatically and manually indent code, quickly move though functions and insert comments.

When a language mode is on, Emacs can automatically indent code as you type. To turn this mode on, type **^C^A**. The same command is used to turn this mode back off.

With this mode active, auto-indenting takes place when certain characters are entered from the keyboard. These characters are the semi-colon, curly braces, and under certain circumstances, the comma and colon.

For example, if auto-indent (or technically **c-toggle-auto-state**) is on and the following code is typed into the buffer:

```
void main ( int argc, char **argv) { while (
```

it will be formatted by Emacs as follows:

```
void main ( int argc, char **argv)
    {
        while (
```

Table 2-9 shows some of the common C-mode commands.

Table 2-9 C-mode Commands

Action	Command
ESC ;	Insert comment
ESC ^A	Go to top of function
ESC ^E	Go to bottom of function
ESC ^H	Mark function
{	Insert bracket and return
}	Return and insert bracket
^C^A	Toggle Auto-indent mode
^\	Auto-indent selected region

2.2.5   Using Tags

As an application grows in size, it also grows in complexity. As the number of subroutines, variables, functions and files increases, it becomes much more difficult to keep track of every piece and to quickly find the portion of code that one needs to work on. To address this issue, Emacs has the ability to read a file that contains a table of tags that reference various parts of an application.

These tags are stored in a TAGS file that is created by the etags command. Once this file is built, Emacs can read this table and use it to quickly locate a specific portion of code, regardless of whether it is in a currently open file or not.

From the command line the etags command is issued with a list of file names to be read:

```
$ etags *.[ch]
```

This command will read all files in the current directory that have a .c or .h extension and build a tags table file in the current directory. The output file is, by default, called TAGS.

To build a single TAGS table for a project that has source code spread through any number of subdirectories, the following command may be used:

```
$ find . -name \*.[ch] | xargs etags -
```

Just be aware if there are too many files, then this command may need to be run several times with varying arguments in order to build a complete table. To do this, you must use the -append option to the etags command as shown:

```
$ find . -name \*.c | xargs etags -
$ find . -name \*.h | xargs etags --append -
```

Any of these commands may be issued from within Emacs itself by using the **M-!** command to issue a shell command. Simply type **ESC ! <command name>** and press return.

Once you have built a TAGS table, it must first be read into Emacs before you can use it to search. To accomplish this, type **M-x visit-tags-table**, specify the location of the TAGS file to be read in, and then the name of the TAGS file. The default value for the location is the current working directory, and the default tags file name is "TAGS".

Once the TAGS file has been read in, you may issue search commands against the table. There are several commands that can be used. The one most commonly used is **ESC .** which searches for a tag that matches the search parameter. The default search parameter is the word at the current pointer position. For example, if the pointer were on the character string search_function, the default search string that Emacs presents would be search_function.

If you are not sure of the name of the function that you are looking for, you can type the first few characters of the function name and press the **TAB** key. This invokes the completion function of Emacs and, if the function is unique, it will display that function name. If the function name is not unique, Emacs will complete as much of the function name as it can and then prompt you for the rest. Pressing **TAB** again after Emacs has completed as much of the function name as it can and will display the matching functions in a new buffer. If, for example, you wanted to edit the **close_files** function, Figure 2-3 shows the results of typing **ESC .** **c<TAB><TAB>.**

If Emacs finds a function that matches your search string, it will replace the current buffer with the contents of the first file in which it found the search string and the pointer will be positioned at the first line of that function. In the above example, completing the file name and pressing ENTER results in the file exit.c being opened and the pointer being positioned on the first line of the close_files function. This is shown in Figure 2-4.

Alternatively, you can initiate the search with the command **ESC x find-tag-other-window** and rather than replacing the current buffer with the found function, a new buffer will be opened instead. Remember that Emacs has a completion function, so after typing the first few characters of a function, you can press the **TAB** key and Emacs will fill in the rest of the command if it is unique. If you are sure that a command is unique, pressing the **ENTER** key will execute that command.

Rather than searching for functions by name, you can also search all of the files referenced in the tags file for a regular expression. To accomplish this, type **ESC x tags-search** and Emacs will prompt you for a regular expression to search for. If it finds a match, the first occurrence of the string found will be displayed in the current buffer. You can search for the next occurrence of the string by issuing the **ESC ,** command.

```
Buffers Files Tools Edit Search Mule Minibuf Help
}


/* Given the mask, find the first available signal that should be serviced. */

static int
next_signal(struct task_struct *tsk, sigset_t *mask)
{
        unsigned long i, *s, *m, x;
        int sig = 0;
--1-:**-F1  signal.c          (C)--L50-- 4%-------------------------------------
In this buffer, type RET to select the completion near point.

Possible completions are:
calc_load                           call_usermodehelper
can_schedule                        cap_bset
cap_emulate_setxuid                 cap_set_all
cap_set_pg                          cascade_timers
check_free_space                    check_resource
child_reaper                        close_files
collect_signal                      console_cmdline
--11:---F1  *Completions*    (Completion List)--L1--Top--------------------------
Find tag: (default int) c
```

Figure 2-3 Emacs tags-search function.

```
Buffers Files Tools Edit Search Mule C Help
                       /* We dont want people slaying init */
                       p->exit_signal = SIGCHLD;
                       p->self_exec_id++;
                       p->p_opptr = reaper;
                       if (p->pdeath_signal) send_sig(p->pdeath_signal, p, 0);
               }
       }
       read_unlock(&tasklist_lock);
}

static inline void close_files(struct files_struct * files)
{
       int i, j;

       j = 0;
       for (;;) {
               unsigned long set;
               i = j * __NFDBITS;
               if (i >= files->max_fdset || i >= files->max_fds)
                       break;
               set = files->open_fds->fds_bits[j++];
--1-:---F1  exit.c              (C)--L177--27%--------------------------------
Mark set
```

Figure 2-4 Finding the function.

Instead of searching for a specific regular expression, the command **ESC tags-apropos** will create a new buffer entitled *Tags List* that contains a listing of all of the tags that match that regular expression. By moving the pointer around this buffer, you can place it on the function that you are looking for and use the **ESC .** command to open that function in the current buffer. A list of TAGS commands is shown in Table 2-10.

Table 2-10 Emacs commands related to TAGS

Action	Command
M-x visit-tags-table	Load a tags file into Emacs
M-.	Search for a function
M-x find-tag-other-window	Search for a function and load the file in a new buffer
M-x tags-search	Search for a regular expression in the files represented by the current tag list
M-,	Repeat regular expression search
M-x tags-apropos	Load a list of all tags into a new buffer

2.2.6   Compiling

Emacs has the facility to call external compilers, parse their output and display the results in a buffer. As the results are displayed, the programmer can then move forward and backward through any error or warnings. As each error or warning is displayed, the appropriate line in the code is displayed and may be edited.

To invoke the compiler from Emacs, type M-X compile; in response, Emacs will ask you for the command to use to compile the program for application. You can either specify make or the command line compiler with all the options. The default is to invoke make with the –k option in order to continue as far into the make as it can when encountering errors.

For example, assume that the following (broken) bit of code is in a buffer entitled 'main.c'.

```
#include <stdio.h>

int main ()
{
  printf('Hello World\n');
}
```

The compiler may be invoked by typing:

```
M-X compile
Compile command: gcc -o main main.c
```

If the buffer being compiled has not been saved, the editor will prompt you to save it. The results of the compilation will appear in the *compilation* buffer as seen in Figure 2-5.

```
Buffers Files Tools Edit Search Mule C Help
#include <stdio.h>

int main ()
{
  printf('Hello World\n');
}




--1-:---F1  main.c            (C)--L1--All-----------------------------------
cd ~/
gcc -o main main.c
main.c: In function `main':
main.c:5: character constant too long
main.c:5: warning: passing arg 1 of `printf' makes pointer from integer without\
 a cast

Compilation exited abnormally with code 1 at Sun Jun 30 15:56:30


--11:**-F1  *compilation*      (Compilation:exit [1])--L1--All----------------
(No files need saving)
```

Figure 2-5 The results of M-X compile.

The main.c buffer is still the active buffer, but it is linked to the *compilation* buffer. As indicated by Figure 2-6, typing **^X-`** the first error in the bottom buffer is highlighted and the pointer in the top buffer is positioned in the line of code that caused the error. Repeating that command moves the pointer forward in the code to the next error.

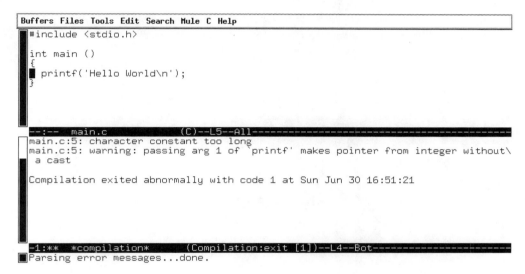

Figure 2-6 Using the built-in functions to debug code.

While navigating through the *compilation* buffer, typing ^C^C will move the code in the window to the line referenced by the error message. Table 2-11 lists the commands used to aid in debugging compiled code.

Table 2-11 Compiling with Emacs

Action	Command
M-X compile	Compile a file or an entire project
^X-`	Find the next error
^C^C	Examine source code that created the error

2.2.7   Xemacs

Xemacs is a project that was spawned from the original source tree of the Emacs project. In many ways it still resembles its ancestor, but when it is run it includes additional features that make use of the X-Window interface. These include toolbars, font faces, image embedding and editing, and similar features.

As you can see in Figure 2-7, the Xemacs interface has taken many commonly used functions and created a tool bar across the top of the display that makes them accessible to the mouse. In addition, most of the user interface is customizable.

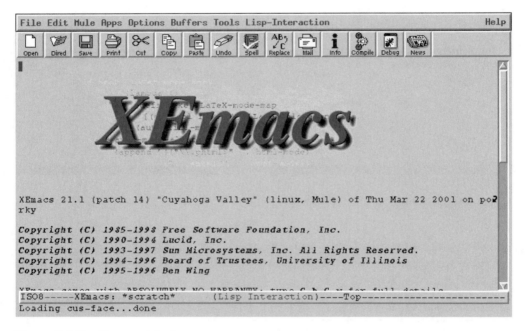

Figure 2-7 The Xemacs interface.

2.3   Jed

Jed was designed as a small, lightweight editor. It has many of the functions required by application programmers and can be set up with one of several different key bindings to aid people transitioning from other editors.

The main Jed configuration file is in JEDROOT/lib/jed.rc (/usr/share/jed/lib/jed.rc if the RedHat RPM was used to install the application). This file contains the default values for all users, but it is only read if the user does not have a local configuration file present in the home directory.

2.3.1   Configuring Jed

Individual users may change their default setting by copying JEDROOT/lib/jed.rc to .jedrc in their home directory:

```
$ cp /usr/share/jed/lib/jed.rc ~/.jedrc
```

This file may be edited to change the initial values and behavior of Jed. Lines beginning with a percent symbol (%) are comments and are ignored when the file is read. Other than conditional statements, all entries must end in a semi-colon (;).

One of the first options that a user may wish to change is the emulation mode of the editor. By default Jed uses Emacs-like key bindings for entering commands. Some other emulation modes available are IDE, CUA and even WordStar. To select a new emulation, edit the .jedrc in the user's home directory, comment out the current emulation and uncomment the one that you wish to use.

Below, the user has changed the application to use the IDE mode instead of the default. These key bindings resemble those used by in Borland's IDE.

```
if (BATCH == 0)
{
%   () = evalfile("emacs");      % Emacs-like bindings
%   () = evalfile("edt");        % EDT emulation
    () = evalfile ("ide");       % Borland IDE
%   () = evalfile ("brief");     % Brief Keybindings
%   () = evalfile("wordstar");   % Wordstar (use ide instead)
%   () = evalfile ("cua");       % CUA-like key bindings
...
}
```

You will also notice that there is a conditional statement in the example above. This is because Jed may also be run in batch mode for processing files unattended. Statements within this block will only be processed if the application is run in interactive mode, not when run in batch mode. While having the statements outside of this block would not effect the application when run in batch mode, having them separated speeds up the load time of the application when they are not needed.

There are many other configuration options available in the .jedrc file that control how the program operates. Some of them are generic to all modes and others are used in only one mode. For example, the variable CASE_SEARCH may be set to force case sensitivity in searches, or C_BRA_NEWLINE may be set to force a newline character to be inserted prior to a curly-bracket when in C-mode.

Jed also has the capability of calling a compiler directly and examining the output. The standard compiler is assumed to be gcc. If you are using a different compiler, you will need to set the Compile_Default_Compiler variable in the .jedrc file.

2.3.2   Using Jed

Jed is called from the command line with an argument telling it which file you would like to edit. If Jed is called without an argument, it will prompt you for the name of the file before you may do any editing. This behavior may be changed by modifying the `Startup_With_File` variable in .jedrc to have a value of 0.

Jed may be called with one or more command line arguments. A –n argument forces Jed to ignore the users' local *.jedrc* file as well as the *jedrc* file. There is also an X version of Jed that allows you to use the mouse to select text and options from the menu. To start Jed, simply type:

    $ **jed** *<filename>*

or

    $ **xjed** *<filename>*

Figure 2-8 shows the initial text-based Jed display when no command-line argument is given. The menu across the top is accessed by pressing the F-10 key. This scratch buffer will disappear when you begin to type and if a filename is given on the command line you will be taken immediately to that buffer to begin editing.

The basic editing features of Jed will be dependent upon the emulation mode that is selected. In this section, it is assumed that you will be using the Emacs emulation mode.

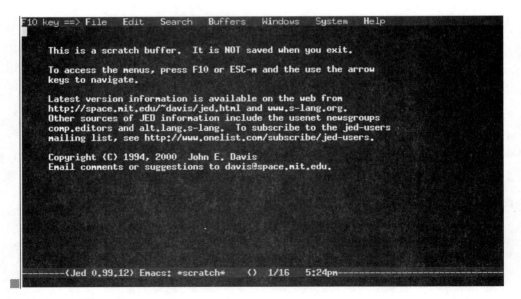

Figure 2-8 The Jed text interface.

2.3.3 Folding Code

The ability to fold buffers in order to view only the parts of a file that are necessary at the time is quite useful when trying to understand program flow and how the application is put together at a very high level.

In order for folding to be used, special markers must be put in the file at the appropriate points. There are two markers, one to denote the beginning of a section to be folded and one to denote the end. In plain text files, these markers must be in the leftmost column; but when an application language that is recognized by Jed is used, they may be inserted in comments.

The opening marker is three left curly braces "{{{" and the closing is three of the right "}}}" To insert marker into a C-language program, place the markers directly after the /* that begins the comment:

```
/*{{{ Deep magic begins here. */
{
    x = n[i];
    a = ((a<<19)^(a>>13)) + n[(i+128)&255];
    n[i] = y = n[x&255] + a + b;
    r[i] = d = n[(y>>8)&255] + x;
    }
/*}}} */
```

When the file is folded up, the above section of code will appear as follows:

```
/*{{{ Deep magic begins here. */...
```

The ellipsis at the end of the line indicates that this line may be unfolded.

Figure 2-9 shows a section of Perl code with the fold markers in place. The comments are placed before and after each section of code and a description of the code included in that fold has been added. Figure 2-10 shows the same file folded.

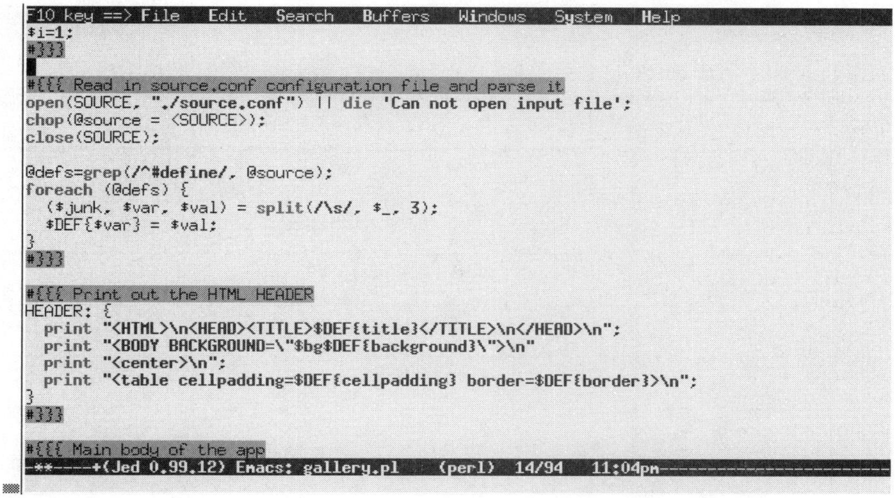

Figure 2-9 The file with the folding markers in place.

```
F10 key ==> File   Edit   Search   Buffers   Windows   System   Help
#!/usr/bin/perl

#{{{ Static Variable Definitions...

#{{{ Read in source.conf configuration file and parse it...

#{{{ Print out the HTML HEADER...

#{{{ Main body of the app...

#{{{ Print out the HTML FOOTER...


sub makepage {
#{{{ ...




--**----+(Jed 0.99.12) Emacs: gallery.pl   (perl)  3/94  11:07pm-------------
folding buffer...done
```

Figure 2-10 The same file folded.

The entire program can be folded and unfolded at once, or individual sections of the file may be unfolded. Several sections from different parts of the program may be unfolded at once.

Jed treats each folded section as a subroutine and it can be edited as such. By moving the pointer to a folded section and pressing ^C> only that section of the program is displayed for editing.

In order to use the folding mode, it must be activated from within Jed. In order to do this, type M-X folding-mode <RETURN>. This will turn the folding mode on and immediately fold up the current buffer.

See Table 2-12 for a list of the available commands in this mode.

Table 2-12 Folding Mode Commands

Action	Command
^C^W	Fold current buffer
^C^O	Unfold current buffer
^C^X	Fold current marked section
^C^S	Unfold current marked section
^C^F	Fold highlighted section
^C>	Edit folded section
^C<	Exit current section being edited

2.4 VIM

VIM stands for Vi IMproved and was developed by Bram Moolenaar. It is based on the functionality of the original, non-open source vi editor. While most open source software is also free-
ware, VIM is distributed as Charityware. In exchange for using the program, the authors request
that users consider donating to the Kibaale Children's Center (KCC), a charity providing food,
health care and education for the children in the area. For further information regarding this
donation program and the KCC, within VIM, type **:help ifcc** or visit http://www.vim.org/
ifcc.

2.4.1 Using VIM

VIM is available in both text-based and graphical modes. The graphical version, shown in Figure 2-11, has the same functionality as the text-based version, but also provides easy access to
many functions through pull-down menus and a button bar. To start the text-based version, use
the command **vim**. The graphical version is started by typing **gvim**. For example, to start VIM
and edit the file main.c, type the following:

```
$ vim main.c
```

Or, for the graphical version, type:

```
$ gvim main.c
```

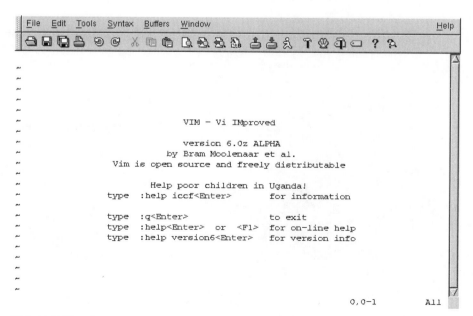

Figure 2-11 gvim.

2.4.1   VIM Concepts

There are two basic modes within VIM that determine VIM's behavior. These two modes are Normal and Insert. In Normal mode, the editor expects the user to enter commands that perform a number of functions. In Insert mode, the editor inserts typed characters into the current document.

The editor starts in Normal mode. To return to that mode from Insert mode, press the **ESC** key.

2.4.2   Basic Editing

As previously noted, VIM is based on the vi editor and anyone familiar with vi's editing keys will immediately be at home with VIM.

VIM uses two methods of entering commands into the application. Simple commands such as those used for navigation and entering Insert mode are one- or two-letter commands that are case sensitive and are not echoed to the screen as they are typed. More complex commands such as those used to perform searches and utilize the tags created by the ctags program are entered and echoed into the last line of the application screen. A colon, slash or question mark character is used to activate the last line mode and enter the command. The character used will depend upon which command is being issued.

Most simple commands can be preceded by a number. When this occurs, the command entered is treated as if it had been entered that many times. For example, the command to delete a line in a buffer is dd. If this command preceded by the number 15, as in 15dd, the next 15 lines in the buffer will be deleted.

To exit VIM, type **:q** if the text has not been changed, **:q!** to abandon all changes made to the file, or **:wq!** to save all changes and exit.

For help on any function, type **:help <name>** where <name> is the name of the function. Typing

```
:help tutor
```

will bring up information about VIMs built in tutor file. This file will walk you through the basics of using VIM.

Navigation

If the terminal that is being used is set up correctly, the arrow keys on the keyboard will often work for simple navigation commands that move the cursor around the screen. If the terminal type is not properly configured, alternate keys may be used to navigate through the text.

The "h", "j", "k", and "l" keys can be used in place of the left, down, up and right arrow keys respectively. Additionally, the cursor may be moved one word, sentence or paragraph at a time by using the keys listed in Table 2-13.

Table 2-13 Navigating VIM

Action	Command
Hjkl	Left, down, up, right
W	Move one word forward
E	Move one word backward
( )	Move to previous, next sentence
{ }	Move to previous, next paragraph

It is also possible to scroll the text on the screen without moving the cursor from its current position. Table 2-14 lists some of the more common commands.

Table 2-14 Folding Mode Commands

Action	Command
^F ^B	Scroll one screen forward, backward
^U ^D	Scroll one half screen up, down
^E ^Y	Scroll one line up, down

Insert Mode

There are numerous ways to enter Insert mode depending on where in the buffer you wish to insert text and how much of the text you wish to change. For example, it is possible to insert text at the beginning of the current line, at the end of the line, to change only the letter or word at the cursor, or to change text from the cursor to the end of the line. All of these commands are accomplished by simple one- and two-letter commands. When you press the "i" key, VIM enters Insert mode and starts inserting the next typed characters at the current cursor position. If "a" (append) is used to enter Insert mode, the insertion point is the character following the cursor.

Pressing "I" will insert characters at the beginning of the line, and "A" will append characters to the end of the current line. The "o" character opens the line after the current one for inserting text, and the "O" key creates a new line above the current one and positions the cursor to enter new text.

Table 2-15 lists these commands.

Table 2-15 Entering Insert mode

Action	Command
i a	Begin inserting characters at the cursor, after the cursor
I A	Begin inserting characters at the beginning, end of the line
o O	Open a new line after, before the current line

In addition to simply entering text into the buffer, vim can change text already in the document. Table 2-16 lists the commands for changing text and their function.

Table 2-16 Commands to change text

Action	Command
cw	Change from the current cursor position to the end of the word
cc	Change the current line
r	Replace the letter at the cursor
R	Replace from cursor on

Also of note are the deletion commands. They are entered from Normal mode and may be used to delete a character, a word or a line at a time. These commands are listed in Table 2-17.

Table 2-17 Deletion commands

Action	Command
x X	Delete the character at, before the cursor
dw	Delete from the cursor to the end of the current word
dd	Delete the current line
D	Delete from cursor to end of the current line

Automatic Indentation

There are several indenting options available with VIM. They are `autoindent`, `smartindent` and `cindent`. The first, `autoindent`, simply copies the indentention from the previous line and uses that as the default for all new lines entered into the buffer. `Smartindent` and `cindent` are similar, but `cindent` is stricter in the way that it handles the formatting and may not be suitable for programming languages other than C.

To turn any of these indent modes on, with the application in Normal mode, type `:set <indent mode>`. To turn off an indent mode, simply preface the mode name with the word "no". For example, to turn on `cindent`, type:

```
:set cindent
```

To turn `cindent` back off, type:

```
:set nocindent
```

2.4.3   Using Tags with VIM

The `ctags` program can be used to build a tags file that is readable by VIM and can be used to quickly navigate among multiple source code files. Building the tags file is done in the same way as described earlier in the chapter for Jed, but you must us the `ctags` program instead of `etags`.

```
$ ctags *.[ch]
```

This builds the *tags* file in the current directory.

To build a tags file for an entire project that spans many subdirectories, from the main project directory, issue the `ctags` command with the –R option to recurse the directories.

```
$ ctags -R
```

From within VIM, if you need to jump to a particular function that is in the current file, place the cursor on the appropriate function and press `^]`. This command uses the tags file to locate the function and reads that file into the buffer.

To open a file and locate a function that is not present in the current buffer, type:

```
:tag <tagname>
```

where `<tagname>` is the name of the function that you are looking for. This will load the file into the buffer and position the cursor at that appropriate tag.

To list the tags that you have jumped to in this editing session, type **:tags**. The output from this command is shown below.

```
:tags
# TO tag            FROM line  in file/text
  1  1 main                 1  ./arch/alpha/boot/tools/mkbb.c
  2  1 perror             116  ./arch/alpha/boot/tools/mkbb.c
>
```

By pressing the number listed in the left column, you can return to previously accessed tags.

In large projects, it would not be uncommon for one function to be referenced in several places. In the event that multiple tags are created with the same name, you can select from the list of similar tags by using the `:tselect` command. To select from a list functions, type **:tselect <tagname>**. When the `tselect` command completes, you will be presented with a list of matching functions from which to choose. When you type in the appropriate number from the left-hand column, that function will be opened in the buffer.

2.4.4   Folding Code

VIM can use several methods for folding code. The most useful of these for application programming is the indent method. The variable `foldmethod` determines how the folding will take place. To indent set the mode by typing:

```
:set foldmethod=indent
```

This command can also be set as a default by entering it in the ~/.vimrc configuration file.

When this option is set and a file is opened, VIM will parse the file looking for initial tab sequences in order to determine the various indent levels and fold the file automatically. In order to open or unfold a section, use **zo** and to close or refold a section, use **zc**.

The commands **zm** and **zr** can also be used to increase and decrease the amount of folding currently being done to a file. By issuing the `zr` command, the amount of folding being done is reduced by one *shiftwidth* level. That is to say, one level of tabbing is revealed in the code. The **zm** command reverses this and folds up one level of indentation every time that it is used.

2.5   References and Resources

1. Learning GNU Emacs, Second Edition, Debra Cameron, Bill Rosenblatt & Eric Raymond, O'Reilly & Associates, Inc., ISBN:1-56592-152-6.
2. GNU Emacs home page, http://www.gnu.org/software/emacs/emacs.html
3. Jed home page, http://space.mit.edu/~davis/jed/
4. GNU Emacs Lisp Reference Manual, http://www.gnu.org/manual/elisp-manual-21-2.8/html_chapter/elisp.html
5. Coffee.el, a fanciful elisp program to have Emacs make coffee, http://www.chez.com/emarsden/downloads/coffee.el
6. Xemacs home page. http://www.xemacs.org/
7. VIM Home page. http://www.vim.org

## CHAPTER 3

Compilers and Assemblers

All development systems are essentially a combination of many tools. Compilers, assemblers and debuggers are integral parts of these development tools. Fortunately Linux has a large number of tools available for software developers. These tools have a very rich set of features that we shall discuss in this and coming chapters. The basic reason for including this chapter is to enable a reader to use compilers and assembler in a development environment in a productive way. However this chapter is not a tutorial on any language or programming technique. Examples of code listings presented in this chapter are very simple and are intended to demonstrate the function of development tools.

GNU C compiler, most commonly known as GCC, is the most important part of this discussion. This compiler can be used to compile programs written in the following languages:

- ANSI C
- Objective C
- C++
- Java
- Fortran
- Pascal, after converting Pascal code to C

GCC recently added the capability to generate object code from Java source code. Work has also been done on Ada support.

GNU assembler is often needed in projects where you want to have tight control over a particular part of code and want to write it in assembly language. Most of the time people also write boot code for embedded systems in assembly language. The compiler uses assembler during the compilation process to generate object code.

In addition to the most common compilers, we shall also discuss the use of some less common languages in the Linux environment. These languages include the following:

- Oberon
- Smalltalk
- Ada

The compilation process is completed in different stages. These stages are:

- Preprocessing
- Compiling to generate assembly language code
- Assembling to generate object code
- Linking to generate executable code

The GNU compiler takes help from many programs during this process and can be used to generate intermediate files. For example, the compiler can generate Assembly language code from a C source code file.

This chapter provides information about the GNU set of compilers and how to build a software development environment using GNU tools. During this process you will also learn the building process for the GNU C library, most commonly known as glibc.

3.1   Introduction to GNU C and C++ Compilers

The GNU compiler, most commonly known as GCC, is not a single program. It is a large set of programs, libraries and other utilities that work together to build source code into executable form. A user, however, mostly interacts with gcc command. The gcc program acts as sort of a front end for compilers and other utilities. This section is an introduction to the compiler and its capabilities.

3.1.1   Languages Supported by GCC

GCC is a family of compilers, also known as the GNU Compiler Collection. GCC supports multiple languages, including:

- C
- C++
- Fortran
- Objective C
- Java

Front-end preprocessors for many other languages also exist for GCC. For example, you can use a Pascal language front end with GCC.

C is the primary language and GCC supports ANSI/ISO standards put forward in 1989-90 and 1995-96. These standards are also sometimes called C90 and C95, respectively. Another revision of the ANSI/ISO C language standard was made in 1999 (known as C99), and GCC does not yet fully support this revision. You can find out the current status of support for this revision at http://gcc.gnu.org/gcc-3.0/c99status.html.

Support for these variations in standards can be selected using command line switches when compiling programs. For example, to compile programs according to original 1989-90 standards, you can use one of the following command line switches:

```
-ansi
-std=c89
-std=iso9899:1990
```

The GCC compiler supports Objective C source code. Information on Objective C can be found in different books and online resources. However there is no standard for Objective C yet. Later in this chapter you will learn how to compile a simple program written in Objective C.

GCC supports GNU Fortran language and we shall discuss later in this chapter how to compile programs written in Fortran.

Support for Java is a new addition to GCC and we shall see how GCC handles Java code with the GCJ compiler. This compiler, which is a part of the GCC family of compilers, can create an executable object from Java source code files.

Standard libraries are not part of the GCC compiler. You have to separately install libraries. The most common library used with the compiler is the GNU C library and we shall see how to get and install this library on Linux systems. The GNU C library (also known as glibc) provides support for:

- ANSI/ISO C
- POSIX
- BSD
- System V
- X/Open

For more information on languages supported by GCC, please see http://gcc.gnu.org/onlinedocs/gcc-3.0.2/gcc_2.html.

3.1.2   New Features in GCC 3.x

There are many new features in GNU compiler starting with version 3.0. Some of these are discussed below briefly. In addition to that, version 3.0.x also includes many fixes for bugs present in 2.x versions.

3.1.2.1   Optimization Improvements

A major improvement in this version is new optimization features. Some of these features greatly improve compile and run-time performance. Important features are listed below.

- Basic block reordering pass is now optimized. In some cases, it improves performance by eliminating a JMP instruction in assembly code. An explanation can be found at http://www.gnu.org/software/gcc/news/reorder.html.
- A new register-renaming pass is included.
- Static Single Assignment or SSA is introduced in GCC. A dead code elimination pass is included in new versions of GCC to improve optimization.
- A global Null pointer elimination test elimination pass is included. Information about this enhancement can be found at http://www.gnu.org/software/gcc/news/null.html.
- New optimizations for `stdio.h`, `string.h` and old BSD functions are added.

3.1.2.2   Support of new Languages

Support of Java is now added through GCJ compiler. It includes a run-time library having non-GUI Java classes.

3.1.2.3   Language Improvements

There are some improvements in the support of different languages and these are listed below.

- New C++ support library is added. Details are available at http://www.gnu.org/software/gcc/libstdc++/.
- A new inliner is added that significantly reduces both memory utilization as well as compile time. Details are present at http://www.gnu.org/software/gcc/news/inlining.html.
- The C preprocessor is rewritten with many improvements. Details are available at http://www.gnu.org/software/gcc/news/dependencies.html.
- More warning messages and a new warning option are added.
- There are many improvements in Fortran language support area and these are listed on http://gcc.gnu.org/onlinedocs/g77_news.html.
- There are other improvements that are not listed here. Go to the GCC home page at http://gcc.gnu.org/ for a complete list.

3.1.2.4   Addition of New Targets

Support for the following platforms is added.

- HP-UX 11
- IA-64
- MCore 210
- MCore 340
- Xscale
- Atmel AVR Micro- controller
- D30V from Mitsubishi
- AM33 from Matsushita
- FR30 from Fujitsu
- 68HC11
- 68HC12
- picoJava from Sun Microsystems

3.1.2.5   Target Specific Improvements

Some of the improvements are as follows:

- New back end is added for x86 targets
- New back end for Arm and Strongarm
- Improvements in PowerPC code generation

3.1.2.6   Improved Documentation

Significant improvements in this area are:

- Many manuals are re-written.
- There are some improvements to man pages.

3.1.2.7   Additional GCC Version 3.0.1 Improvements

This version includes some bug fixes in version 3.0. It also addresses some bugs for exception handling. A port to IBM S/390 is added and some improvements in cross-compiling are made.

3.1.2.8   Additional GCC Version 3.0.2 Improvements

This version mostly contains some bug fixes.

3.1.2.9   GCC Version 3.0.3 Improvements

This version contains some more bug fixes as well as improvement in generation of debugging information.

At the time of revision of this book, GCC 3.1 is released and it has all of these features, among others.

3.2   Installing GNU Compiler

In most cases, GCC comes with all Linux distributions. However you can download the latest version, and build and install it according to your requirements. You may also need to build your compiler if you are building a cross-compiling development system. The best way to build a new version of the compiler is to have some pre-installed and pre-configured Linux distribution on your system that will be used to build the new compiler. For the purpose of writing this book, we have used Red Hat 7.1 but the process is the same on any distribution of Linux.

The installation process is done in multiple steps. After downloading, you have to untar the source code and build it in a directory. This directory should be separate from the source code directory tree. The building process includes configuration and compiling stages. Once you have successfully created the new compiler, you can install it in a directory of your choice. It is advised to keep this installation directory separate from the location where the original compiler is installed.

3.2.1   Downloading

You can download the latest version of GCC from ftp://ftp.gnu.org/gnu/gcc/. I downloaded GCC 3.0.4 and it is about 17.5 MB. You can also find a mirror site near you to get GCC. A list of mirror sites is available on http://www.gnu.org/order/ftp.html.

3.2.2   Building and Installing GCC

The GCC installation process can be divided into four steps for simplicity and understanding.

1. Download and extract
2. Configure
3. Build
4. Install

3.2.2.1   Download and Extract

First create a directory where you will unpack the source code. Use the `tar` command to unpack the code. For our purpose, I have created a directory `/gcc3` to compile and build the GCC compiler. The untar process looks like the following and it creates a directory `gcc-3.0.4` under `/gcc3` directory.

```
[root@laptop /gcc3]# tar zxvf gcc-3.0.4.tar.gz
gcc-3.0.4/
gcc-3.0.4/INSTALL/
gcc-3.0.4/INSTALL/index.html
gcc-3.0.4/INSTALL/README
gcc-3.0.4/INSTALL/specific.html
gcc-3.0.4/INSTALL/download.html
gcc-3.0.4/INSTALL/configure.html
```

```
gcc-3.0.4/INSTALL/build.html
gcc-3.0.4/INSTALL/test.html
gcc-3.0.4/INSTALL/finalinstall.html
gcc-3.0.4/INSTALL/binaries.html
gcc-3.0.4/INSTALL/gfdl.html
gcc-3.0.4/.cvsignore
gcc-3.0.4/COPYING
gcc-3.0.4/COPYING.LIB
gcc-3.0.4/ChangeLog
gcc-3.0.4/MAINTAINERS
gcc-3.0.4/Makefile.in
gcc-3.0.4/README
```

This is a partial output of the command. Most of the output is truncated to save space.

3.2.2.2   Running `configure` Script

After uncompressing the source code, the first thing is to run the `configure` script. This script is found in `/gcc3/gcc-3.0.4` directory. You can specify three major things when you run the `configure` script.

1. Build machine. This is the machine where you compile and build the compiler.
2. Host machine. This is the machine where compiler will be installed. This is usually the same as the build machine.
3. Target machine. This is the machine for which the newly built compiler will generate executable code. If you are building a native compiler, this is the same machine as the host machine. If you are building a cross-compiler, this machine will be different than the host machine.

Each of these machines names are used in the following format:

CPUname-CompanyName-SystemName

For example, if you want to build a compiler that will run on a sparc processor made by Sun Microsystems and on SunOS 4.1 operating system, the command line for `configure` script will be as follows:

```
./configure -host=sparc-sun-sunos4.1
```

Please see a list of supported systems at http://gcc.gnu.org/onlinedocs/gcc-3.0.4/gcc_4.html .

For a native compiler (a compiler that runs on the same machine where it is built and generates code for the same machine), you don't need to specify any options on the command line when you run the `configure` script. However, if you are building a cross-compiler, you must specify the target machine. Similarly, if you are building a compiler that will be installed on some other machine, you have to specify the host machine.

N O T E   There may be some other requirements when you are
building a non-native compiler.

It is recommended to run the `configure` script in a directory other than the source code
directory so that the source code tree is completely separate from the place where you build the
compiler. For the sake of this example, I have created a directory `/gcc3/objdir` and I ran the
`configure` script from that directory. As you already know, the source code tree is under the `/
gcc3/gcc-3.0.4` directory. You may need to add a prefix for GCC installation files. The pre-
fix shows the directory where GCC files will be finally installed. The default prefix is `/usr/
local`. This means that GCC binary files will be installed in `/usr/local/bin` directory.
For installation purposes, I have selected `/opt/gcc-3.0.4` directory as the prefix. In a typical development environment, you would do something similar to that. Just create a directory
under `/opt` and install all of your tools and applications under `/opt`. The following command
line will configure the GCC compilation process and will create many files under `/gcc3/
objdir`. These files will be used later on to build the compiler. When you start the `config-
ure` script, the following messages will start scrolling up.

```
[root@laptop objdir]# ../gcc-3.0.4/configure --prefix=/opt/
gcc-3.0.4
Configuring for a i686-pc-linux-gnu host.
Created "Makefile" in /gcc3/gcc-3.0.4 using "mt-frag"
Configuring libiberty...
creating cache ../config.cache
checking host system type... i686-pc-linux-gnu
checking build system type... i686-pc-linux-gnu
checking for ar... ar
checking for ranlib... ranlib
checking for gcc... gcc
checking whether we are using GNU C... yes
checking whether gcc accepts -g... yes
checking for POSIXized ISC... no
checking for working const... yes
checking for inline... inline
checking for a BSD compatible install... /usr/bin/install -c
checking how to run the C preprocessor... gcc -E
checking for sys/file.h... yes
checking for sys/param.h... yes
checking for limits.h... yes
checking for stdlib.h... yes
checking for string.h... yes
```

Most of the output is truncated from the configure script to save space. When the configure script is completed, you will get back the command prompt. Now you may start building the
compiler.

If you want to enable threads on Linux systems, you can use `--enable-threads=posix` as a command line option.

3.2.2.3 Building GCC

It is recommended that you use GNU `make` for building purpose. Running the `make bootstrap` command will build the compiler, libraries and related utilities. Following is part of the output when you start the building process.

```
[root@laptop objdir]# make bootstrap
make[1]: Entering directory `/gcc3/objdir/libiberty'
if [ x"" != x ] && [ ! -d pic ]; then \
  mkdir pic; \
else true; fi
touch stamp-picdir
if [ x"" != x ]; then \
  gcc -c -DHAVE_CONFIG_H -g -O2 -I. -I../../gcc-3.0.4/
libiberty/../include  -W -Wall -Wtraditional -pedantic  ../../
gcc-3.0.4/libiberty/argv.c -o pic/argv.o; \
else true; fi
gcc -c -DHAVE_CONFIG_H -g -O2 -I. -I../../gcc-3.0.4/libiberty/
../include  -W -Wall -Wtraditional -pedantic ../../gcc-3.0.4/
libiberty/argv.c
if [ x"" != x ]; then \
  gcc -c -DHAVE_CONFIG_H -g -O2 -I. -I../../gcc-3.0.4/
libiberty/../include  -W -Wall -Wtraditional -pedantic  ../../
gcc-3.0.4/libiberty/choose-temp.c -o pic/choose-temp.o; \
else true; fi
gcc -c -DHAVE_CONFIG_H -g -O2 -I. -I../../gcc-3.0.4/libiberty/
../include  -W -Wall -Wtraditional -pedantic ../../gcc-3.0.4/
libiberty/choose-temp.c
if [ x"" != x ]; then \
  gcc -c -DHAVE_CONFIG_H -g -O2 -I. -I../../gcc-3.0.4/
libiberty/../include  -W -Wall -Wtraditional -pedantic  ../../
gcc-3.0.4/libiberty/concat.c -o pic/concat.o; \
else true; fi
gcc -c -DHAVE_CONFIG_H -g -O2 -I. -I../../gcc-3.0.4/libiberty/
../include  -W -Wall -Wtraditional -pedantic ../../gcc-3.0.4/
libiberty/concat.c
if [ x"" != x ]; then \
  gcc -c -DHAVE_CONFIG_H -g -O2 -I. -I../../gcc-3.0.4/
libiberty/../include  -W -Wall -Wtraditional -pedantic  ../../
gcc-3.0.4/libiberty/cplus-dem.c -o pic/cplus-dem.o; \
else true; fi
```

Again most of the output is truncated. The building process may take a long time depending upon how powerful a computer you are using for building GCC. The process is completed in three stages. Stage 1 and stage 2 binaries are deleted as soon as they are no longer needed. Typically this building process will do the following:

- Build some basic tools like bison, gperf and so on. These tools are necessary to continue the compilation process.
- Build target tools like gas, ld, binutils and so on.
- Perform a three-stage bootstrap of the compiler.
- Perform comparison of stage 2 and stage 3.
- Build run-time libraries.
- Remove unnecessary files.

You should have enough disk space to build GCC. If you are short of disk space, you can use the `bootstrap-lean` option on the command line instead of `bootstrap`.

3.2.2.4   Final Install

The final installation process is necessary to move GCC binaries under the directory used as a prefix during the `configure` script execution. We have used `/opt/gcc-3.0.4` as the prefix directory. Executing the following command in `/gcc3/objdir` will move GCC binaries in a tree structure under `/opt/gcc-3.0.4`.

```
make install
```

A typical directory tree after installation is shown below.

```
[root@conformix gcc-3.0.4]# tree -d |more
.
|-- bin
|-- include
|   |-- g++-v3
|   |   |-- backward
|   |   |-- bits
|   |   |-- ext
|   |   `-- i686-pc-linux-gnu
|   |       `-- bits
|   |-- gcj
|   |-- gnu
|   |   |-- awt
|   |   |   `-- j2d
|   |   |-- classpath
|   |   |-- gcj
|   |   |   |-- awt
|   |   |   |-- convert
|   |   |   |-- io
|   |   |   |-- jni
|   |   |   |-- math
|   |   |   |-- protocol
```

```
|    |    |    |    |-- file
|    |    |    |    |-- http
|    |    |    |    `-- jar
|    |    |    |-- runtime
|    |    |    |-- text
|    |    |    `-- util
|    |    `-- java
|    |         |-- beans
|    |         |    |-- editors
|    |         |    `-- info
|    |         |-- io
|    |         |-- lang
|    |         |    `-- reflect
|    |         |-- locale
|    |         `-- security
|    |              `-- provider
|    `-- java
|         |-- applet
|         |-- awt
|         |    |-- color
|         |    |-- datatransfer
|         |    |-- event
|         |    |-- geom
|         |    |-- image
|         |    `-- peer
|         |-- beans
|         |    `-- beancontext
|         |-- io
|         |-- lang
|         |    |-- ref
|         |    `-- reflect
|         |-- math
|         |-- net
|         |-- security
|         |    |-- cert
|         |    |-- interfaces
|         |    `-- spec
|         |-- sql
|         |-- text
|         `-- util
|              |-- jar
|              `-- zip
|-- info
|-- lib
|    `-- gcc-lib
|         `-- i686-pc-linux-gnu
|              `-- 3.0.4
|                   `-- include
```

```
|                                    |-- SDL
|                                    |-- X11 -> root/usr/X11R6/include/X11
|                                    |-- linux
|                                    |-- mozilla
|                                    |-- ncurses
|                                    |-- objc
|                                    |-- openssl
|                                    |-- pcap
|                                    |   `-- net
|                                    |-- pgsql
|                                    |   `-- utils
|                                    |-- root
|                                    |   `-- usr
|                                    |       `-- X11R6
|                                    |           `-- include
|                                    |               `-- X11
|                                    |-- schily
|                                    |   `-- scg
|                                    |-- slang
|                                    |-- ucd-snmp
|                                    |-- w3c-libwww
|                                    |-- wnn
|                                    `-- wnn6
|-- man
|   |-- man1
|   `-- man7
`-- share

95 directories
[root@conformix gcc-3.0.4]#
```

N O T E   Detailed instructions for compiling and installing GCC
are available at http://gcc.gnu.org/onlinedocs/gcc-3.0.4/gcc_4.html
as well as at http://gcc.gnu.org/install/.

3.2.3   Environment Variables

The GCC compiler relies on many environment variables for its operation. These variables are used for different purposes including location of library and header files, location of helping programs and so on. Some important variables and their respective use are introduced in this section.

TMPDIR   This variable shows location of temporary file location. GCC uses
                              this location to store temporary files during the compiling and
                              linking processes.

GCC_EXEC_PREFIX	If this variable is set, GCC will look into the directory to find sub programs.
COMPILER_PATH	This is a colon-separated list of directories that GCC uses to find out sub programs if search fails using GCC_EXEC_PREFIX variable.
LIBRARY_PATH	This is a colon-separated list of directories that is used to find out libraries for linking process.
C_INCLUDE_PATH	Colon separated list of directories to find out header files for C programs.
OBJC_INCLUDE_PATH	Colon separated list of directories to find out header files for Objective C programs.
CPLUS_INCLUDE_PATH	Colon separated list of directories to find out header files for C++ programs.
LD_LIBRARY_PATH	Path for shared libraries.

There are other environment variables and settings that GCC uses while building a target. You can display these using the –v command line switch with the gcc command when you compile a program. This will show you the path including files, programs used during the compilation process, and command line arguments and switches passed to each of these programs. The following is the output of the command when you compile the hello.c program.

```
[rr@conformix 4]$ gcc -v hello.c
Reading specs from /opt/gcc-3.0.4/lib/gcc-lib/i686-pc-linux-
gnu/3.0.4/specs
Configured with: ../gcc-3.0.4/configure --prefix=/opt/gcc-
3.0.4 --enable-threads=posix
Thread model: posix
gcc version 3.0.4
 /opt/gcc-3.0.4/lib/gcc-lib/i686-pc-linux-gnu/3.0.4/cc1 -lang-
c -v -D__GNUC__=3 -D__GNUC_MINOR__=0 -D__GNUC_PATCHLEVEL__=4 -
D__ELF__ -Dunix -Dlinux -D__ELF__ -D__unix__ -D__linux__ -
D__unix -D__linux -Asystem=posix -D__NO_INLINE__ -
D__STDC_HOSTED__=1 -Acpu=i386 -Amachine=i386 -Di386 -D__i386 -
D__i386__ -D__tune_i686__ -D__tune_pentiumpro__ hello.c -quiet
-dumpbase hello.c -version -o /tmp/ccJsUmYa.s
GNU CPP version 3.0.4 (cpplib) (i386 Linux/ELF)
GNU C version 3.0.4 (i686-pc-linux-gnu)
compiled by GNU C version 3.0.4.
ignoring nonexistent directory "/opt/gcc-3.0.4/i686-pc-linux-
gnu/include"
#include "..." search starts here:
#include <...> search starts here:
 /usr/local/include
```

```
/opt/gcc-3.0.4/include
/opt/gcc-3.0.4/lib/gcc-lib/i686-pc-linux-gnu/3.0.4/include
/usr/include
End of search list.
 as --traditional-format -V -Qy -o /tmp/ccn7wLgw.o /tmp/
ccJsUmYa.s
GNU assembler version 2.10.91 (i386-redhat-linux) using BFD
version 2.10.91.0.2
 /opt/gcc-3.0.4/lib/gcc-lib/i686-pc-linux-gnu/3.0.4/collect2 -
m elf_i386 -dynamic-linker /lib/ld-linux.so.2 /usr/lib/crt1.o
/usr/lib/crti.o /opt/gcc-3.0.4/lib/gcc-lib/i686-pc-linux-gnu/
3.0.4/crtbegin.o -L/opt/gcc-3.0.4/lib/gcc-lib/i686-pc-linux-
gnu/3.0.4 -L/opt/gcc-3.0.4/lib/gcc-lib/i686-pc-linux-gnu/
3.0.4/../../.. /tmp/ccn7wLgw.o -lgcc -lc -lgcc /opt/gcc-3.0.4/
lib/gcc-lib/i686-pc-linux-gnu/3.0.4/crtend.o /usr/lib/crtn.o
[rr@conformix 4]$
```

If you examine the output of this command, you can find out which helper programs gcc uses and what command line switches are passed to these programs.

3.2.4   Post-Installation Tasks

There are a few tasks that you need to carry out after the installation process of the compilers.

3.2.4.1   Setting PATH Variable

This is the first important task. Your PATH variable must include the directory where GCC binaries are installed. We have installed these in /opt/gcc-3.0.4/bin directory because we used /opt/gcc-3.0.4 as the prefix while running the configure script. This directory should come before the directories where the old compiler is installed. A typical command to do this in bash or other POSIX-compliant shells to include our installation location is as follows:

```
export PATH=/opt/gcc-3.0.4/bin:$PATH
```

where /opt/gcc-3.0.4/bin is the path to newly installed compilers.

It is also extremely important that you make sure the GCC in the path is the correct one. The 'which gcc' command will provide this.

3.2.4.2   Setting the Location of Libraries

There are two steps to set up the location of libraries. First edit /etc/ld/so.config and add the path of any newly created libraries. This directory is /opt/gcc-3.0.4/lib because we used –prefix=/opt/gcc-3.0.4 while building the compiler. Typical contents of this file after adding the new directory are as follows:

```
/opt/gcc-3.0.4/lib
/usr/lib
/usr/kerberos/lib
/usr/X11R6/lib
/usr/lib/sane
```

```
/usr/lib/qt-2.3.0/lib
/usr/lib/mysql
/usr/lib/qt-1.45/lib
```

After editing this file, execute the `ldconfig` program, which will configure dynamic linker binding. You can use the −v command line option to get more information when you run this command. Note that the order of commands is important.

The next step is to setup the `LD_LIBRARY_PATH` variable. You can do this by adding the following line at the end of `/etc/profile` file so that it is set for all users at login time.

```
export LD_LIBRARY_PATH=/opt/gcc-3.0.4/lib
```

Again note that this is the path where new library files are installed. Please note that if you make these changes, some older programs that are compiled for some other set of shared libraries may not function properly.

3.2.4.3   Setting Location of include Files

The default search path for include files can be found by executing the following command:

```
[rr@conformix 4]$ gcc -v -E -
Reading specs from /opt/gcc-3.0.4/lib/gcc-lib/i686-pc-linux-
gnu/3.0.4/specs
Configured with: ../gcc-3.0.4/configure --prefix=/opt/gcc-
3.0.4 --enable-threads=posix
Thread model: posix
gcc version 3.0.4
 /opt/gcc-3.0.4/lib/gcc-lib/i686-pc-linux-gnu/3.0.4/cpp0 -
lang-c -v -D__GNUC__=3 -D__GNUC_MINOR__=0 -
D__GNUC_PATCHLEVEL__=4 -D__ELF__ -Dunix -Dlinux -D__ELF__ -
D__unix__ -D__linux__ -D__unix -D__linux -Asystem=posix -
D__NO_INLINE__ -D__STDC_HOSTED__=1 -Acpu=i386 -Amachine=i386 -
Di386 -D__i386 -D__i386__ -D__tune_i686__ -
D__tune_pentiumpro__ -
GNU CPP version 3.0.4 (cpplib) (i386 Linux/ELF)
ignoring nonexistent directory "/opt/gcc-3.0.4/i686-pc-linux-
gnu/include"
#include "..." search starts here:
#include <...> search starts here:
 /usr/local/include
 /opt/gcc-3.0.4/include
 /opt/gcc-3.0.4/lib/gcc-lib/i686-pc-linux-gnu/3.0.4/include
 /usr/include
End of search list.
```

The last part of the output shows that include files will be searched in the following directories by default.

```
/usr/local/include
```

```
/opt/gcc-3.0.4/include
/opt/gcc-3.0.4/lib/gcc-lib/i686-pc-linux-gnu/3.0.4/
include
/usr/include
```

You can place include files in other directories if you have set the C_INCLUDE_PATH environment variable. Setting this variable to /opt using the following command will include / opt directory also in the search list. Also note that order is once again extremely important.

```
export C_INCLUDE_PATH=/opt
```

If you again execute the gcc -v -E - command, /opt path will be included in the last part of the output.

To set additional include paths permanently for all users, it is a good idea to add a line with the export command in /etc/profile file.

3.2.4.4   Setting Manual Pages Path

To be able to use manual pages installed with GCC, you have to add a line in the /etc/ man.config file. This will enable the man command to also look into the /opt/gcc-3.0.4/man directory when searching for manual pages. The line looks like the following:

```
MANPATH /opt/gcc-3.0.4/man
```

Location of this line with respect to other MANPATH entries is important. If you put this line after other entries, you will still get the same old man pages. That is why it is recommended to put this entry BEFORE any other line that starts with MANPATH keyword in this file.

3.2.5   What Not to Do when Installing Development Tools

When building GCC, don't build it into the source directory. I would also recommend not installing your development tools in the default location (under /usr/local). Instead use some place under the /opt directory. This way if something goes wrong, you can just delete this directory under /opt without making any other change in the system. If you install these tools in the default location, you may overwrite some existing files and may not be able to reverse the installation process.

3.3   Compiling a Program

The GCC compiler is commonly invoked using the gcc command. The command accepts many command line switches that can be used to invoke different options for the compilation process. You can use the same command line switch multiple times. For example, if you need to specify multiple include paths, you can use -I option multiple times. However you can't combine two switches into one. For example -c and -o can't be combined as -co. This section provides information about different methods of compilation and things you need to consider in the compilation process. Please note that in most of software development projects, you don't invoke gcc from the command line. Instead, the GNU make utility that reads one or many Makefiles is used. These Makefiles contain information about how the compiler will be invoked and what command line switches will be used. Information about GNU `make` and Makefiles is presented in Chapter 5.

3.3.1 Simple Compilation

Consider the following C source code file, which is named `hello.c`. We shall frequently refer to this program in this as well as coming chapters.

```
#include <stdio.h>
main ()
{
   printf("Hello world\n");
}
```

To compile this file, you just need to run the following command.

```
[rr@conformix 4]$ gcc hello.c
[rr@conformix 4]$
```

By default, this command will generate an output file named `a.out`, which can be executed on the command line as follows:

```
[rr@conformix 4]$ ./a.out
Hello world
[rr@conformix 4]$
```

Note that regardless of the name of your source code file, the name of the output file is always `a.out`. You may actually know what an ordinary `a.out` file is, but this isn't one of them. It is an `elf` file, despite its name. If you want to create an output file with a different name, you have to use the –o command line option. The following command creates an output file with name `hello`.

```
gcc hello.c -o hello
```

As you may have noted, the above commands do both the compiling and linking processes in a single step. If you don't want to link the program, then simple compilation of `hello.c` file can be done with the following command. The output file will be `hello.o` and will contain object code.

```
gcc -c hello.c
```

Note that both –c and –o command line switches can be used simultaneously. The following command compiles `hello.c` and produces an output file `test.o` which is not yet linked.

```
gcc -c hello.c  -o test.o
```

Usually when you compile many files in a project, you don't create `a.out` files. Either you compile many files into object files and then link them together into an application or make executables with the same name as the source code file.

3.3.2   Default File Types

GCC can recognize an input file by the last part of its name, sometimes called an extension. Table 3-1 shows file types and the extensions used with them. Depending upon a particular extension, gcc takes appropriate action to build the output file.

Table 3-1 File types used with GCC

File Extension	File Type
.c	C source code file.
.cc	C++ source code file.
.cp	C++ source code file.
.cxx	C++ source code file.
.cpp	C++ source code file.
.c+	C++ source code file.
.C	C++ source code file.
.m	Objective C source code file.
.F	Fortran source code file.
.fpp	Fortran source code file.
.FPP	Fortran source code file.
.h	C header file.
.i	C source code file. GCC does not preprocess it.
.ii	C++ source code file. GCC does not preprocess it.
.mi	Objective C source code file. GCC does not preprocess it.
.f	Fortran source code file. GCC does not preprocess it.
.for	Fortran source code file. GCC does not preprocess it.
.FOR	Fortran source code file. GCC does not preprocess it.
.s	Assembler code. GCC does not preprocess it.
.S	Assembler file.

This means that if you use command gcc hello.c, GCC will consider hello.c as a C program and will invoke appropriate helper programs to build the output. However, if you use gcc hello.cpp command, GCC will consider hello.cpp as a C++ program and will compile it accordingly. You can also select a language type with a particular file using –x command line option. Table 3-2 lists languages that can be selected with this option.

Table 3-2 Selecting languages with –x option.

Option	Language
-x c (lowercase c)	C language selection
-x c++	C++ file
-x objective-c	Objective C
-x assembler	Assembler file
-x f77	Fortran file
-x java	Java language file

Note that –x option applies to all the files that follow until you turn it off using the –x none option on the command line. This is especially important when you use the GNU make utility discussed in Chapter 5.

By default, the object file created by GCC has .o extension, replacing the original extension of the file. You can create output file with a particular name using –o command line option. The following command creates test.o file from hello.c.

```
gcc –c hello.c –o test.o
```

3.3.3   Compiling to Intermediate Levels

The compilation process involves many steps like preprocessing, assembling and linking. By default GCC carries out all of these processes and generates executable code as you have seen earlier. However, you can force GCC not to do all of these steps. For example, using the –c command line option, the gcc command will only compile a source code file and will not generate executable object code. As you already know, the following command compiles file hello.c and creates an object file hello.o.

```
gcc –c hello.c
```

If you look at the type of the newly created object file using the file command, you can see that this is not a linked file. This is shown in the following command output.

```
[root@conformix chap-03]# file hello.o
hello.o: ELF 32-bit LSB relocatable, Intel 80386, version 1,
not stripped
[root@conformix chap-03]#
```

3.3.3.1   Creating Assembler Code

Using the −S (uppercase S) command line option, you can stop the GCC compiler just before the assembler process. The output is an assembler file with a .s extension. The following command creates an output file hello.s from source code file hello.c.

```
gcc -S hello.c
```

If you look at the output file, you can see the assembler code. Contents of the input file are as follows:

```
#include <stdio.h>
main()
{
  printf ("Hello world\n");
}
```

The output assembler code is shown below:

```
[root@conformix chap-03]# cat hello.s
        .file   "hello.c"
        .version        "01.01"
gcc2_compiled.:
                .section        .rodata
.LC0:
        .string "Hello world\n"
.text
        .align 4
.globl main
        .type   main,@function
main:
        pushl   %ebp
        movl    %esp, %ebp
        subl    $8, %esp
        subl    $12, %esp
        pushl   $.LC0
        call    printf
        addl    $16, %esp
        leave
        ret
.Lfe1:
        .size   main,.Lfe1-main
        .ident  "GCC: (GNU) 2.96 20000731 (Red Hat Linux 7.1
2.96-81)"
[root@conformix chap-03]#
```

This assembler code may be used with some assembler, like GNU as. Here *as* is not word "as" but name of the GNU Assembler which is often written as *GNU as as*, later on. It can also be assembled and linked to create and execute. Please note that for the above command, the compiler that is included in RedHat distribution was used.

3.3.4 Compilation with Debug Support

If you want to debug a program after compiling with `gcc`, you have to include debug information in the compiled program. The debug information is included in object file using the –g command line switch with `gcc`. The following command creates the `hello.o` file that contains debug information.

```
[rr@conformix 4]$ gcc -g -c hello.c
[rr@conformix 4]$
```

Note that when you compile a program with debug information, the size may be quite large as compared to a file compiled without debug information. In the example program of `hello.c`, the size of `hello.o` is 908 bytes when compiled without debug information. The size of `hello.o` is 10780 bytes when it is compiled with debug information.

You can use multiple debug levels with –g option. The default debug level is 2 which is equivalent to using –g2 command line option. If you use –g3 command line option, information about macros is also included which makes it easier to debug macros.

N O T E You can use the debug option with optimization options. Optimization options are discussed later in this chapter.

With the –a option on the command line, you can also include some profiling information in the object code.

You can also use some command line switches to provide extra information. For example, one useful thing is to print out a list of directories that the `gcc` command searches to find files. The following command will print all directories that `gcc` uses to search libraries, programs and so on.

```
[rr@conformix 4]$ gcc -print-search-dirs hello.c -o hello
install: /usr/lib/gcc-lib/i386-redhat-linux/2.96/
programs: =/usr/lib/gcc-lib/i386-redhat-linux/2.96/:/usr/lib/
gcc-lib/i386-redhat-linux/2.96/:/usr/lib/gcc-lib/i386-redhat-
linux/:/usr/lib/gcc/i386-redhat-linux/2.96/:/usr/lib/gcc/i386-
redhat-linux/:/usr/lib/gcc-lib/i386-redhat-linux/2.96/../../
../../i386-redhat-linux/bin/i386-redhat-linux/2.96/:/usr/lib/
gcc-lib/i386-redhat-linux/2.96/../../../../i386-redhat-linux/
bin/
libraries: =/usr/lib/gcc-lib/i386-redhat-linux/2.96/:/usr/lib/
gcc/i386-redhat-linux/2.96/:/usr/lib/gcc-lib/i386-redhat-
linux/2.96/../../../../i386-redhat-linux/lib/i386-redhat-
linux/2.96/:/usr/lib/gcc-lib/i386-redhat-linux/2.96/../../../
../i386-redhat-linux/lib/:/usr/lib/gcc-lib/i386-redhat-linux/
2.96/../../../i386-redhat-linux/2.96/:/usr/lib/gcc-lib/i386-
redhat-linux/2.96/../../../:/lib/i386-redhat-linux/2.96/:/lib/
:/usr/lib/i386-redhat-linux/2.96/:/usr/lib/
[rr@conformix 4]$
```

Here I have used GCC version 2.96 that came with RedHat Linux 7.1 and you can see directories and references to this version information also.

You can also find the amount of time taken by each process during compilation. The following command displays time taken during each step of building the output file.

```
[rr@conformix 4]$ gcc -time hello.c -o hello
# cpp0 0.06 0.00
# cc1 0.08 0.01
# as 0.02 0.00
# collect2 0.12 0.03
[rr@conformix 4]$
```

It is also evident from the output of the above command that GCC has used four other programs (cpp0, cc1, as and collect2) during the compilation process.

3.3.5   Compilation with Optimization

The first objective of a compiler is to generate output code swiftly. The compiler does not do any code optimization to make the compile time short. However you can instruct gcc to compile code with code optimization. This is done using –O (uppercase O, not zero) on the command line. Different optimization levels can be designated by using a number suffix with this option. For example, –O2 will do code optimization at level 2. If you specifically don't want to do any code optimization, you can use zero with option as –O0.

So what does optimization mean? Consider the following C source code file sum.c that calculates the sum of two numbers and prints the result. Of course this is not the best code for this purpose and it is used only to demonstrate a point.

```
1   #include <stdio.h>
2   main ()
3   {
4     int a, b, sum;
5
6     a=4;
7     b=3;
8     sum = a+b;
9
10    printf("The sum is: %d\n", sum);
11  }
```

If you compile this program without any optimization, the compiler will generate code for all lines starting from line number 6 to line number 10. This can be verified by loading the file in a debugger and tracing through it. However, if you optimize the compilation process, lines 6 to 10 can be replaced by a single line as shown below. This can be done without affecting the output of the program.

```
printf("The sum is: 7\n", );
```

This is because the compiler can easily determine that all of the variables are static and there is no need to assign values and then calculate the sum at the run time. All of this can be done at the compile time. You can also verify this fact in a debugger. The optimized code will skip over assignment lines (lines 6 to 8) and will directly jump to the `printf` statement when you step through.

However in the following code, the compiler can't make such decisions because the numbers a and b are entered interactively.

```
1   #include <stdio.h>
2   main ()
3   {
4      int a, b, sum;
5
6      printf("Enter first number: ");
7      scanf("%d", &a);
8      printf("Enter second number: ");
9      scanf("%d", &b);
10
11     sum = a+b;
12
13     printf("The sum is: %d\n", sum);
14  }
```

If you compile this code with different levels of optimization (e.g., –O1 and –O2), and then trace it through a debugger, you will see a difference in execution sequence because of the way the compiler makes decisions at the compile time.

It may be mentioned that optimization is not always beneficial. For example, code optimization changes timings or clock cycles when the code is executed. This especially may create some problems on embedded systems if you have debugged your code by compiling without optimization. The rule of thumb is that you should create optimized code instead of relying on the compiler to make optimization for you.

For a detailed list of optimization options, please see all options starting with –f command line option. However options starting with –O are the most commonly used in the optimization process.

3.3.6   Static and Dynamic Linking

A compiler can generate static or dynamic code depending upon how you proceed with the linking process. If you create static object code, the output files are larger but they can be used as stand-alone binaries. This means that you can copy an executable file to another system and it does not depend on shared libraries when it is executed. On the other hand, if you chose dynamic linking, the final executable code is much smaller but it depends heavily upon shared libraries. If you copy the final executable program to another system, you have to make sure that the shared libraries are also present on the system where your application is executed. Please note that version inconsistencies in dynamic libraries can also cause problems.

To create static binaries, you have to use −static command line option with gcc. To created dynamically linked output binary files, use −shared on the command line.

For example, if we compile the hello.c program used earlier in this chapter with shared libraries, size of the output executable file is 13644 bytes (this can be further reduced using the strip utility discussed later in Chapter 7 of this book). However, if you compile it statically, the size of the output binary file is 1625261 bytes, which is very large compared to the shared binary. Note that this size can also be reduced using the strip utility.

To identify the dependencies of a dynamically linked binary file, you can use the ldd command. The following command shows that linked output file hello depends upon two dynamic libraries.

```
[rr@conformix 4]$ ldd hello
  libc.so.6 => /lib/i686/libc.so.6 (0x4002c000)
  /lib/ld-linux.so.2 => /lib/ld-linux.so.2 (0x40000000)
[rr@conformix 4]$
```

If you copy hello to some other host, you also need to make sure that libc.so.6 and ld-linux.so.2 exist on the target system.

On most of the Linux systems, dynamic linking is done by default.

3.3.7   Compiling Source Code for Other Languages

As mentioned earlier, the GCC set of compilers supports many languages. It can be used to compile programs other than C language. Following is an introduction to compiling programs from other languages.

3.3.7.1   Compiling C++ Code

C++ source code files have suffixes such as .C, .cpp, .cc, .c++, .cxx or .cp. The gcc compiler recognizes these extensions and can compile C++ code. However you can also use g++ or c++ compilers, which are part of the GCC compilers family and are installed with it. These programs invoke gcc with appropriate options to compile C++ code and location of class files. Using these programs, you can also compile C++ source code files that don't have the standard suffixes listed earlier.

3.3.7.2   Compiling Objective C Code

Objective files have suffixes such as .m and gcc recognizes Objective C files with that suffix. When you compile Objective C code, you have to pass an option to the linker. This is done using −lobjc. By this option, the linker uses Objective C libraries during the linking process. Consider the following sample Objective C code (stored in hello.m file) to print "Hello World" on the standard output.

```
#include "objc/Object.h"

@interface HelloWorld : Object
{
```

```
  STR msg;
}

+ new;
- print;
- setMessage: (STR) str;

@end

@implementation HelloWorld

+ new
{
  self = [super new];
  [self setMessage : ""];
  return self;
}

- print
{
  printf("%s\n", msg);
  return self;
}

- setMessage: (STR) str
{
  msg = str;
  return self;
}

@end


int main(int argc, char**argv) {
  id msg;

  msg = [HelloWorld new];

  [msg setMessage: "Hello World"] ;
  [msg print];
  return 0;
}
```

You can compile and link it using the gcc hello.m -lobjc command. The output is again a.out file that can be executed on the command line.

This is sort of a long "Hello World" program. There are much shorter Objective C "Hello World" programs available on the Internet.

3.3.7.3 Compiling Java Code

Information about the GCC Java compiler gcj is available at http://gcc.gnu.org/java/. Before you can build Java programs, you also need to have libgcj installed. With old compilers, you had to install it separately from source code. When you build and install new versions of GCC, libgcj is installed automatically. If you are still using an old compiler and want to have libgcj installed, information is available at http://gcc.gnu.org/java/libgcj2.html. Briefly the process is as follows:

Download libgcj from ftp://sourceware.cygnus.com/pub/java/ or another web site on the Internet. Untar it in /opt directory and a new directory will be created under /opt which will contain source code for libgcj. Create a directory /opt/libgcj-build and move into this directory. After that you have to perform the following sequence of commands:

- ../libgcj/configure
- make
- make install

Note that your new compiler must be in PATH before you build libgcj.

Now let us see how to compile a Java program. Consider the following simple Java program that prints the message "Hello World". The source code filename is hello.java.

```
class HelloWorld {
  public static void main (String args[]) {
    System.out.print("Hello World ");
  }
}
```

Traditionally you have to invoke the javac program to build a byte code. After that you have to run the byte code using the java program on Linux. However if you use gcj, you can create a binary output file hello using the following command:

```
gcj -main=HelloWorld -o hello hello.java
```

The output file is hello, which is an executable binary. The -main switch is used for the entry point when the program is executed.

The compiler uses some information to build Java code. This information includes reading the gcj specification file and libraries. The following command displays this information.

```
[rr@conformix 4]$ gcj -v
Reading specs from /opt/gcc-3.0.4/lib/gcc-lib/i686-pc-linux-
gnu/3.0.4/specs
Reading specs from /opt/gcc-3.0.4/lib/gcc-lib/i686-pc-linux-
gnu/3.0.4/../../../libgcj.spec
rename spec lib to liborig
rename spec startfile to startfileorig
```

```
Configured with: ../gcc-3.0.4/configure --prefix=/opt/gcc-
3.0.4 --enable-threads=posix
Thread model: posix
gcc version 3.0.4
[rr@conformix 4]$
```

The compilation of Java programs is completed in many steps. Let us compile the
hello.java program to build a statically linked hello output binary using the following
command. The –v switch shows all of the steps during this process.

```
[rr@conformix 4]$ gcj hello.java --main=HelloWorld  -o hello -
static -v
Reading specs from /opt/gcc-3.0.4/lib/gcc-lib/i686-pc-linux-
gnu/3.0.4/specs
Reading specs from /opt/gcc-3.0.4/lib/gcc-lib/i686-pc-linux-
gnu/3.0.4/../../../libgcj.spec
rename spec lib to liborig
rename spec startfile to startfileorig
Configured with: ../gcc-3.0.4/configure --prefix=/opt/gcc-
3.0.4 --enable-threads=posix
Thread model: posix
gcc version 3.0.4
 /opt/gcc-3.0.4/lib/gcc-lib/i686-pc-linux-gnu/3.0.4/jc1
hello.java -fuse-divide-subroutine -fuse-boehm-gc -fnon-call-
exceptions -quiet -dumpbase hello.java -g1 -version -o /tmp/
ccHj5WMY.s
GNU Java version 3.0.4 (i686-pc-linux-gnu)
  compiled by GNU C version 3.0.4.
 as --traditional-format -V -Qy -o /tmp/cchm92Nc.o /tmp/
ccHj5WMY.s
GNU assembler version 2.10.91 (i386-redhat-linux) using BFD
version 2.10.91.0.2
 /opt/gcc-3.0.4/lib/gcc-lib/i686-pc-linux-gnu/3.0.4/jvgenmain
HelloWorldmain /tmp/ccTlFcXz.i
 /opt/gcc-3.0.4/lib/gcc-lib/i686-pc-linux-gnu/3.0.4/cc1 /tmp/
ccTlFcXz.i -quiet -dumpbase HelloWorldmain.c -g1 -version -
fdollars-in-identifiers -o /tmp/ccHj5WMY.s
GNU CPP version 3.0.4 (cpplib) (i386 Linux/ELF)
GNU C version 3.0.4 (i686-pc-linux-gnu)
  compiled by GNU C version 3.0.4.
 as --traditional-format -V -Qy -o /tmp/ccBgJjpa.o /tmp/
ccHj5WMY.s
GNU assembler version 2.10.91 (i386-redhat-linux) using BFD
version 2.10.91.0.2
 /opt/gcc-3.0.4/lib/gcc-lib/i686-pc-linux-gnu/3.0.4/collect2 -
m elf_i386 -static -o hello /usr/lib/crt1.o /usr/lib/crti.o /
opt/gcc-3.0.4/lib/gcc-lib/i686-pc-linux-gnu/3.0.4/crtbegin.o -
L/opt/gcc-3.0.4/lib/gcc-lib/i686-pc-linux-gnu/3.0.4 -L/opt/
```

```
gcc-3.0.4/lib/gcc-lib/i686-pc-linux-gnu/3.0.4/../../.. /tmp/
ccBgJjpa.o /tmp/cchm92Nc.o -lgcc -lgcj -lm -lgcjgc -lpthread -
lzgcj -ldl -lgcc -lc -lgcc /opt/gcc-3.0.4/lib/gcc-lib/i686-pc-
linux-gnu/3.0.4/crtend.o /usr/lib/crtn.o
[rr@conformix 4]$
```

As you can see, different programs have been executed to get the output binary file. These programs include:

- The `jcl` program
- GNU assembler as. Again as is the name of the assembler. `as`
- The `jvgenmain` program
- The `cc1` compiler
- The `collect2` program

You can also see various command line switches used with these programs.

3.3.8   Summary of gcc Options

Hundreds of options can be used with `gcc` on command line. Explanation of all of these options is beyond the scope of this book. However, following is a summary list of these options as displayed by `gcc` man page (using `man gcc` command). Options are grouped in different sections which will be helpful for you if you are looking for options related to a particular task.

3.3.8.1   Overall Options

```
-c
-S
-E
-o file
-pipe
-pass-exit-codes
-x language
-v
--target-help
--help
```

3.3.8.2   C Language Options

```
-ansi
-std=standard
-aux-info filename
-fno-asm
-fno-builtin
-fhosted
-ffree-standing
-trigraphs
-traditional
```

```
-traditional-cpp
-fallow-single-precision
-fcond-mismatch
-fsigned-bitfields
-fsigned-char
-funsigned-bitfields
-funsigned-char

-fwritable-strings
-fshort-wchar
```

3.3.8.3   C++ Language Options

```
-fno-access-control
-fcheck-new
-fconserve-space
-fno-const-strings
-fdollars-in-identifiers
-fno-elide-constructors
-fno-enforce-eh-specs
-fexternal-templates

-falt-external-templates
-ffor-scope
-fno-for-scope
-fno-gnu-keywords
-fno-implicit-templates
-fno-implicit-inline-templates
-fno-implement-inlines
-fms-extensions
-fno-nonansi-builtins
-fno-operator-names
-fno-optional-diags
-fpermissive
-frepo
-fno-rtti
-fstats
-ftemplate-depth-n
-fuse-cxa-atexit
-fno-weak
-nostdinc++
-fno-default-inline
-Wctor-dtor-privacy
-Wnon-virtual-dtor
-Wreorder
-Weffc++
-Wno-deprecated
-Wno-non-template-friend
```

```
-Wold-style-cast
-Woverloaded-virtual
-Wno-pmf-conversions
-Wsign-promo
-Wsynth
```

3.3.8.4   Objective-C Language Options

```
-fconstant-string-class=class-name
-fgnu-runtime
-fnext-runtime
-gen-decls
-Wno-protocol
-Wselector
```

3.3.8.5   Language Independent Options

```
-fmessage-length=n
-fdiagnostics-show-location=[once|every-line]
```

3.3.8.6   Warning Options

```
-fsyntax-only
-pedantic
-pedantic-errors
-w
-W
-Wall
-Waggregate-return
-Wcast-align
-Wcast-qual
-Wchar-subscripts
-Wcomment
-Wconversion
-Wdisabled-optimization

-Werror
-Wfloat-equal
-Wformat
-Wformat=2
-Wformat-nonliteral
-Wformat-security
-Wid-clash-len
-Wimplicit
-Wimplicit-int
-Wimplicit-function-declaration
-Werror-implicit-function-declaration
-Wimport
-Winline
-Wlarger-than-len
```

```
-Wlong-long
-Wmain
-Wmissing-braces
-Wmissing-declarations
-Wmissing-format-attribute
-Wmissing-noreturn
-Wmultichar
-Wno-format-extra-args
-Wno-format-y2k
-Wno-import
-Wpacked
-Wpadded
-Wparentheses
-Wpointer-arith
-Wredundant-decls
-Wreturn-type
-Wsequence-point
-Wshadow
-Wsign-compare
-Wswitch
-Wsystem-headers
-Wtrigraphs
-Wundef
-Wuninitialized
-Wunknown-pragmas
-Wunreachable-code
-Wunused
-Wunused-function
-Wunused-label
-Wunused-parameter
-Wunused-value
-Wunused-variable
-Wwrite-strings
```

3.3.8.7   C-only Warning Options

```
-Wbad-function-cast
-Wmissing-prototypes
-Wnested-externs
-Wstrict-prototypes
-Wtraditional
```

3.3.8.8   Debugging Options

```
-a
-ax
-dletters
-dumpspecs
-dumpmachine
```

```
-dumpversion
-fdump-unnumbered
-fdump-translation-unit[-n]
-fdump-class-hierarchy[-n]
-fdump-ast-original[-n]
-fdump-ast-optimized[-n]
-fmem-report
-fpretend-float
-fprofile-arcs
-ftest-coverage

-ftime-report -g
-glevel
-gcoff
-gdwarf
-gdwarf-1
-gdwarf-1+
-gdwarf-2
-ggdb
-gstabs
-gstabs+
-gxcoff
-gxcoff+
-p
-pg
-print-file-name=library
-print-libgcc-file-name
-print-multi-directory
-print-multi-lib
-print-prog-name=program
-print-search-dirs
-Q
-save-temps
-time
```

3.3.8.9   Optimization Options

```
-falign-functions=n
-falign-jumps=n
-falign-labels=n
-falign-loops=n
-fbranch-probabilities
-fcaller-saves
-fcse-follow-jumps
-fcse-skip-blocks
-fdata-sections
-fdce -fdelayed-branch
-fdelete-null-pointer-checks
```

```
-fexpensive-optimizations

-ffast-math
-ffloat-store
-fforce-addr
-fforce-mem
-ffunction-sections

-fgcse
-finline-functions
-finline-limit=n
-fkeep-inline-functions

-fkeep-static-consts
-fmove-all-movables
-fno-default-inline
-fno-defer-pop
-fno-function-cse
-fno-guess-branch-probability
-fno-inline
-fno-math-errno
-fno-peephole
-fno-peephole2
-fomit-frame-pointer
-foptimize-register-move

-foptimize-sibling-calls
-freduce-all-givs
-fregmove
-frename-registers

-frerun-cse-after-loop
-frerun-loop-opt
-fschedule-insns
-fschedule-insns2

-fsingle-precision-constant
-fssa
-fstrength-reduce
-fstrict-aliasing
-fthread-jumps
-ftrapv
-funroll-all-loops
-funroll-loops --param name=value -O
-O0
-O1
-O2
-O3
-Os
```

3.3.8.10   Preprocessor Options

```
-$
-Aquestion=answer
-A-question[=answer]
-C
-dD
-dI
-dM
-dN
-Dmacro[=defn]
-E
-H
-idirafter dir
-include file
-imacros file
-iprefix file
-iwithprefix dir
-iwithprefixbefore dir
-isystem dir
-M
-MM
-MF
-MG
-MP
-MQ
-MT
-nostdinc
-P
-remap
-trigraphs
-undef
-Umacro
-Wp,option
```

3.3.8.11   Assembler Option

```
-Wa,option
```

3.3.8.12   Linker Options

```
 object-file-name
-llibrary
-nostartfiles
-nodefaultlibs
-nostdlib
-s
-static
-static-libgcc
-shared
```

```
-shared-libgcc
-symbolic
-Wl,option
-Xlinker option
 -u symbol
```

3.3.8.13   Directory Options

```
-Bprefix
-Idir
-I-
-Ldir
-specs=file
```

3.3.8.14   Target Options

```
-b machine
-V version
```

3.3.8.15   Machine Dependent Options

M680x0 Options

```
-m68000
-m68020
-m68020-40
-m68020-60
-m68030
-m68040
-m68060
-mcpu32
-m5200
-m68881
-mbitfield
-mc68000
-mc68020
-mfpa
-mnobitfield
-mrtd
-mshort
-msoft-float
-mpcrel
-malign-int
-mstrict-align
```

M68hc1x Options

```
-m6811
-m6812
-m68hc11
-m68hc12
-mauto-incdec
```

```
-mshort
-msoft-reg-count=count
```

VAX Options

```
-mg
-mgnu
-munix
```

SPARC Options

```
-mcpu=cpu-type
-mtune=cpu-type
-mcmodel=code-model
-m32
-m64
-mapp-regs
-mbroken-saverestore

-mcypress
-mepilogue
-mfaster-structs
-mflat
-mfpu
-mhard-float
-mhard-quad-float
-mimpure-text
-mlive-g0
-mno-app-regs
-mno-epilogue
-mno-faster-structs
-mno-flat
-mno-fpu
-mno-impure-text
-mno-stack-bias
-mno-unaligned-doubles
-msoft-float
-msoft-quad-float
-msparclite
-mstack-bias
-msupersparc
-munaligned-doubles
-mv8
```

Convex Options

```
-mc1
-mc2
-mc32
-mc34
```

```
-mc38
-margcount
-mnoargcount
-mlong32
-mlong64
-mvolatile-cache
-mvolatile-nocache
```

AMD29K Options

```
-m29000
-m29050
-mbw
-mnbw
-mdw
-mndw
-mlarge
-mnormal
-msmall
-mkernel-registers

-mno-reuse-arg-regs
-mno-stack-check
-mno-storem-bug
-mreuse-arg-regs
-msoft-float
-mstack-check
-mstorem-bug
-muser-registers
```

ARM Options

```
-mapcs-frame
-mno-apcs-frame
-mapcs-26
-mapcs-32
-mapcs-stack-check
-mno-apcs-stack-check
-mapcs-float
-mno-apcs-float
-mapcs-reentrant
-mno-apcs-reentrant
-msched-prolog
-mno-sched-prolog
-mlittle-endian
-mbig-endian
-mwords-little-endian
-malignment-traps
-mno-alignment-traps
-msoft-float
```

```
-mhard-float
-mfpe
-mthumb-interwork
-mno-thumb-interwork
-mcpu=name
-march=name
-mfpe=name
-mstructure-size-boundary=n
-mbsd
-mxopen
-mno-symrename
-mabort-on-noreturn
-mlong-calls
-mno-long-calls
-msingle-pic-base
-mno-single-pic-base
-mpic-register=reg
-mnop-fun-dllimport
-mpoke-function-name
-mthumb
-marm
-mtpcs-frame
-mtpcs-leaf-frame
-mcaller-super-interworking
-mcallee-super-interworking
```

MN10200 Options

```
-mrelax
```

MN10300 Options

```
-mmult-bug
-mno-mult-bug
-mam33
-mno-am33
-mno-crt0
-mrelax
```

M32R/D Options

```
-mcode-model=model-type
-msdata=sdata-type -G num
```

M88K Options

```
-m88000
-m88100
-m88110
-mbig-pic
-mcheck-zero-division
```

```
-mhandle-large-shift
-midentify-revision
-mno-check-zero-division
-mno-ocs-debug-info
-mno-ocs-frame-position
-mno-optimize-arg-area
-mno-serialize-volatile
-mno-underscores
-mocs-debug-info
-mocs-frame-position
-moptimize-arg-area
-mserialize-volatile

-mshort-data-num
-msvr3
-msvr4
-mtrap-large-shift
-muse-div-instruction
-mversion-03.00
-mwarn-passed-structs
```

RS/6000 and PowerPC Options

```
-mcpu=cpu-type
-mtune=cpu-type
-mpower
-mno-power
-mpower2
-mno-power2
-mpowerpc

-mpowerpc64
-mno-powerpc
-mpowerpc-gpopt
-mno-powerpc-gpopt
-mpowerpc-gfxopt

-mno-powerpc-gfxopt
-mnew-mnemonics
-mold-mnemonics
-mfull-toc
-mminimal-toc

-mno-fop-in-toc
-mno-sum-in-toc
-m64
-m32
-mxl-call
-mno-xl-call
```

```
-mthreads
-mpe
-msoft-float
-mhard-float
-mmultiple
-mno-multiple
-mstring
-mno-string
-mupdate
-mno-update
-mfused-madd
-mno-fused-madd
-mbit-align
-mno-bit-align
-mstrict-align
-mno-strict-align
-mrelocatable
-mno-relocatable
-mrelocatable-lib
-mno-relocatable-lib
-mtoc
-mno-toc
-mlittle
-mlittle-endian
-mbig
-mbig-endian
-mcall-aix
-mcall-sysv
-mcall-netbsd
-mprototype
-mno-prototype-

-msim
-mmvme
-mads
-myellowknife
-memb
-msdata
-msdata=opt
-mvxworks -G num
```

RT Options

```
-mcall-lib-mul
-mfp-arg-in-fpregs
-mfp-arg-in-gregs
-mfull-fp-blocks
-mhc-struct-return
-min-line-mul
```

```
-mminimum-fp-blocks
-mnohc-struct-return
```

MIPS Options

```
-mabicalls
-mcpu=cpu-type
-membedded-data
-muninit-const-in-rodata
-membedded-pic-

-mfp32
-mfp64
-mgas
-mgp32
-mgp64
-mgpopt
-mhalf-pic
-mhard-float
-mint64
-mips1
-mips2
-mips3
-mips4
-mlong64
-mlong32
-mlong-calls
-mmemcpy
-mmips-as
-mmips-tfile
-mno-abicalls
-mno-embedded-data
-mno-uninit-const-in-rodata
-mno-embedded-pic
-mno-gpopt
-mno-long-calls
-mno-memcpy
-mno-mips-tfile
-mno-rnames
-mno-stats
-mrnames
-msoft-float
-m4650
-msingle-float
-mmad
-mstats
-EL
-EB
-G num
```

```
-nocpp
-mabi=32
-mabi=n32
-mabi=64
-mabi=eabi -mfix7000
-mno-crt0
```

i386 Options

```
-mcpu=cpu-type
-march=cpu-type
-mintel-syntax
-mieee-fp
-mno-fancy-math-387
-mno-fp-ret-in-387
-msoft-float
-msvr3-shlib
-mno-wide-multiply
-mrtd
-malign-double
-mreg-alloc=list
-mregparm=num
-malign-jumps=num
-malign-loops=num
-malign-functions=num
-mpreferred-stack-boundary=num
-mthreads
-mno-align-stringops
-minline-all-stringops
-mpush-args
-maccumulate-outgoing-args

-m128bit-long-double
-m96bit-long-double
-momit-leaf-frame-pointer
```

HPPA Options

```
-march=architecture-type
-mbig-switch
-mdisable-fpregs
-mdisable-indexing
-mfast-indirect-calls
-mgas
-mjump-in-delay
-mlong-load-store
-mno-big-switch
-mno-disable-fpregs
-mno-disable-indexing
-mno-fast-indirect-calls
```

```
-mno-gas
-mno-jump-in-delay
-mno-long-load-store
-mno-portable-runtime
-mno-soft-float
-mno-space-regs
-msoft-float
-mpa-risc-1-0
-mpa-risc-1-1
-mpa-risc-2-0
-mportable-runtime
-mschedule=cpu-type
-mspace-regs
```

Intel 960 Options

```
-mcpu-type
-masm-compat
-mclean-linkage
-mcode-align
-mcomplex-addr
-mleaf-procedures
-mic-compat
-mic2.0-compat
-mic3.0-compat
-mintel-asm
-mno-clean-linkage
-mno-code-align
-mno-complex-addr
-mno-leaf-procedures
-mno-old-align
-mno-strict-align
-mno-tail-call
-mnumerics
-mold-align
-msoft-float
-mstrict-align
-mtail-call
```

DEC Alpha Options

```
-mfp-regs
-mno-fp-regs
-mno-soft-float
-msoft-float
-malpha-as
-mgas
-mieee
-mieee-with-inexact
-mieee-conformant
```

```
-mfp-trap-mode=mode
-mfp-rounding-mode=mode

-mtrap-precision=mode
-mbuild-constants
-mcpu=cpu-type
-mbwx
-mno-bwx
-mcix
-mno-cix
-mmax
-mno-max
-mmemory-latency=time
```

Clipper Options

```
-mc300
-mc400
```

H8/300 Options

```
-mrelax
-mh
-ms
-mint32
-malign-300
```

SH Options

```
-m1
-m2
-m3
-m3e
-m4-nofpu
-m4-single-only
-m4-single
-m4
-mb
-ml
-mdalign
-mrelax
-mbigtable
-mfmovd
-mhitachi
-mnomacsave
-mieee
-misize
-mpadstruct
-mspace
-mprefergot
-musermode
```

System V Options

```
-Qy
-Qn
-YP,paths
-Ym,dir
```

ARC Options

```
-EB
-EL
-mmangle-cpu
-mcpu=cpu
```
-mtext=text-section
-mdata=data-section
-mrodata=readonly-data-section

TMS320C3x/C4x Options

```
-mcpu=cpu
-mbig
-msmall
-mregparm
-mmemparm
-mfast-fix
-mmpyi
-mbk
-mti
-mdp-isr-reload -mrpts=count
-mrptb
-mdb
-mloop-unsigned
-mparallel-insns
-mparallel-mpy
-mpreserve-float
```

V850 Options

```
-mlong-calls
-mno-long-calls
-mep
-mno-ep
-mprolog-function
-mno-prolog-function

-mspace
-mtda=n
-msda=n
-mzda=n
-mv850
-mbig-switch
```

NS32K Options

```
-m32032
-m32332
-m32532
-m32081
-m32381
-mmult-add
-mnomult-add
-msoft-float
-mrtd
-mnortd
-mregparam
-mnoregparam
-msb
-mnosb
-mbitfield
-mnobitfield
-mhimem
-mnohimem
```

AVR Options

```
-mmcu=mcu
-msize
-minit-stack=n
-mno-interrupts
-mcall-prologues
-mno-table-jump

-mtiny-stack
```

MCore Options

```
-mhardlit
-mno-hardlit
-mdiv
-mno-div
-mrelax-immediates
-mno-relax-immediates
-mwide-bitfields
-mno-wide-bitfields
-m4byte-functions
-mno-4byte-functions
-mcallgraph-data
-mno-callgraph-data
-mslow-bytes
-mno-slow-bytes
-mno-lsim
-mlittle-endian
```

```
-mbig-endian
-m210
-m340
-mstack-increment
```

IA-64 Options

```
-mbig-endian
-mlittle-endian
-mgnu-as
-mgnu-ld
-mno-pic
-mvolatile-asm-stop
-mb-step
-mregister-names
-mno-sdata
-mconstant-gp
-mauto-pic
-minline-divide-min-latency

-minline-divide-max-throughput
-mno-dwarf2-asm
-mfixed-range=register-range
```

S/390 and zSeries Options

```
-mhard-float
-msoft-float
-mbackchain
-mno-backchain
-msmall-exec
-mno-small-exec
-mmvcle
-mno-mvcle
-m64
-m31
-mdebug
-mno-debug
```

Xtensa Options

```
-mbig-endian
-mlittle-endian
-mdensity
-mno-density
-mmac16
-mno-mac16
-mmul16
-mno-mul16
-mmul32
```

```
-mno-mul32
-mnsa
-mno-nsa
-mminmax
-mno-minmax
-msext
-mno-sext
-mbooleans
-mno-booleans
-mhard-float
-msoft-float
-mfused-madd
-mno-fused-madd
-mserialize-volatile
-mno-serialize-volatile
-mtext-section-literals
-mno-text-section-literals
-mtarget-align
-mno-target-align
-mlongcalls
-mno-long-calls
```

3.3.8.16   Code Generation Options

```
-fcall-saved-reg
-fcall-used-reg
-ffixed-reg
-fexceptions
-fnon-call-exceptions
-funwind-tables
-finhibit-size-directive
-finstrument-functions
-fcheck-memory-usage

-fprefix-function-name
-fno-common
-fno-ident
-fno-gnu-linker
-fpcc-struct-return
-fpic
-fPIC
-freg-struct-return
-fshared-data
-fshort-enums
-fshort-double
-fvolatile
-fvolatile-global
-fvolatile-static
```

```
-fverbose-asm
-fpack-struct
-fstack-check
-fstack-limit-register=reg
-fstack-limit-symbol=sym
-fargument-alias
-fargument-noalias
-fargument-noalias-global

-fleading-underscore
```

3.4   Linking a program

As mentioned earlier, building an executable binary file from a source code file is a multi-stage process.

The gcc compiler usually carries all these steps for you by default. However you can stop gcc at any of these stages for various reasons. You have already seen how to create assembler code from a C source code file. In most software projects, output binaries are built from many source code files. For this purpose you have to compile these source code files to object files one by one before you can generate the output binary file. After creating these object files, you can link these files using gcc to the final executable.

The gcc compiler gets help from different programs during the four steps listed earlier in this chapter. During the linking part, the ld program is invoked with appropriate arguments to link one or many object files together with libraries to generate an executable. Command line switches used with ld can be found using manual pages.

The linker is a part of GNU binary utilities package also known as binutils. You can download and install the latest version of GNU linker if you need to do so.

3.5   Assembling a Program

GNU assembler is part of GNU binary utilities package. To get the latest binutils packages, you can download it from ftp://ftp.gnu.org/gnu/binutils/. After downloading you have to use the tar command to extract source code files. The latest version at the time of writing this chapter is 2.12 and the tar command will create a directory binutils-2.12 automatically. I have extracted it in /opt directory, so the source code directory is /opt/binutils-2.12. I created another directory /opt/binutils-build to build the package. Running the configure script is the first step towards building binary utilities package. The following sequence of commands does all of these steps.

```
[root@conformix /opt]# cd /opt
[root@conformix /opt]# tar zxvf binutils-2.12.tar.gz
[root@conformix /opt]# mkdir binutils-build
[root@conformix /opt]# cd binutils-build/
[root@conformix binutils-build]# ../binutils-2.12/configure --
prefix=/opt/gcc-3.0.4 --enable-shared
```

```
[root@conformix /opt]# make LDFLAGS=-all-static tooldir=/opt/
gcc-3.0.4
[root@conformix /opt]# make tooldir=/opt/gcc-3.0.4 install
```

Note that since we have used /opt/gcc/3.0.4 as a prefix and tooldir as the destination for installation, the binary utilities will be installed in /opt/gcc-3.0.4/bin directory. As you may have noted, I have installed all software under /opt/gcc-3.0.4 so that I can use one directory for all of my tools.

3.6   Handling Warning and Error messages

The GNU compiler generates two types of messages when compiling source code. Warning messages are non-critical messages and the compiler can build the output code even if there are warning messages. Error messages are fatal messages and compiler is not able to generate output files when an error occurs. By default, the compiler does not display many warning messages. You may like to see these messages, for example, when you want to get a release of a software package. Usually the release version of software should be compiled without any warning message. Using options that start with –W, you can control which types of messages should be displayed. It is a good idea to always use –Wall option in your Makefiles. The reason is that warnings often signify problems in code that you will want to see. Please see gcc man pages to get a feel of options controlling warning messages.

3.7   Include files

During the compilation process, the compiler should know where include files will be located. This can be done in different ways. The compiler looks into some default locations when searching for include files and you have already seen in this chapter how to display that information. You can also use the –I command line switch with the gcc command to set additional paths to locate include files. The third method is the use of environment variables. Please see the environment variables section earlier in this chapter for more information.

3.8   Creating Libraries

Libraries are files containing commonly used functions needed for all programs. For example, printf() is a function used in most of the C programs. When the program is linked, the linker must know where the code for the printf() function is located. Knowledge of location of library files is a must at this stage. The location can be passed to the linker using command line options or environment variables. In large software projects, this is done inside Makefiles. The environment variable that shows the location of library files is LD_LIBRARY_PATH. Please see the list of command line options in this chapter or use manual pages to find out which options are appropriate.

3.9 Standard Libraries

In addition to the compiler, assembler, linker and other tools, you also need standard library files. All Linux distributions come with the GNU C library which is installed as `glibc`. However, when you are building your development environment, you may need to get the library in source code format and install the latest version. You may also need the library in source code format in order to cross compile it when you are building a cross-compilation environment. The standard GNU C library provides functions for the following major areas.

- Memory management
- Error handling
- Character handling
- Strings and arrays
- Locales and international specific things, like character handling and date and time specific functions
- Searching
- Sorting
- Pattern matching
- Input and output
- File system support
- Pipes
- Fifos
- Sockets
- Terminal I/O
- Mathematics functions
- Date and time functions
- Signal and exception handling
- Process management
- Job control
- User and groups
- System related tasks

Information about `glibc` is available on http://www.gnu.org/software/libc/libc.html. You can download it from ftp://ftp.gnu.org/gnu/glibc/ where you can find the latest as well as old versions. The current version at the time of writing this book is 2.2.5.

After downloading the library, you have to untar it. For the sake of this book, I untarred the library file in `/opt` directory. The following `tar` command extracts library files in `/opt/glibc-2.2.5` directory.

```
tar zxvf glibc-2.2.5.tar.gz
```

Now you have to extract any other components or add-ons of the library. I have added one component, Linux threads. File `glibc-linuxthreads-2.2.5.tar.gz` can also be downloaded from the same location from which you downloaded the main `glibc-2.2.5.tar.gz` file. The following commands are used to extract files from these two archives:

```
cd glibc-2.2.5
tar zxvf ../ glibc-linuxthreads-2.2.5.tar.gz
```

In old versions of `glibc`, you had to install add-ons like locale data and crypt library. These are included in the latest version of `glibc`.

Now you have to configure the library after creating a build directory. Basically this is the same process that you have done while installing GCC and binutils. This is done using the following set of commands:

```
[root@conformix glibc-2.2.5]# mkdir build
[root@conformix glibc-2.2.5]# cd build
[root@conformix build]# ../configure --enable-add-
ons=linuxthreads --prefix=/opt/gcc-3.0.4
```

The actual compilation and testing is done using the following two commands:

```
make
make check
```

The final install command is the following:

```
make install
```

This command will install components of GNU C library under `/opt/gcc-3.0.4/lib` because we had chosen `/opt/gcc/3.0.4` as our prefix when we ran the `configure` script. Now you can set the appropriate paths in your Makefiles to use the new library.

3.10 Compiling Pascal Programs

Pascal programs can be converted to C language programs and then compiled in the usual way. The `p2c` command on Linux does this for you. Consider the following Pascal program `hello.pas`.

```
(* Program to demonstrate Pascal compilation *)
program Hello ;
begin
   writeln ('Hello world')
end.
```

The following command will create a file `hello.c` which is the equivalent C version of the `hello.pas` program.

```
[rr@conformix 4]$ p2c hello.pas
Hello

Translation completed.
[rr@conformix 4]$
```

The output `hello.c` file is shown below:

```
/* Output from p2c 1.21alpha-07.Dec.93, the Pascal-to-C
translator */
/* From input file "hello.pas" */


/* Program to demonstrate Pascal compilation */

#include <p2c/p2c.h>


main(argc, argv)
int argc;
Char *argv[];
{
  PASCAL_MAIN(argc, argv);
  printf("Hello world\n");
  exit(EXIT_SUCCESS);
}



/* End. */
```

You may need some libraries with `p2c` program and C compiler to successfully complete this process.

Many Pascal compilers are also available in the open source world. These compilers can be used to generate executable code from Pascal source directly without any help from GCC.

3.10.1 Using Free Pascal (fpc)

The Free Pascal Project has created a 32-bit Pascal compiler which is available for Linux, among other operating systems. You can download it from http://www.freepascal.org. This software is licensed under GPL like other open source projects. At the time of writing this book version 1.0.4 is available for download. After download, you can install the compiler as follows on a RedHat system:

```
[root@conformix rr]# rpm --install fpc-1.0.4.i386.rpm
Write permission in /etc.
Found libgcc.a in /usr/lib/gcc-lib/i386-redhat-linux/2.96
Writing sample configuration file to /etc/ppc386.cfg
[root@conformix rr]#
```

The best thing about this compiler is that you don't need to convert source code files to C language and then compile these. The fpc compiler creates binary executable files. The following command creates an executable file `hello` from `hello.pas` program listed earlier.

```
[rr@conformix 4]$ fpc hello.pas
Free Pascal Compiler version 1.0.4 [2000/12/18] for i386
Copyright (c) 1993-2000 by Florian Klaempfl
Target OS: Linux for i386
Compiling hello.pas
Assembling hello
Linking hello
6 Lines compiled, 0.1 sec
[rr@conformix 4]$
```

The output hello program can be executed like any other program.

3.10.2 Using GNU Pascal

A GNU Pascal compiler is available from http://agnes.dida.physik.uni-essen.de/~gnu-pascal/ for download and can be installed on many platforms like gcc. The web site contains all manuals and downloadable files for this compiler. This compiler also creates executable files from Pascal source code.

3.11 Compiling Fortran Programs

The GCC family of compilers also includes g77 which acts as a front end to invoke gcc. The gcc compiler is used to compile Fortran programs. Consider the following simple hello.for Fortran program that write "Hello world" on standard output.

```
c This program is to display a string and then end
c Written to demonstrate Fortran program compilation
c
c Rafeeq Rehman, March 18, 2002

      program hello
      write (*,*) 'Hello world'
      stop
      end
```

Note that statements in Fortran start from column 7. All lines starting with c in column 1 are comment lines. You can compile this program using the following command:

```
g77 hello.for
```

The g77 compiler, like gcc, creates a.out as a default output executable. You can create output file with a different name using –o command line option. The following command creates "kaka" as output binary executable file.

```
g77 hello.for -o kaka
```

The g77 program uses many programs to generate output binary. You can display version information by using g77 –v command. Output of this command is shown below.

```
[rr@conformix 4]$ g77 -v
g77 version 2.96 20000731 (Red Hat Linux 7.1 2.96-81) (from
FSF-g77 version 0.5.26 20000731 (Red Hat Linux 7.1 2.96-81))
Driving: g77 -v -c -xf77-version /dev/null -xnone
Reading specs from /usr/lib/gcc-lib/i386-redhat-linux/2.96/
specs
gcc version 2.96 20000731 (Red Hat Linux 7.1 2.96-81)
 /usr/lib/gcc-lib/i386-redhat-linux/2.96/tradcpp0 -lang-
fortran -v -D__GNUC__=2 -D__GNUC_MINOR__=96 -
D__GNUC_PATCHLEVEL__=0 -D__ELF__ -Dunix -Dlinux -D__ELF__ -
D__unix__ -D__linux__ -D__unix -D__linux -Asystem(posix) -
Acpu(i386) -Amachine(i386) -Di386 -D__i386 -D__i386__ -
D__tune_i386__ /dev/null /dev/null
GNU traditional CPP version 2.96 20000731 (Red Hat Linux 7.1
2.96-81)
 /usr/lib/gcc-lib/i386-redhat-linux/2.96/f771 -fnull-version -
quiet -dumpbase g77-version.f -version -fversion -o /tmp/
ccr29cz4.s /dev/null
GNU F77 version 2.96 20000731 (Red Hat Linux 7.1 2.96-81)
(i386-redhat-linux) compiled by GNU C version 2.96 20000731
(Red Hat Linux 7.1 2.96-81).
GNU Fortran Front End version 0.5.26 20000731 (Red Hat Linux
7.1 2.96-81)
 as -V -Qy -o /tmp/ccqJAAN9.o /tmp/ccr29cz4.s
GNU assembler version 2.10.91 (i386-redhat-linux) using BFD
version 2.10.91.0.2
 ld -m elf_i386 -dynamic-linker /lib/ld-linux.so.2 -o /tmp/
ccijxxjb /tmp/ccqJAAN9.o /usr/lib/gcc-lib/i386-redhat-linux/
2.96/../../../crt1.o /usr/lib/gcc-lib/i386-redhat-linux/2.96/
../../../crti.o /usr/lib/gcc-lib/i386-redhat-linux/2.96/
crtbegin.o -L/usr/lib/gcc-lib/i386-redhat-linux/2.96 -L/usr/
lib/gcc-lib/i386-redhat-linux/2.96/../../.. -lg2c -lm -lgcc -
lc -lgcc /usr/lib/gcc-lib/i386-redhat-linux/2.96/crtend.o /
usr/lib/gcc-lib/i386-redhat-linux/2.96/../../../crtn.o
 /tmp/ccijxxjb
__G77_LIBF77_VERSION__: 0.5.26 20000731 (prerelease)
@(#)LIBF77 VERSION 19991115
__G77_LIBI77_VERSION__: 0.5.26 20000731 (prerelease)
@(#) LIBI77 VERSION pjw,dmg-mods 19991115
__G77_LIBU77_VERSION__: 0.5.26 20000731 (prerelease)
@(#) LIBU77 VERSION 19980709
[rr@conformix 4]$
```

As you can see, it takes the help of gcc to compile programs. Note that Fortran programs have .for or .f at the end of the name of the program file.

As with gcc, you can create intermediate assembled or object code with g77. See manual pages of g77 for more information.

3.12 Other Compilers

A major benefit of using Linux as a development platform is that you have so many tools and compilers available in the open source community that you can develop in virtually any standard language. This section provides short information about a few more languages that can be easily integrated into the Linux development platform.

3.12.1 Smalltalk

Smalltalk is an object oriented language and a GNU version of Smalltalk can be downloaded from ftp://ftp.gnu.org/gnu/smalltalk/. The latest version at the time of writing this book is 1.95.9. The compilation and installation is quite easy and is similar to other GNU tools. You can also go to www.smalltalk.org for more information.

3.12.2 Oberon

Oberon is the successor to the Pascal and Modula languages and it is an object-oriented language. It is mostly used in educational environments for teaching programming language concepts. For detailed information, please refer to http://www.oberon.ethz.ch/.

3.12.3 Ruby

Ruby is an interpreted language. Information about this language can be found at http://www.ruby-lang.org/en/.

3.13 References and Resources

1. GNU web site at http://www.gnu.org/
2. Languages supported by GCC at http://gcc.gnu.org/onlinedocs/gcc-3.0.2/gcc_2.html
3. Status of C99 support on GCC at http://gcc.gnu.org/gcc-3.0/c99status.html
4. Object Oriented Programming and Objective C at http://developer.apple.com/techpubs/macosx/Cocoa/ObjectiveC/
5. Object Programming and Objective Language at http://www.toodarkpark.org/computers/objc/
6. The GNU C Library at http://www.delorie.com/gnu/docs/glibc/libc_toc.html
7. Using as at http://www.objsw.com/docs/as_toc.html
8. Using and porting GNU cc at http://www.delorie.com/gnu/docs/gcc/gcc_toc.html
9. GNU C++ Library at http://www.delorie.com/gnu/docs/libg++/libg++_toc.html
10. NetBSD Library source code at http://www.ajk.tele.fi/libc/code.html
11. Free Pascal project at http://www.freepascal.org
12. GNU Pascal at http://agnes.dida.physik.uni-essen.de/~gnu-pascal/
13. GNU Smalltalk download site at ftp://ftp.gnu.org/gnu/smalltalk/
14. Smalltalk information at http://www.smalltalk.org

15. Bob Nevlen, Linux Assembly Language Programming ISBN 0-13-0877940-1, Prentice Hall PTR 2000.

16. Oberon Home page at http://www.oberon.ethz.ch/

17. Ruby Home Page at http://www.ruby-lang.org/en/

CHAPTER 4

Using GNU make

All serious software projects are built in pieces by many developers. These pieces consist of source code and header files, libraries and different tools. To combine these pieces into a product is a process commonly known as a *build*. The GNU *make* utility is one of the many available utilities used to build these software projects. Large software projects often have hundreds and even thousands of files. Compiling these files and linking them into final executable product files is done by a careful and well-defined automated process. This automated process, also known as the *software build* process, is controlled by the make utility through *makefiles*. The make utility reads one or more of these makefiles containing information about how to build a project. Makefiles contain different types of information, including variables, control structures and rules to compile and link source files, build libraries and so on. In the most common makefiles, rules are present to remove object and executable files from the source code directory to clean it up, if required. These rules are enforced based upon time stamps on different files. For example, if an existing object file is newer than the corresponding source code file, it is not recompiled. However if the object file is older than the source file, it shows that someone modified the source file after the object file was last built. In such a case, make detects it and rebuilds the object file. Depending upon the requirements of a project, someone can create different types of rules and commands to build software projects.

This chapter contains information on how to write makefiles for software projects and provides sufficient information for a reader to write makefiles for fairly complex projects. You can also refer to the reference at the end of this chapter for more comprehensive information about the make utility.

To demonstrate the use of make, several examples are presented in this chapter. These examples demonstrate how make can be used for different objectives. These examples are simple and easy to understand and are explained in the text. However you may write makefiles in many different ways for the same object. Features of make that are discussed in this chapter are those most commonly used. Make has many additional, less commonly used, features that are not covered here and you may want to use these as well while designing your makefiles.

4.1 Introduction to GNU make

The make utility has been used for a very long time in all types of software development projects. There are open-source as well as commercial variants available from many vendors. The most common and popular distribution of make is the GNU make, which is open source and is available for almost all UNIX and Microsoft Windows platforms. All of the Linux distributions have the GNU make as a standard package with the development system. If you have installed development software from a distribution, you don't need to install any additional software for make to work. The version of make currently installed can be displayed using the following command.

```
[root@conformix make]# make -v
GNU Make version 3.79.1, by Richard Stallman and Roland
McGrath.
Built for i386-redhat-linux-gnu
Copyright (C) 1988, 89, 90, 91, 92, 93, 94, 95, 96, 97, 98,
99, 2000
        Free Software Foundation, Inc.
This is free software; see the source for copying conditions.
There is NO warranty; not even for MERCHANTABILITY or FITNESS
FOR A PARTICULAR PURPOSE.

Report bugs to <bug-make@gnu.org>.

[root@conformix make]#
```

Since this is one of the most widely used software packages in the development community, there is a wealth of information available about it on the Internet. This chapter is intended to provide sufficient information to use `make` in all types of software projects.

Simply put, `make` reads a text input file that contains information about how to compile, link and build target files. Make uses commands and rules specified in this file to carry out its operation. We shall discuss in detail the contents of these files, commonly known as *makefiles*.

4.1.1 Basic Terminology

Before we move ahead with more information about `make` and how to use it, let us get familiar with some basic terminology about the software build process and the `make` utility. The terms defined below will be used throughout this chapter as well as in the chapters that follow.

Input Files

The `make` utility uses input files to build software projects. These input files, also known as *makefiles*, contain information about when and how to compile, assemble or link files. These input files also contain commands and rules to carry out these tasks.

Rules

A rule in an input file provides information about how to build an individual target (defined next). A rule has three parts:

1. The target
2. Dependencies
3. Commands

A target is rebuilt whenever a dependency file has a timestamp that is newer than the target. A target may have no dependency, in which case it is always rebuilt. The commands in the rule are executed to build the target from dependencies. The general format of a rule is as follows:

```
Target: Dependencies
    Commands
```

The commands part always starts with a TAB character. There are two types of rules that will be explained later in this chapter. These are types are:

1. The explicit rules
2. The implicit rules

The rules defined above fall into explicit rules category. Implicit rules are predefined rules that `make` uses when it does not find an implicit rule to build a target.

Target

A target is usually a file or set of files that is the result of some operation on one or more other files. A target may be an object file, a final executable file or some intermediate file. Targets may be fake or phony, in which case no files are actually rebuilt. One such example is the phony target to remove all object and executable files from the source files directory. This process is often called a *cleaning process*. As a convention, all makefiles have a rule to clean the source code so that everything can be rebuilt freshly.

Dependency

The dependencies are files that determine when to build a target. The decision to rebuild a target is made if the timestamp on any dependency is newer than the target. This usually shows that a dependency file has been modified after the target was built the last time. Consider the example of an object file that was built from a C source file. After building the object file, if someone modifies the source code file, we need to rebuild the object file because it is no longer current. When the make utility scans the input files, it verifies this rule and rebuilds the object file automatically if it finds a change in the source file. If multiple machines are used, they need to be in time sync.

A target may have multiple dependencies separated by space characters. In case of multiple dependencies, the target is rebuilt if any of the dependencies has changed. If the list of dependencies is very long, you can write multiple lines for dependencies by using a backslash character at the end of a line to continue to the next line. For example, the following lines show that tftp.o has dependencies spanning three lines.

```
tftp.o: tftp.c tftp.h file1.c file2.c file3.c file4.c\
        file5.c file6.c file7.c file1.h file2.h file3.h\
        file4.h file5.h
```

Note that the starting character in the second and third line should not be a TAB character; otherwise make will consider these lines as command lines and will try to execute these.

Default Goal

An input file (makefile) usually contains many rules. Each of these rules has a target. However the make utility does not build all of these targets. It only tries to build the first target specified in the input makefile. This target is called the *default* goal of the makefile. However, note that if dependencies to this default goal are targets of some other rules, the make utility can also build those targets in an effort to build the default goal. This happens when dependencies of the default goal are out of date.

If you want to build a target that is not the default goal, you have to specify the target at the command line when starting make. This will be explained later in this chapter.

Phony Target

Some targets may have no dependencies. A common example is the clean target that removes some files from the source directory tree. A typical clean target is shown below:

```
clean:
    rm *.o
```

Whenever you invoke `make` to build this target, the `rm` command is always executed. This is because the target has no dependency. These types of targets are called phony targets.

However there is a problem with such targets. Sometimes if there is a file with the same name as the phony target, the `make` utility may get confused while building it and execute the command in the phony target when it is not required to do so. To avoid this problem, you can specify which targets are phony targets in the makefile. The following line in the makefile defines clean as a phony target.

```
.PHONY: clean
clean:
    rm *.o
```

4.1.2 Input Files

The `make` command, when invoked without a command line argument, expects certain file names as input. These files names are searched in the current directory in the following order.

1. GNUmakefile
2. makefile
3. Makefile

If none of these files is present, `make` will not take any action and displays the following error message:

```
[root@conformix make]# make
make: *** No targets specified and no makefile found.  Stop.
[root@conformix make]#
```

However there is a way to specify files with non-standard names as explained later. The common practice is to use "Makefile" as the name of the input file because it easy to distinguish from other files due to upper case M.

> **NOTE** If you have multiple input files in the same directory with names GNUmakefile, makefile and Makefile, only the GNUmakefile will be used. As a rule of thumb, make will use only the first available file in its priority list to build a project. This means that if we have two files with names makefile and Makefile, only the file named makefile will be used.

You can specify any other filename using command line switch –f with the make command. For example, if you have a file named myrules.make, you can use it as input file to the make utility as follows:

```
make -f myrules.make
```

From now on in this book, we shall use only "Makefile" as the name of the input file for the make command. This is a usual convention in most of the software development projects. Input files with any other name will be used as include files in the Makefile. The common conventional name for include file is Makefile.in.

4.1.3   Typical Contents of a Makefile

The makefiles that are used as input to the make command have similar types of contents. Some of the typical contents of a makefile are as follows.

Variables

Variables are usually the first part of any makefile. Variables are used to associate a name to a text string in the makefiles. These variables are then substituted into other targets, dependencies or commands later in the makefile. A simple equal sign can associate a text string to a name. The following line defines a variable *targets* in the makefile. This variable is equal to two target files tftp.o and fto.o.

```
targets = tftp.o ftp.o
```

To use this variable later on, you enclose the variable name in parentheses and use a dollar sign with it. The targets variable will be used as $(targets) in the makefile to refer to these two object files. A typical use of this variable is shown in the following three lines.

```
$(targets): tftp.c tftp.h ftp.c ftp.h
  gcc -c tftp.c
  gcc -c ftp.c
```

This rule tells make command that if any of the four dependency files (tftp.c, tftp.h, ftp.c, ftp.h) has a timestamp newer than the object files, the object files should be rebuilt.

Now you may have noticed that this is not a wise rule. If only tftp.c is changed, then we need to build only tftp.o but with this rule we are also building ftp.o which may not be required. However this type of rule may be useful when a single dependency may affect many targets. For example, both ftp.o and tftp.o may be dependent on common.h file and the following rule will make sense.

```
$(targets): common.h
  gcc -c tftp.c
  gcc -c ftp.c
```

We shall discuss more about these things and how to write wiser and more comprehensive rules in makefiles later in this chapter.

Rule to Build the Default Goal

After defining the variables, the first rule defines the default goal. This is usually used to build one or more final executable from all of the source, object and library files.

Rules to Build Other Goals

After defining the default goal, you can define as many other rules as you like. These other rules are used to build individual parts of a big project. For example, if a project consists of three main parts, the FTP server, the TFTP server and the DNS resolver, you can have three individual rules for all of these individual parts. The default goal may be used to build all of these three targets in a single step.

Rules to Build Individual Objects

In addition to defining rules to build goals, you may have to define rules to build individual objects or intermediate files. One example of these rules is to build object files from the source files. These object files may then be used to build executable or library files.

Rules to Install

Some rules may be required to install the files into appropriate directories created by other rules. For example, after building library files, you may want to install them into /lib or /usr/lib directory. Similarly, after building executable files, you may want to install them into /bin, /usr/bin or /sbin directory or any other directory of your choice. For this reason, one or more rules may be defined in the makefiles so that make copies the appropriate files into their target location.

Rules to Clean Previous Builds

As mentioned earlier, the rule to clean previous builds is usually a phony rule to clean up the source code tree from the previously built intermediate and target files. This rule is useful when you want to hand over a clean directory to someone or to force everything to be rebuilt, perhaps with new options.

Comments and Blank Lines

As a good convention, you can insert some comment lines in makefiles so that you and others can make sense of what is there. All comments start with a hash (#) symbol. You can also put a comment after a command. The rule of thumb is that anything after the hash character will be considered a comment. If this character is the first character in a line, all of the line is a comment line.

C A U T I O N Any empty line that begins with a TAB is not really an empty line. It is considered an empty command. Empty commands are sometimes useful when you don't want to take any action for a particular dependency.

4.1.4   Running make

In its basic and most widely used form, simply entering "make" on the command line invokes the make program. Upon invocation, it reads its input file, in a priority order as explained earlier, and executes different commands in it to build the default goal. In this chapter, we are using a hypothetical project that builds three applications: ftp, tftp and dnsresolver. Reference to this project will be used in many parts of the remaining chapter. See section 4.4 for a complete listing of the makefiles used.

Building a Default Goal

If we have a Makefile in the current directory and the default goal is to build all of the ftp, tftp, and dnsresolver, specified by "all" rule, a typical session will be as follows:

```
[root@rr2 test]# make
gcc -g -O2 -c ftp.c
gcc -g -O2 -c common.c
gcc -static ftp.o common.o -o ftp
gcc -g -O2 -c tftp.c
gcc -static tftp.o common.o -o tftp
gcc -g -O2 -c dnsresolver.c
gcc -static dnsresolver.o common.o -o dnsresolver
[root@rr2 test]#
```

Building a Non-Default Goal

If you have multiple goals in a Makefile and you don't want to build a default goal, you have to specify the goal you want to build on the command line. The following line builds only the ftp server.

```
[root@rr2 test]# make ftp
gcc -g -O2 -c ftp.c
gcc -g -O2 -c common.c
gcc -static ftp.o common.o -o ftp
[root@rr2 test]#
```

When a Target is Updated

There are certain rules about when a target will be built or rebuilt. These are as listed below.

- *Target is not present.* If a target is not present and a rule is executed, the target will always be rebuilt.
- *Target is outdated.* This means that one or more dependencies of a target are newer than the target. This happens when someone changed a dependency after the target was built last time.
- *Target is forced to be rebuilt.* You can define rules to force a target to be rebuilt whether a dependency has changed or not. This is also true for phony targets.

4.1.5   Shell to Execute Commands

All commands in a makefile are executed in a subshell invoked by the `make` command. It is important to know which shell will be used to execute commands in the makefile. By default the shell name is `/bin/sh`. However this can be changed using the `SHELL` variable in the makefile. Please note that this is not the environment variable `SHELL`, but is set within the makefile. This is to avoid conflict with someone's personal preference of using a particular shell.

Each line that starts with TAB character represents a command and is executed by a single instance of shell. So, for example, the following line will cause a directory change to `tftp` and the command `rm *.o` to be executed from that directory. After executing this command, the `next` command is executed in the original directory because a new subshell is invoked and the effect of the `cd tftp` command is gone.

```
tftp: tftp/Makefile
   cd tftp; rm *.o
   @echo "Rebuilding . . ."
```

As mentioned earlier, one line can be split into multiple lines by placing a backslash at the end of the line. The above three lines can be written as follows without any change in their result:

```
tftp: tftp/Makefile
   (cd tftp;\
rm *.o)
   @echo "Makefile changed. Rebuilding …"
```

4.1.6   Include Files

In case of large projects, makefile rules can be split into many files. These smaller files can then be included into a makefile. When the `make` utility is scanning through the makefile and it finds an `include` file, it will go through the `include` file before going to the next line in the makefile. Logically, you can think of contents of the `include` file being inserted into the makefile at the place where the file is included.

Files can be included using the *include* directive inside a makefile. The following line includes a file `myrules.in` in a makefile.

```
include myrules.in
```

Multiple files can be included into a makefile on the same line. The following line includes two files `myrules.in` and `bootarules.in` into a makefile.

```
include myrules.in bootarules.in
```

When multiple files are included, these are read in the order they are present in the makefile. In the above example, first `myrules.in` will be read by the `make` utility and then `bootarules.in` will be read.

You can also use wildcards and variables to specify file names with the include directives. The following include directive includes all files with last part as ".in" and files specified by the variable MKINCS.

```
include *.in $(MKINCS)
```

4.2   The make Rules

Rules are the most important part of a makefile. Rules control how a project should be built. Each rule has a common structure which is discussed in this section. A typical makefile is introduced as an example to show you how rules are written in makefiles.

4.2.1   Anatomy of a Rule

As mentioned earlier, a typical rule looks like the following:

```
Target: Dependencies
    Commands
```

A target is the objective of the rule that depends upon a list of dependencies. Commands are used to build the target. The target name is followed by a colon. Commands start with a TAB character.

> **C A U T I O N** Each line containing commands starts with a TAB character. The TAB character distinguishes command lines from other lines. A common error is to replace the TAB character with a multiple space character. The result is that commands on this line are not executed.

Multiple Commands in the Same Line

A rule can have multiple commands to build target. These commands can be listed in multiple lines or in a single line. If commands are listed in a single line, they are separated by a semicolon. It should be noted that the difference is whether or not they are executed in the same subshell. Commands listed in one line are executed in the same subshell. If each command is listed in a separate line, each line starts with a TAB character in the start of the line. The following rule, used to remove some files from the current directory, has two commands. The first is echo and the second is the rm command.

```
clean:
    @echo "Deleting files ..."
    rm -f $(OBJS) *~
```

These two commands can also be listed as follows:

```
clean:
    @echo "Deleting files ..." ; rm -f $(OBJS) *~
```

Command Echoing

By default all commands in the makefile are echoed to standard output as these are executed. This provides information about the activity of make as it is going through the makefile. However you can suppress the command echo by starting commands with the character @.

This is especially useful in printing information from within the makefile using the echo command. For example, you can create a makefile that prints information before it starts executing. A typical rule in the makefile that displays information about the object before executing any other command follows. It displays a line showing that make is going to build FTP:

```
ftp: $(SRCS) $(HDRS)
        @echo "Building FTP"
        @$(CC) $(CFLAGS) $(INCLUDES) ftp.c
        @$(CC) $(LDFLAGS) $(COMMON) $(OBJS) -lcommon -o ftp
```

When make reads this file, it displays the following output:

```
[root@conformix ftp-dir]# make ftp
Building FTP
[root@conformix ftp-dir]#
```

If you don't insert the @ characters in this file, the result will be as follows. You can easily find the difference between this and the earlier output of the make command.

```
[root@conformix ftp-dir]# make ftp
echo "Building FTP"
Building FTP
gcc -g -O2 -c -I../common-dir ftp.c
gcc -static -L../common-dir  ftp.o  -lcommon -o ftp
[root@conformix ftp-dir]#
```

N O T E There are other ways to suppress the command echo. One of these is the use of -s or -silent flag on the command line. However the most common method is the use of the @ character.

Rules with no Dependencies

Many rules are used with no dependencies. These rules are used to execute commands without looking into any dependencies. Commands in these rules are guaranteed to be executed.

4.2.2 A Basic Makefile

Let us start with a simple makefile shown below. This makefile is used to build ftp, which is the default target.

```
################################################
# Makefile created to demonstrate use of the make
# utility in the "Linux Development Platform" book.
#
# Author: Rafeeq Ur Rehman
#         rr@conformix.net
################################################

# Variable definition
OBJS = ftp.o common.o
HDRS = ftp.h common.h
CFLAGS = -g -O2
TARGETS = ftp
CC = gcc

# Default Target

ftp: $(OBJS) $(HDRS)
  $(CC) $(OBJS) -o ftp

ftp.o: ftp.c $(HDRS)
  $(CC) $(CFLAGS) -c ftp.c

common.o: common.c common.h
  $(CC) $(CFLAGS) -c common.c

clean:
  rm -f $(TARGETS) $(OBJS)
```

This makefile has initial comments that show information about the file. After that, variables are defined. The rule to build default target is listed next. This rule has two dependencies which are defined by variables $(OBJS) and $(HDRS). Rules to build the object files are listed after the default rule. The last rule, clean, is used to remove files created during the make process so that the directory contains only the initial source code files when you invoked this rule for the first time. This rule has no dependency, so the rm command is guaranteed to be executed.

When building the default target ftp, make checks the dependencies. For this it expands two variables $(OBJS) and $(HDRS). After expansion, make finds out that the target is dependent upon the following four files.

1. ftp.o
2. ftp.h
3. common.o
4. common.h

Now make also finds out that there are other rules to build ftp.o and common.o files. If these two files are not up-to-date, make rebuilds these object files using corresponding rules. For example, if common.c file has been changed since make built common.o last time, make will rebuild it. After checking dependencies, make will build ftp if any of the dependency is newer than the ftp file or ftp file does not exist.

If you want to remove the target file and the object files, you can use the make clean command that invokes the clean rule. This rule has no dependency so the rm command will always execute, removing the ftp and any object files.

4.2.3   Another Example of Makefile

The following Makefile is a little bit bigger and is used to build three targets. These are as follows:

1. The ftp server
2. The tftp server
3. The dnsresolver

Before going into detail of how it is done, let us look at the Makefile itself. It is listed below.

```
##################################################
# Makefile created to demonstrate use of the make
# utility in the "Linux Development Platform" book.
#
# Author: Rafeeq Ur Rehman
#          rr@conformix.com
##################################################

# Variable definition
SRCS = ftp.c tftp.c dnsresolver.c common.c
OBJS = ftp.o tftp.o dnsresolver.o common.o
FTPOBJS = ftp.o common.o
FTPHDRS = ftp.h common.h
TFTPOBJS = tftp.o common.o
TFTPHDRS = tftp.h common.h
DNSRESOLVEROBJS =  dnsresolver.o common.o
DNSRESOLVERHDRS =  dnsresolver.h common.h
CC = gcc
CFLAGS = -g -O2
LDFLAGS = -static
TARGETS = ftp tftp dnsresolver
INSTALLDIR = /root

# Default Target
```

```
all: $(TARGETS)

# Rule to build object files

$(OBJS): $(SRCS)
  $(CC) $(CFLAGS) -c $(@:.o=.c)

# Rules to build individual targets

ftp: $(FTPOBJS) $(FTPHDRS)
  $(CC) $(LDFLAGS) $(FTPOBJS) -o ftp

tftp: $(TFTPOBJS) $(TFTPHDRS)
  $(CC) $(LDFLAGS) $(TFTPOBJS) -o tftp

dnsresolver: $(DNSRESOLVEROBJS) $(DNSRESOLVERHDRS)
  $(CC) $(LDFLAGS) $(DNSRESOLVEROBJS) -o dnsresolver

clean:
  rm -f $(TARGETS) $(OBJS)

install:
  cp $(TARGETS) $(INSTALLDIR)
# Additional Dependencies

ftp.o: $(FTPHDRS) tftp.o: $(TFTPHDRS)
dnsresolver.o: $(DNSRESOLVERHDRS)
```

After comments in the start of the makefile, the first part of the file defines variables used in this file. As you shall see, defining variables is very helpful if you need any modification in the Makefile or want to add or remove more files later on. After defining variables, the default target is defined with the name "all" as follows:

```
all: $(TARGETS)
```

This in turn has dependencies on the three targets that we want to make. Please note that we don't have any command to build this default target. When make reaches the default target, it tries to meet dependencies to make sure that these are up-to-date. If any of these dependencies is not up-to-date, make will try to recreate it.

The three dependencies to the default target (ftp, tftp and dnsresolver) have their own rules to build. For example, the following ftp rule shows that it depends upon two variables $(FTPOBJS) and $(FTPHDRS).

```
ftp: $(FTPOBJS) $(FTPHDRS)
  $(CC) $(LDFLAGS) $(FTPOBJS) -o ftp
```

This means that if any of the files listed in these two variables has changed, the ftp target will be rebuilt. These files defined in the two variables are as follows:

- `ftp.o`
- `common.o`
- `ftp.h`
- `common.h`

We have another rule to build object files from source files. This rule is as follows:

```
$(OBJS): $(SRCS)
    $(CC) $(CFLAGS) -c $(@:.o=.c)
```

It will build any of the `.o` object file, which is not up-to-date from its corresponding `.c` source code file. The @ sign is used to substitute the name of the target by replacing `.o` with `.c` so that if we want to build the target `common.o`, the @ symbol will replace `.o` with `.c` in the target, making it `common.c`. This way the compiler gets the correct argument after the `-c` switch in the command line. This technique is especially useful if you are dealing with files with different extensions. For example, if the source code files are C++ files ending with `.cpp`, the above rule may be written as follows:

```
$(OBJS): $(SRCS)
    $(CC) $(CFLAGS) -c $(@:.o=.cpp)
```

Now the @ will replace `.o` with `.cpp` for each file in the target.

The `clean` rule will delete all of the object and executable files. The install rule will copy files into the /root directory. Both of these rules have no dependency. This means that the commands in these rules don't depend on anything and will always be executed whenever this rule is invoked.

The last part of the makefile lists some additional dependencies not covered by earlier rules. Note that these three rules in the end have no command to execute. You can have as many rules to build a target as you like, but only one of these rules should contain commands to build it.

Now you can see how the use of variables is useful in this Makefile. If you add or remove some files or dependencies, you need to modify only the upper part of the makefile where variables are defined, without worrying about the rest of the `makefile`. For example, if you add a new header file to the dependency list of ftp, you just need to modify the variable FTPHDRS. Similarly to add a new source code file `common.c` that is being used by ftp, you need to add it to the following two variables:

1. FTPOBJS
2. OBJS

By modifying these two variables, this will automatically be used by `ftp`, `$(OBJS)` and `clean` rules.

Now is the time to use this makefile and see how the `make` program executes different commands. The output of the `make` command is shown below that needs some attention to understand how the `make` program checks dependencies and builds different targets.

```
[root@rr2 test]# make
gcc -g -O2 -c ftp.c
gcc -g -O2 -c common.c
gcc -static ftp.o common.o -o ftp
gcc -g -O2 -c tftp.c
gcc -static tftp.o common.o -o tftp
gcc -g -O2 -c dnsresolver.c
gcc -static dnsresolver.o common.o -o dnsresolver
[root@rr2 test]#
```

The default target is "all" which has dependency upon the variable $(TARGETS). This variable has three words: ftp, tftp and dnsresolver. First make tries to verify that ftp is up-to-date. For this it finds that ftp file does not exist so it tries to build it using some other rule. It finds the following rule to build ftp:

```
ftp: $(FTPOBJS) $(FTPHDRS)
    $(CC) $(LDFLAGS) $(FTPOBJS) -o ftp
```

Now it tries to find if dependencies of this rule are up-to-date. The object files are not present, so first it tries to build the object file. To build the object files, it looks for another rule and finds the following rule to build two object files (ftp.o and common.o) in the dependency list.

```
$(OBJS): $(SRCS)
    $(CC) $(CFLAGS) -c $(@:.o=.c)
```

When make executes the command in this rule, you see the following two lines in the output of the make command.

```
gcc -g -O2 -c ftp.c
gcc -g -O2 -c common.c
```

Now it has all of the dependencies for the ftp target up-to-date and it builds ftp using the corresponding rule. At this point you see the following line in the output of the make command:

```
gcc -static ftp.o common.o -o ftp
```

By building ftp, make has satisfied one dependency in the default goal. Now it will try to meet the second dependency, which is tftp. Since the tftp file is not present, it will locate a rule that can be used to build tftp. In the tftp rule dependencies, the common.o file is already up-to-date, so it will not recompile it. However since it does not find tftp.o, it will rebuild tftp.o. At this point you see the following line in the output:

```
gcc -g -O2 -c tftp.c
```

Now it has successfully built dependencies for tftp and it will build the tftp target and display the following line in the output:

```
gcc -static tftp.o common.o -o tftp
```

The same process is repeated for the dnsresolver and the following two lines are displayed:

```
gcc -g -O2 -c dnsresolver.c
gcc -static dnsresolver.o common.o -o dnsresolver
```

After building dnsresolver, nothing is left in the default target rule "all," so make will stop at this point.

Now let us see what happens if you modify the ftp.h file and run make again. The output will be as follows:

```
[root@rr2 test]# make
gcc -g -O2 -c ftp.c
gcc -static ftp.o common.o -o ftp
[root@rr2 test]#
```

This time make only rebuilt ftp because ftp.h is a dependency only for the target ftp. However if you modify common.h, it will rebuild ftp, tftp and dnsresolver as follows:

```
[root@rr2 test]# make
gcc -g -O2 -c ftp.c
gcc -static ftp.o common.o -o ftp
gcc -g -O2 -c tftp.c
gcc -static tftp.o common.o -o tftp
gcc -g -O2 -c dnsresolver.c
gcc -static dnsresolver.o common.o -o dnsresolver
[root@rr2 test]#
```

Modifying common.c will cause rebuilding of all object files as well. This result of make after modification in common.c is as follows:

```
[root@rr2 test]# make
gcc -g -O2 -c ftp.c
gcc -g -O2 -c common.c
gcc -static ftp.o common.o -o ftp
gcc -g -O2 -c tftp.c
gcc -static tftp.o common.o -o tftp
gcc -g -O2 -c dnsresolver.c
gcc -static dnsresolver.o common.o -o dnsresolver
[root@rr2 test]#
```

You can also use rules to build individual targets. For example, if you want to build only ftp, you use the following command line instead:

```
[root@rr2 test]# make ftp
gcc -g -O2 -c ftp.c
gcc -g -O2 -c common.c
gcc -static ftp.o common.o -o ftp
[root@rr2 test]#
```

Now let us clean the files we have created using the following rule.

```
clean:
   rm -f $(TARGETS) $(OBJS)
```

The result of running the command make clean will be as follows:

```
[root@rr2 test]# make clean
rm -f ftp tftp dnsresolver ftp.o tftp.o dnsresolver.o common.o
[root@rr2 test]#
```

As you can see from the above output, make has replaced variables with values present in the variables before running the rm command. This is what is done every time make invokes a command.

4.2.4   Explicit Rules

There are two types of rules: *explicit* rules and *implicit* rules. All of the rules that we have been using in this chapter until now are explicit rules. An explicit rule has three parts: target, dependencies and commands. Explicit rules are defined in detail and they perform exactly as they are written. In general, all rules present in a makefile are explicit rules.

4.2.5   Implicit Rules

Implicit rules are used by make to build certain targets by itself. These rules are usually language-specific and operate depending upon file extension. For example, make can build .o files from .c files using an implicit rule for C language compilation. Consider the basic makefile we used earlier in this chapter as shown below:

```
# Variable definition
OBJS = ftp.o common.o
HDRS = ftp.h common.h
CFLAGS = -g -O2
TARGETS = ftp
CC = gcc

# Default Target

ftp: $(OBJS) $(HDRS)
  $(CC) $(OBJS) -o ftp

ftp.o: ftp.c $(HDRS)
  $(CC) $(CFLAGS) -c ftp.c

common.o: common.c common.h
  $(CC) $(CFLAGS) -c common.c

clean:
   rm -f $(TARGETS) $(OBJS)
```

You can modify this file so that it uses implicit rules to build object files. The modified file is shown below:

```
# Variable definition
OBJS = ftp.o common.o
HDRS = ftp.h common.h
CFLAGS = -g -O2
TARGETS = ftp
CC = gcc

# Default Target

ftp: $(OBJS) $(HDRS)
  $(CC) $(OBJS) -o ftp

clean:
  rm -f $(TARGETS) $(OBJS)
```

Note that we have completely taken out two rules that are used to build the object files. Now when make needs to build these object files, it uses its implicit rule for this purpose. Running make on this makefile produces the following result.

```
[root@conformix make]# make
gcc -g -O2    -c -o ftp.o ftp.c
gcc -g -O2    -c -o common.o common.c
gcc ftp.o common.o -o ftp
[root@conformix make]#
```

Note that the first two lines of the output create object files using implicit rules. You may also have noted that the CFLAGS variable is also used in this process. Like CFLAGS, implicit rules use other variables while building targets. For a more detailed discussion, please see the reference at the end of this chapter.

While using implicit rules, you should be careful about the process, because make can build a target using explicit rule depending upon which source files are available. For example, make can produce an object file from a C source code file as well as Pascal source code file. In the above example, if common.c file is not present but common.p (Pascal source code file) is present in the current directory, make will invoke Pascal compiler to create common.o file, which may be wrong. You also have less control over options on implicit rules.

4.3 Using Variables

Variables are an important part of all makefiles used in a project. Variables are used for many purposes; the most important of which is to have structured and easily understandable makefiles. This section contains more information about variables used in makefiles.

4.3.1   Defining Variables

Variables can be defined in a usual way by typing in the variable name, followed by an equal sign. The equal sign is followed by the value that is assigned to the variable. Note that there may be space characters on one or both sides of the equal sign. A typical variable assignment may be as follows:

```
CFLAGS = -g -O2
```

Another example of defining the C compiler name is as follows:

```
CC = gcc
```

This variable than can be used in other parts of the makefile by placing a $ sign and a pair of parenthesis or braces. The following line in a makefile is used to compile a file `tftp.c` and create an object file `tftp.o` with the help of above two variables;

```
$(CC) $(CFLAGS) -o tftp.o  tftp.c
```

This line can also be written as follows:

```
${CC} ${CFLAGS} -o tftp.o  tftp.c
```

N O T E   Variables are case sensitive in makefiles. A variable `$(OUTFILES)` is different from a variable `$(OutFiles)`.

4.3.2   Types of Variables

There are two types of variables. Variables defined using the = sign are *recursively expanded variables*. This means that a variable may be expanded depending upon value of a variable at a later stage in the makefile. Consider the following lines in a makefile.

```
OBJ1 = ftp.o
OBJ2 = common.o
OBJS = $(OBJ1) $(OBJ2)
printobjs:
  @echo $(OBJS)
OBJ1 = ftp.o tftp.o
```

Variable `OBJS` will contain a list of three files, `ftp.o`, `tftp.o` and `common.o`, although `tftp.o` was added *after* the echo command. Output of this makefile is as follows.

```
[root@conformix make]# make
ftp.o tftp.o common.o
[root@conformix make]#
```

This is because `make` used the default target rule and executed the `echo` command. Before printing out the value of the `OBJS` variable, it scanned the makefile to the end to re-evaluate the value of the `OBJ1` variable and hence the `OBJS` variable.

The other types of variables are *simply expanded* variables and the value of these variables is determined at the time of their definition. These variables are defined using the `:=` symbol instead of just the = symbol. If we change the OBJS line in the above makefile to this type of variable, the value printed by the makefile will be as follows:

```
[root@conformix make]# make
ftp.o common.o
[root@conformix make]#
```

Now make did not take into consideration the changed value of the OBJ1 variable later in the makefile.

There are advantages and disadvantages to both types of variables. You can decide which type of variable to use in a particular situation.

4.3.3   Pre-Defined Variables

The make utility can also take variables from the shell environment. For example, the CFLAGS variable can be set through shell startup file (e.g. /etc/profile). If this variable is not redefined inside the makefile, its value will be taken from the environment.

4.3.4   Automatic Variables

Some variables are pre-defined and are called *automatic variables*. They are usually very short in length but play a very important role in the decision-making process. The most commonly used automatic variables are listed below.

- The $@ variable contains the value of the target of a rule.
- The $< variable always contains the first dependency of a rule.
- The $? variable contains a list of modified files in the dependency list. If the target is being built for the first time, it contains a list of all dependencies. Consider the following makefile.

```
# Variable definition
OBJS = ftp.o common.o
HDRS = ftp.h common.h

CFLAGS = -g -O2
TARGETS = ftp
CC = gcc

# Default Target

ftp: $(OBJS) $(HDRS)
  @echo $?
  @echo $@
  @echo $<
  $(CC) $(OBJS) -o ftp
```

```
[root@conformix make]# make
gcc -g -O2    -c -o ftp.o ftp.c
gcc -g -O2    -c -o common.o common.c
ftp.o common.o ftp.h common.h
ftp
ftp.o
gcc ftp.o common.o -o ftp
[root@conformix make]#
```

The first two lines in the output use implicit rules to build object files. The third line in the output is generated by the first echo command and it has a list of all the dependencies. The second echo command displays the fourth line in the output, which is just the name of the target, i.e. ftp. The last echo command prints the first dependency in the fifth line of the output.

Now let us modify the common.c file and run make once again. The output will be as follows:

```
[root@conformix make]# make
gcc -g -O2    -c -o common.o common.c
common.o
ftp
ftp.o
gcc ftp.o common.o -o ftp
[root@conformix make]#
```

This time make used an implicit rule to build common.o. The important thing to note is the second line in the output, which is displayed by the first echo command in the makefile. This time it displayed only one file in the dependency list because common.o is the only file that is changed in the dependencies.

Automatic variables are very useful in control structures and in the decision-making process when you carry out an operation based upon the result of some comparison.

4.4   Working with Multiple Makefiles and Directories

Until now we have used simple makefiles to build projects or targets. We used only one makefile in the project and all of the source files were present in the same directory. In real-life software development projects, we have multiple directories containing different parts of a software product. For example, one directory may contain all library files, another header files and a third one common files used by different parts. Similarly every part of the software project may have its own subdirectory.

This section deals with the same source files and targets that we used earlier in this chapter. The project contains three targets to be built. These targets are ftp, tftp and dnsresolver. We are using the same set of source files. However to demonstrate the use of multiple directories and multiple makefiles, we have created each component in a separate directory. This may not be the best example for a real-life situation, but it is well suited to demonstrate one of many possible ways to handle such a situation. The following directory tree shows the arrangement of these files in different directories.

```
[root@conformix make]# tree
.
|-- Makefile
|-- common-dir
|   |-- Makefile
|   |-- common.c
|   `-- common.h
|-- dns-dir
|   |-- Makefile
|   |-- dnsresolver.c
|   `-- dnsresolver.h
|-- ftp-dir
|   |-- Makefile
|   |-- ftp.c
|   `-- ftp.h
`-- tftp-dir
    |-- Makefile
    |-- tftp.c
    `-- tftp.h

4 directories, 13 files
[root@conformix make]#
```

As you can see, you have four directories, each having its own makefile as well as source files. There is a makefile in the top directory that is used with the make command. This top-level makefile used makefiles in sub-directories. We can carry out the common tasks of building, installing and cleaning different targets while sitting in the top directory. Let's have a look at makefile in each directory.

4.4.1 Makefile in The Top Directory

Makefile in the top directory is used to build all of the targets using different rules. To build a particular target, we move to the directory where source files for that target are present and run make in that directory. This makefile is shown below.

```
##################################################
# Makefile created to demonstrate use of the make
# utility in the "Linux Development Platform" book.
#
# Author: Rafeeq Ur Rehman
#         rr@conformix.com
##################################################

# Variable definition
```

```
FTPDIR = ftp-dir
TFTPDIR = tftp-dir
DNSDIR = dns-dir
COMDIR = common-dir

SUBDIRS = $(COMDIR) $(FTPDIR) $(TFTPDIR) $(DNSDIR)

# Default Target

all:
  @echo
  @echo "####################################"
  @echo "###       BUILDING ALL TARGETS     ###"
  @echo "####################################"
  @echo
  for i in $(SUBDIRS) ; do     \
        ( cd $$i ; make ) ;          \
  done

# Rules to build individual targets

libs:
  @cd $(COMDIR) ; make

ftp:
  @cd $(FTPDIR) ; make

tftp:
  @cd $(TFTPDIR) ; make

dnsresolver:
  @cd $(DNSDIR) ; make

clean:
  rm -f *~
  for i in $(SUBDIRS) ; do     \
        ( cd $$i ; make clean) ;  \
        done

install:
  for i in $(SUBDIRS) ; do     \
        ( cd $$i ; make install); \
  done
```

N O T E   Please note that the following lines:

```
ftp:
  @cd $(FTPDIR) ; make
```

are not equal to the following three lines:

```
ftp:
  @cd $(FTPDIR)
make
```

In the first case, `make` changes the directory to $(FTPDIR) and then executes the `make` command in that directory, which is the right thing to do. However in the second case, the cd command is executed and after that the next `make` command is again executed in the current directory. The effect of the cd command is lost when `make` goes to the next line to execute the next command. This is because of a new instance of sub-shell. that executes commands in each line as discussed earlier in this chapter.

After defining variables, we have a rule for each target. This rule basically has two commands on the same line. The first command, `cd,` is used to change the directory where source files for that target are located. In the second command, `make` uses makefile in that directory to build that target. Please note that we can also use the $(MAKE) variable for this purpose.

In the `clean` and `install` rules, we use the for loop to go into each directory and execute some commands. The `for` loop is explained later in this chapter.

4.4.2   Makefile in common-dir Directory

The files in the `common-dir` directory are used to build a simple library that is used by other targets at link time. The makefile in this directory is listed below:

```
# Variable definition
SRCS = common.c
OBJS = common.o
HDRS = common.h
LIBCOMMON = libcommon.a
INSTALLDIR = /root

CC = gcc
CFLAGS = -g -O2 -c

# Default Target

$(LIBCOMMON): $(SRCS) $(HDRS)
  $(CC) $(CFLAGS) common.c
  ar -cr $(LIBCOMMON) $(OBJS)
  ranlib $(LIBCOMMON)
```

```
install:
    cp $(LIBCOMMON) $(INSTALLDIR)
clean:
    rm -f $(OBJS) $(LIBCOMMON) *~
```

This makefile builds an archive library file libcommon.a, which is the default target. Note that this makefile can also be used as a standalone in this directory so that if someone is working only on the library part of the project, he/she can use this makefile to test only the compilation and library building process. This is useful because each developer can stay in his/her own directory without building all parts of the project from the main makefile in the top directory.

4.4.3   Makefile in the ftp-dir Directory

The makefile in the ftp-dir directory builds the ftp target. It compiles and then statically links the object files using the library we built in common-dir directory. This makefile is shown below.

```
# Variable definition
SRCS = ftp.c
OBJS = ftp.o
HDRS = ftp.h

CC = gcc
CFLAGS = -g -O2 -c
INCLUDES = -I../common-dir
LDFLAGS = -static -L$(LIBSDIR)
LIBSDIR = ../common-dir
INSTALLDIR = /root

# Default Target

ftp: $(SRCS) $(HDRS)
    $(CC) $(CFLAGS) $(INCLUDES) ftp.c
    $(CC) $(LDFLAGS) $(COMMON) $(OBJS) -lcommon -o ftp

install:
    cp ftp $(INSTALLDIR)

clean:
    @echo "Deleting files ..."
    rm -f ftp $(OBJS) *~
```

4.4.4 Makefile in the tftp-dir Directory

The makefile in the `tftp-dir` directory builds the `tftp` target. It compiles and then statically links the object files using the library we built in the `common-dir` directory. This makefile is shown below. It also has rules to install the target and clean the directory.

```
# Variable definition
SRCS = tftp.c
OBJS = tftp.o
HDRS = tftp.h

CC = gcc
CFLAGS = -g -O2 -c
INCLUDES = -I../common-dir
LIBSDIR = ../common-dir
LDFLAGS = -static -L$(LIBSDIR)
INSTALLDIR = /root

# Default Target

tftp: $(SRCS) $(HDRS)
  $(CC) $(CFLAGS) $(INCLUDES) tftp.c
  $(CC) $(LDFLAGS) $(COMMON) $(OBJS) -lcommon -o tftp

install:
  cp tftp $(INSTALLDIR)

clean:
  @echo "Deleting files ..."
  rm -f tftp $(OBJS) *~
```

4.4.5 Makefile in the dns-dir Directory

The makefile in the `dns-dir` directory builds the `dnsresolver` target. It compiles and then statically links the object files using the library we built in the `common-dir` directory. This makefile is shown below.

```
# Variable definition
SRCS = dnsresolver.c
OBJS = dnsresolver.o
HDRS = dnsresolver.h

CC = gcc
CFLAGS = -g -O2 -c
INCLUDES = -I../common-dir
LIBSDIR = ../common-dir
LDFLAGS = -static -L$(LIBSDIR)
INSTALLDIR = /root
```

```
# Default Target

dnsresolver: $(SRCS) $(HDRS)
  $(CC) $(CFLAGS) $(INCLUDES) dnsresolver.c
  $(CC) $(LDFLAGS) $(COMMON) $(OBJS) -lcommon -o dnsresolver

install:
  cp dnsresolver $(INSTALLDIR)

clean:
  @echo "Deleting files ..."
  rm -f dnsresolver $(OBJS) *~
```

4.4.6   Building Everything

After going through these makefiles, you are ready to build the targets. Go to the top directory and run the make command from there. It will read the makefile in the top directory and will try to build all targets. A typical output of this action is as follows:

```
[root@conformix make]# make

#######################################
###        BUILDING ALL TARGETS      ###
#######################################

for i in common-dir ftp-dir tftp-dir dns-dir  ; do   \
        ( cd $i ; make ) ;        \
done
make[1]: Entering directory `/root/make/common-dir'
gcc -g -O2 -c common.c
ar -cr libcommon.a common.o
ranlib libcommon.a
make[1]: Leaving directory `/root/make/common-dir'
make[1]: Entering directory `/root/make/ftp-dir'
gcc -g -O2 -c -I../common-dir ftp.c
gcc -static -L../common-dir  ftp.o  -lcommon -o ftp
make[1]: Leaving directory `/root/make/ftp-dir'
make[1]: Entering directory `/root/make/tftp-dir'
gcc -g -O2 -c -I../common-dir tftp.c
gcc -static -L../common-dir  tftp.o  -lcommon -o tftp
make[1]: Leaving directory `/root/make/tftp-dir'
make[1]: Entering directory `/root/make/dns-dir'
gcc -g -O2 -c -I../common-dir dnsresolver.c
gcc -static -L../common-dir  dnsresolver.o  -lcommon -o
dnsresolver
make[1]: Leaving directory `/root/make/dns-dir'
[root@conformix make]#
```

During the process of building all targets, you can see how make enters and leaves each directory and builds targets in each directory.

4.4.7 Cleaning Everything

The cleaning process is done the same way as we built all targets. Output of this process is shown below. Again you can see that make enters each directory, runs the make clean command and then leaves the directory. The clean rule in makefiles present in each subdirectory is used to remove files.

```
[root@conformix make]# make clean
rm -f *~
for i in common-dir ftp-dir tftp-dir dns-dir  ; do   \
        ( cd $i ; make clean) ;  \
        done
make[1]: Entering directory `/root/make/common-dir'
rm -f common.o  libcommon.a *~
make[1]: Leaving directory `/root/make/common-dir'
make[1]: Entering directory `/root/make/ftp-dir'
Deleting files ...
rm -f ftp ftp.o  *~
make[1]: Leaving directory `/root/make/ftp-dir'
make[1]: Entering directory `/root/make/tftp-dir'
Deleting files ...
rm -f tftp tftp.o  *~
make[1]: Leaving directory `/root/make/tftp-dir'
make[1]: Entering directory `/root/make/dns-dir'
Deleting files ...
rm -f dnsresolver dnsresolver.o  *~
make[1]: Leaving directory `/root/make/dns-dir'
[root@conformix make]#
```

The make clean command finishes its operation after going through all subdirectories.

4.4.8 Making Individual Targets

Instead of using a single big makefile, you can also build individual targets using smaller makefiles. While building only one target, make will go into only that directory and build that target. The following output shows the output of the make command when you build only the ftp target.

```
[root@conformix make]# make ftp
make[1]: Entering directory `/root/make/ftp-dir'
gcc -g -O2 -c -I../common-dir ftp.c
gcc -static -L../common-dir  ftp.o  -lcommon -o ftp
make[1]: Leaving directory `/root/make/ftp-dir'
[root@conformix make]#
```

4.5   Special Features of make

In addition to the normal use of the make utility, it has some special features. Two of these features are discussed here that may be of interest for a common user of make. These features are running make commands in *parallel* and running make in *non-stop* mode.

Running multiple commands in parallel enhances the efficiency of make. Running make in non-stop mode is useful for very large projects where you want make to go through everything while running a command without stopping, even in case of errors. You can redirect the output of make to a log file which can be viewed later to find out what error occurred during the make processes of the whole project.

4.5.1   Running Commands in Parallel

Usually make runs commands in serial fashion. This means that one command is executed and when that command is finished, the next command is executed. You can ask make to run many commands in parallel. This is especially useful in multi-processor systems to make execution fast. The only problem with this is that when multiple commands are running in parallel, output from different commands is displayed simultaneously and can get mixed up. To run multiple commands in parallel, use the -j (jobs) command line switch with make.

If you want to specify a maximum number of concurrent commands, a number with the -j switch may be specified. For example, -j5 on the command line will force make to invoke at the maximum five commands simultaneously. It is useful to note that in general the most efficient builds can be done with -j equal to one or two times the total number of processors on the system. Also note that make rules are followed such that all dependencies are satisfied before a target is built. This means you won't always have the maximum number of jobs running simultaneously, depending upon the way makefile is written.

4.5.2   Non-Stop Execution

The make utility executes each command while building a target. After executing the command, it checks the result of that command. If the command was executed successfully, it goes to the next command and executes it. However if the command does not execute successfully, make exits without executing any further commands. It displays an error message to show that the target can't be built.

Sometime, however, it is not important that each command should succeed. As an example, look at the following lines in the clean rule.

```
clean:
  rm ftp
  rm ftp.o common.o
```

If the ftp file is not there, the rm command will return a failure code. However we still want to remove other files using the rm command in the next line. If the rule is listed in this way and the ftp file is not present, the output of the make clean will be as follows:

```
[root@conformix make]# make clean
rm ftp
rm: cannot remove `ftp': No such file or directory
make: *** [clean] Error 1
[root@conformix make]#
```

Now you can see that make did not attempt to execute the second rm command. To overcome this situation, you can use a hyphen at the start of the command whose result code should not be checked. This way make displays an error message but continues to the next command. The same rule with hyphen added to the first rm command will be as follows:

```
clean:
  -rm ftp
  rm ftp.o common.o
```

Now when you invoke this rule and ftp file is not present, make will do something like the following:

```
[root@conformix make]# make clean
rm ftp
rm: cannot remove `ftp': No such file or directory
make: [clean] Error 1 (ignored)
rm ftp.o common.o
[root@conformix make]#
```

As you can see from the above output, make ignored the error and continued to the next line to remove object files.

There are other ways to ignore errors during the make process. You can also use the -i command line switch to ignore errors during the make process. Another method is to use .IGNORE special built-in rule to ignore errors.

4.6   Control Structures and Directives

Control structures inside makefiles enable you to make some logical decisions depending upon certain conditions. Make supports four types of decision-making directives as listed below:

1. The ifeq directive
2. The ifneq directive
3. The ifdef directive
4. The ifndef directive

These directives are explained next. In addition to these directives, you can also use the for control structure to execute a loop a specified number of times. Let us have a look at each of these.

4.6.1   The ifeq Directive

The ifeq directive is used to compare two values and make a decision based upon the result. The general format of this directive is as follows:

```
ifeq (value1, value2)
  block if value 1 is equal to value2
else
  block if value 1 is not equal to value2
endif
```

The else part is optional and may not be present. This structure is useful if you want to make a decision on the basis of some criteria. For example, based upon the value of type of build (temporary or final) you want to use different levels of optimization. The following code in a makefile does that.

```
ifeq ($(BUILD), final)
  $(CC) -c -O2 ftp.c
else
  $(CC) -c -O1 ftp.c
endif
```

Please note that there is no TAB character before ifeq, else and endif words.

4.6.2   The ifneq Directive

The ifneq directive is similar to ifeq directive. The only difference is that sense of equality is reversed. The general syntax is as follows:

```
ifneq (value1, value2)
  block if value 1 is not equal to value2
else
  block if value 1 is equal to value2
endif
```

4.6.3   The ifdef Directive

The ifdef directive checks if the value of the variable is empty or not. If the variable is not empty, the ifdef block is executed, otherwise the else part is executed. The general structure of the directive is as follows:

```
ifdef  variable
  block if variable is non-empty
else
  block if variable is empty
endif
```

This directive is useful to verify if a variable is defined or not. The else part is optional.

4.6.4   The ifndef Directive

The `ifndef` directive is similar to the `ifdef` directive. However selection of a block of commands is reversed as compared to `ifdef` directive. Its format is as follows:

```
ifndef  variable
   block if variable is empty
else
   block if variable is not empty
endif
```

4.6.5   The for Control Structure

You have already used the `for` directive in the example of using `make` with multiple directories. This directive is used to perform repeated operation on multiple items. The following rule in the makefile is used to go into multiple directories and remove object files in each of these directories:

```
SUBDIRS = ftp-dir tftp-dir common-dir
clean:
   for dir in $(SUBDIRS) ; do  \
         ( cd $$dir ; rm *.o) ;  \
   done
```

Each time a new value is assigned to variable `dir` from the values listed by the `SUBDIRS` variable until all of the values are used.

4.7   Getting the Latest Version and Installation

Almost all of the Linux distributions come with `make`. The Red Hat 7.1 distribution that we have used for this book already has the latest version of `make`. However if you want to get the latest version of GNU `make`, it is available at the following FTP site.

```
ftp://ftp.gnu.org/pub/gnu/make/
```

This FTP site has multiple versions of the `make` utility. Download the latest version, which will be a zipped `tar` file. The latest version at the time of writing this book is 3.79.1 and the filename is `make-3.79.1.tar.gz`.

4.7.1   Compilation

After downloading this file, just un-tar it into a directory using the following command:

```
tar zxvf make-3.79.1.tar.gz
```

The source files will be extracted into directory `make-3.79.1`. Change to this directory and run the `configure` script. It will create the makefiles appropriate for you. You should have some previous version of `make` in order to build the latest version. Use the `make` command; the default rule contains information about how to build `make`. Use the following command to verify that the build process for make was successful. This command will show a long list of tests and the output is truncated to save space.

```
[root@conformix make-3.79.1]# ./make check
Making check in i18n
make[1]: Entering directory `/opt/make-3.79.1/i18n'
make[1]: Nothing to be done for `check'.
make[1]: Leaving directory `/opt/make-3.79.1/i18n'
make[1]: Entering directory `/opt/make-3.79.1'
/opt/make-3.79.1/./make  check-local
make[2]: Entering directory `/opt/make-3.79.1'
cd tests && perl ./run_make_tests.pl -make ../make
-----------------------------------------------------
    Running tests for GNU make on Linux conformix.net 2.4.2-2
i686
                        GNU Make version 3.79.1
-----------------------------------------------------

Clearing work...
Finding tests...

features/comments ............................. ok
features/conditionals ......................... ok
features/default_names ........................ ok
features/double_colon.......................... ok
features/echoing .............................. ok
features/errors ............................... ok
features/escape ......,........................ ok
features/include .............................. ok
```

If these tests are successful, you have created the latest and greatest make utility. If some of the tests fail, it is an indication that some of the features are missing from this build of make.

4.7.2   Installation

You can install the newly created make utility using the following command.

```
make install
```

The command should be executed in the same directory in which you did the build process.

4.8   References and Resources

1. GNU Make, Richard M. Stallman and Ronald McGrath, Free Software Foundation, ISBN:1-8822114-80-9. It is also available on many websites in Postscript form.
2. GNU make web site at http://www.gnu.org/software/make/make.html
3. GNU make manual at http://www.gnu.org/manual/make/index.html

Working with GNU Debugger

The debugger is one of the most important components of any development system. No programmer writes a code that works on the first attempt or that does not have any bugs in it. Most of the time you have to go through debugging processes of your programs time and again. Therefore no development system is complete without a debugger. The GNU compiler, Emacs editor and other utilities work very closely with GNU debugger, also known as gdb, which is the debugger of choice of all open source developers community as well as for many commercial products. Many commercial debuggers are also built on top of GNU debugger.

In addition to command line debugging features, you can find many GUI front ends to the GNU debugger. These front ends include the famous xxgdb.

There are many other debuggers available in the open source community. Some of these debuggers are also introduced at the end of this chapter. This chapter provides a comprehensive working knowledge of gdb and how to use it. The text is accompanied by many examples to elaborate concepts presented here. After going through this chapter you should be able to debug many types of programs.

5.1   Introduction to GDB

GNU debugger or more commonly known as GDB is the most commonly used debugger in open source as well as commercial development on UNIX type platforms. It can be used as a native as well as cross debugger. GNU debugger supports many object file formats. The most commonly used formats are as follows:

- ELF
- a.out
- S-record

It is part of almost all of the Linux distributions available these days. In its command line form, it is started using the gdb command. The command provides an interactive text based prompt for the user. The default prompt for the debugger is (gdb). You can use commands available on this command prompt. Most of the commands can be abbreviated as long as they are not confused with any other command. For example, the next command can be used as single character n. This abbreviation will be more clear when you go through examples in this book.

All examples in this book use the GNU debugger that came with RedHat 7.1. The chapter also includes information about how to get the latest version of the debugger and install it on your system.

5.2   Getting Started with GDB

The GNU debugger is started using the gdb command. Upon startup, it displays initial information about the platform. It stops at the (gdb) command prompt where GDB commands can be used. A typical GDB screen is as shown below:

```
[rrehman@laptop gdb]$ gdb
GNU gdb 5.0rh-5 Red Hat Linux 7.1
Copyright 2001 Free Software Foundation, Inc.
GDB is free software, covered by the GNU General Public
License, and you are
welcome to change it and/or distribute copies of it under
certain conditions.
Type "show copying" to see the conditions.
There is absolutely no warranty for GDB.  Type "show warranty"
for details.
This GDB was configured as "i386-redhat-linux".
(gdb)
```

General help about GDB commands can be displayed using the help command on (gdb) prompt as shown below:

```
(gdb) help
List of classes of commands:
```

```
aliases -- Aliases of other commands
breakpoints -- Making program stop at certain points
data -- Examining data
files -- Specifying and examining files
internals -- Maintenance commands
obscure -- Obscure features
running -- Running the program
stack -- Examining the stack
status -- Status inquiries
support -- Support facilities
tracepoints -- Tracing of program execution without stopping
the program
user-defined -- User-defined commands
Type "help" followed by a class name for a list of commands in
that class.
Type "help" followed by command name for full documentation.
Command name abbreviations are allowed if unambiguous.
(gdb)
```

You can stop gdb using quit command on (gdb) prompt. You can also stop gdb or the current running command by pressing the Ctrl and C keys simultaneously.

You need to open a file for debugging after starting gdb using file command. You can also start gdb by providing a file name on the command line. The following command starts gdb and uses a.out file for debugging purpose.

```
gdb a.out
```

Please note that a.out must be compiled using the –g command line switch with gcc compiler. If you don't use the command line switch –g, no debug information will be stored in the a.out file. The typical command line to compile a file with debug support is as follows:

```
gcc -g hello.c -o hello
```

The above command creates an output file hello that can be used to debug hello.c program using the following command:

```
gdb hello
```

If you have started gdb without any command line argument, you can load a file into gdb at any time using file command at the (gdb) prompt.

5.2.1 Most Commonly Used gdb Commands

The most commonly used GDB commands are listed in Table 5-1. These commands are used to start and stop gdb debugging, executing a program and displaying results. Note that you start gdb using the gdb [filename] command and then you get the (gdb) prompt where you can use these commands.

Note that there is a difference between the next and the step commands. The next command will move you to the next line in the current function. If the current line is a function

Table 5-1 Common gdb commands

Command	Description
run	Start a program execution inside gdb from the beginning
quit	Quit gdb
print expr	Print expression, where expression may be a variable name
next	Go to next line
step	Step into next line
continue	Continue from the current place until end of program reaches or you find a break point

call, it will not go into the function code and you will not see what happens inside the function code. This is equivalent to the *step over* action used in many debuggers. On the other hand if you use the step command, it will move to the next line but if the current line is a function call, it will go into the function code and will take you to the first line inside the function. This is also called a *step into* action in some debuggers.

5.2.2   A Sample Session with gdb

In this section you go through a sample gdb session. You will use the following C code in this session and will step through the code from top to bottom. This code is saved in a file sum.c and the output executable file is sum. The sum.c file is listed below.

```
#include <stdio.h>
main ()
{
  int num1, num2, total ;

  printf("Enter first number : ");
  scanf("%d", &num1);
  printf("Enter second number : ");
  scanf("%d", &num2);

  total = num1 + num2;

  printf("\nThe sum is : %d\n", total);
}
```

As you can see, the sum.c file takes two numbers as input. It then calculates the sum and displays it as standard output. The compilation is done using the following command.

```
gcc -g sum.c -o sum
```

Now let us debug the output file. Note that when starting `gdb`, you use the output file `sum` on the command line and `gdb` will automatically find out the source code file name (`sum.c`) from the information stored inside the executable file. An explanation of different `gdb` commands is provided at the end of this debug session. Note that the `next` command is abbreviated as n in this session.

```
[rr@conformix 5]$ gdb sum
GNU gdb 5.0rh-5 Red Hat Linux 7.1
Copyright 2001 Free Software Foundation, Inc.
GDB is free software, covered by the GNU General Public
License, and you are
welcome to change it and/or distribute copies of it under
certain conditions.
Type "show copying" to see the conditions.
There is absolutely no warranty for GDB.  Type "show warranty"
for details.
This GDB was configured as "i386-redhat-linux"...
(gdb) list
1   #include <stdio.h>
2   main ()
3   {
4     int num1, num2, total ;
5
6     printf("Enter first number : ");
7     scanf("%d", &num1);
8     printf("Enter second number : ");
9     scanf("%d", &num2);
10
(gdb) list
11    total = num1 + num2;
12
13    printf("\nThe sum is : %d\n", total);
14  }
(gdb) list 1,14
1   #include <stdio.h>
2   main ()
3   {
4     int num1, num2, total ;
5
6     printf("Enter first number : ");
7     scanf("%d", &num1);
8     printf("Enter second number : ");
9     scanf("%d", &num2);
10
11    total = num1 + num2;
12
13    printf("\nThe sum is : %d\n", total);
```

```
    }
(gdb) list 5
1   #include <stdio.h>
2   main ()
3   {
4     int num1, num2, total ;
5
6     printf("Enter first number : ");
7     scanf("%d", &num1);
8     printf("Enter second number : ");
9     scanf("%d", &num2);
10
(gdb) list 9
4     int num1, num2, total ;
5
6     printf("Enter first number : ");
7     scanf("%d", &num1);
8     printf("Enter second number : ");
9     scanf("%d", &num2);
10
11    total = num1 + num2;
12
13    printf("\nThe sum is : %d\n", total);
gdb) break sum.c:6
Breakpoint 1 at 0x8048496: file sum.c, line 6.
(gdb) run
Starting program: /home/rr/5/sum

Breakpoint 1, main () at sum.c:6
6     printf("Enter first number : ");
(gdb) n
7     scanf("%d", &num1);
(gdb) n
Enter first number : 45
8     printf("Enter second number : ");
(gdb) n
9     scanf("%d", &num2);
(gdb) n
Enter second number : 56
11    total = num1 + num2;
(gdb) n
13    printf("\nThe sum is : %d\n", total);
(gdb) n

The sum is : 101
14 }
(gdb) n
```

```
Program exited with code 022.
(gdb) quit
[rr@conformix 5]$
```

Here are some observations about this session.

- The `list` command lists lines in the source code file and moves the pointer for listing. So the first `list` command lists lines from 1 to 10. The next `list` command lists lines from 11 to 14 where 14 is the last line.

- You can use a number with the `list` command. The `list` command displays the line with the number in the middle. So the command `list 9` will list lines from 4 to 13 trying to keep line number 9 in the middle.

- To list a range of lines, you can specify that range as an argument to the `list` command using a comma. For example, `list 1,14` will list lines from line number 1 to line number 14.

- You can set a break point using the `break` command at a particular line number. When you use the `run` command, the execution will stop at the break point. It is important that you create at least one break point before using the `run` command. If you don't do so, the program will continue to run until it reaches the end and you may not be able to debug it. More on `break` points will be discussed later.

- After setting a break point, you can use the `run` command to start execution of the program. Note that simply loading a file into `gdb` does not start execution. When `gdb` comes across a break point, it will stop execution and you will get a `(gdb)` command prompt. At this point you can start tracing the program line by line or using some other method.

- The `next` command (or simply n) executes the current line and moves execution pointer to the next line. Note that the line number and the contents of line are displayed each time you use the `next` command.

- When the running program needs an input, `gdb` will stop and you can enter the required value. For example, I have entered 45 and 56 as values for num1 and num2.

- `gdb` will print any output when a command is executed that prints something on the output device. You can see the result of addition printed.

- When `gdb` reaches the end of execution, it will print the exit code. After that you can use the `quit` command to end `gdb` session.

This was a simple `gdb` session. In next sections, you will go through more examples of how to use `gdb`.

5.2.3 Passing Command Line Arguments to the Program Being Debugged

Many program need command line arguments to be passed to them at the time of execution. There are multiple ways to pass these command line arguments when you debug a program. Let us look at the following program that prints two command line arguments. The program prints a message if exactly two command line arguments are not specified. Note that this may not be the best program for this purpose and is used only to demonstrate a debugging process. The program name is arg.c and it is listed below.

```
#include <stdio.h>
#include <string.h>
main (int argc, char **argv)
{
  if (argc != 3) {
    printf("You have to use two command line arguments\n");
    exit(-1);
  }
  printf("This program prints two command line arguments\n");
  printf("The first argument is : %s\n", argv[1]);
  printf("The second argument is : %s\n", argv[2]);
}
```

You have to create an executable file, arg, from arg.c source code file. If you run this program in gdb using the run command, it complains about command line arguments and terminates as expected. This is shown below.

```
[rr@conformix 5]$ gdb arg
GNU gdb 5.0rh-5 Red Hat Linux 7.1
Copyright 2001 Free Software Foundation, Inc.
GDB is free software, covered by the GNU General Public
License, and you are
welcome to change it and/or distribute copies of it under
certain conditions.
Type "show copying" to see the conditions.
There is absolutely no warranty for GDB.  Type "show warranty"
for details.
This GDB was configured as "i386-redhat-linux"...
(gdb) run
Starting program: /home/rr/5/arg
You have to use two command line arguments

Program exited with code 0377.
(gdb)
```

Note that no break point is set as we are not interested in stepping through the program line by line at this point.

The following lines of another gdb session output show that you can specify command line arguments with the run command. Any arguments for the run command are considered as program arguments. These arguments are "test1" and "test2" and are printed on the screen when you run the program.

```
[rr@conformix 5]$ gdb arg
GNU gdb 5.0rh-5 Red Hat Linux 7.1
Copyright 2001 Free Software Foundation, Inc.
GDB is free software, covered by the GNU General Public
License, and you are
welcome to change it and/or distribute copies of it under
certain conditions.
Type "show copying" to see the conditions.
There is absolutely no warranty for GDB.  Type "show warranty"
for details.
This GDB was configured as "i386-redhat-linux"...
(gdb) run test1 test2
Starting program: /home/rr/5/arg test1 test2
This program prints two command line arguments
The first argument is : test1
The second argument is : test2

Program exited with code 037.
(gdb)
```

Another method is to set the arguments using the set command as done in the following gdb session. You can display current arguments using the show command, which is also present in this gdb session. After setting the arguments, you can use the run command to start executing the program.

```
[rr@conformix 5]$ gdb arg
GNU gdb 5.0rh-5 Red Hat Linux 7.1
Copyright 2001 Free Software Foundation, Inc.
GDB is free software, covered by the GNU General Public
License, and you are
welcome to change it and/or distribute copies of it under
certain conditions.
Type "show copying" to see the conditions.
There is absolutely no warranty for GDB.  Type "show warranty"
for details.
This GDB was configured as "i386-redhat-linux"...
(gdb) set args test1 test2
(gdb) show args
Argument list to give program being debugged when it is
started is "test1 test2".
(gdb) run
Starting program: /home/rr/5/arg test1 test2
This program prints two command line arguments
The first argument is : test1
The second argument is : test2

Program exited with code 037.
(gdb)
```

5.3   Controlling Execution

Now you are already familiar with some of the gdb commands used for controlling execution of a program. The commands you have already used are run, quit and next commands. In this section you will learn some more commands that can be used to control execution of the program. The most commonly used commands to control execution of a program in gdb are as follows:

- The run command is used to start execution of a program. If the program is already running, you can restart the execution right from the beginning using the run command.
- The quit command will quit the debugger.
- The kill command stops debugging but does not quit the debugger.
- The continue command starts executing program from the current position. The difference between the continue and run commands is that the run commands starts execution from the entry point of the program while the continue command starts execution from the current location.
- The next command goes to the next line in the code. If the current line is a function call, it completes the function call without going into the function code.
- The step command goes to the next line in the code. If the current line is a function call, it goes to the first line inside that function.
- The finish command takes you out of the function call, if you are already inside one.
- The return command returns to the caller of the current frame in the stack. This means that you can return from a function without actually completing the function code execution.

There are many ways to control execution of a program. Mastery of these methods is necessary to debug a program more efficiently.

5.3.1   The step and finish Commands

Here we have a short demonstration of how to use finish and step commands when you are dealing with a function. Consider the following sumf.c program that adds two numbers and prints the result of addition. The addition is completed inside a function called sum().

```
#include <stdio.h>

int sum(int num1, int num2);

main ()
{
  int num1, num2, total ;

  printf("Enter first number : ");
  scanf("%d", &num1);
```

```
  printf("Enter second number : ");
  scanf("%d", &num2);

  total = sum(num1, num2);
  printf("\nThe sum is : %d\n", total);
}

int sum(int num1, int num2)
{
  int result;
  result = num1 + num2 ;
  printf("\nCalculation complete. Returning ...\n");
  return (result);
}
```

Let us create an executable `sumf` from this source code using the `gcc` compiler. This executable then can be debugged using GNU debugger as shown in the next session. Note that we use the `step` command (abbreviated as `s`) to step into the function code. We use the `finish` command to complete execution of code in the function `sum()` instead of tracing it line by line. After the `finish` command is executed, you go to the next line in the `main()` function just after the call to the `sum()` function.

```
[rr@conformix 5]$ gdb sumf
GNU gdb 5.0rh-5 Red Hat Linux 7.1
Copyright 2001 Free Software Foundation, Inc.
GDB is free software, covered by the GNU General Public
License, and you are
welcome to change it and/or distribute copies of it under
certain conditions.
Type "show copying" to see the conditions.
There is absolutely no warranty for GDB.  Type "show warranty"
for details.
This GDB was configured as "i386-redhat-linux"...
(gdb) bre main
Breakpoint 1 at 0x8048496: file sumf.c, line 9.
(gdb) run
Starting program: /home/rr/5/sumf

Breakpoint 1, main () at sumf.c:9
9  printf("Enter first number : ");
(gdb) n
10  scanf("%d", &num1);
(gdb) n
Enter first number : 4
11  printf("Enter second number : ");
(gdb) n
12  scanf("%d", &num2);
(gdb) n
```

```
Enter second number : 5
14   total = sum(num1, num2);
(gdb) s
sum (num1=4, num2=5) at sumf.c:21
21   result = num1 + num2 ;
(gdb) finish
Run till exit from #0  sum (num1=4, num2=5) at sumf.c:21

Calculation complete. Returning ...
0x080484ec in main () at sumf.c:14
14   total = sum(num1, num2);
Value returned is $1 = 9
(gdb) n
15   printf("\nThe sum is : %d\n", total);
(gdb) n

The sum is : 9
16}
(gdb) n

Program exited with code 020.
(gdb)
```

As you can see from the above example, all gdb commands can be abbreviated as long as they can't be confused with any other command. You can use n for next, bre for the break command and s for the step command. Also note that when you return from the function call, the return value of the function is displayed.

5.4   Working with the Stack

One of the most important tasks during the debugging process is to deal with the stack. The stack provides a lot of information about what happened in the past. You can backtrace to higher levels in the stack using gdb. Using the backtrace feature, you can move step-by-step backward to find out how you reached the current position. To demonstrate some of the commands used with stack, let us take the example of sumf.c program that you used in the last section. The program takes two numbers as input and then calls a function to sum() to add these two numbers. The function returns the result back to the main function.

When you start debugging this program, first you set up a break point right at the beginning of the main function and then use the next command repeatedly until you reach the line where the function is called. At this point you use the step command instead of the next command to move into the function code. After entering the function code, some other commands related to stack are used in the following gdb session. These commands are explained at the end of this session listing.

```
[rr@conformix 5]$ gdb sumf
GNU gdb 5.0rh-5 Red Hat Linux 7.1
Copyright 2001 Free Software Foundation, Inc.
GDB is free software, covered by the GNU General Public
License, and you are
welcome to change it and/or distribute copies of it under
certain conditions.
Type "show copying" to see the conditions.
There is absolutely no warranty for GDB.  Type "show warranty"
for details.
This GDB was configured as "i386-redhat-linux"...
(gdb) break main
Breakpoint 1 at 0x8048496: file sumf.c, line 9.
(gdb) run
Starting program: /home/rr/5/sumf

Breakpoint 1, main () at sumf.c:9
9   printf("Enter first number : ");
(gdb) next
10  scanf("%d", &num1);
(gdb) next
Enter first number : 30
11  printf("Enter second number : ");
(gdb) next
12  scanf("%d", &num2);
(gdb) next
Enter second number : 40
14  total = sum(num1, num2);
(gdb) step
sum (num1=30, num2=40) at sumf.c:21
21  result = num1 + num2 ;
(gdb) next
22  printf("\nCalculation complete. Returning ...\n");
(gdb) frame
#0  sum (num1=30, num2=40) at sumf.c:22
22  printf("\nCalculation complete. Returning ...\n");
(gdb) info frame
Stack level 0, frame at 0xbffffa08:
 eip = 0x804851b in sum (sumf.c:22); saved eip 0x80484ec
 called by frame at 0xbffffa38
 source language c.
 Arglist at 0xbffffa08, args: num1=30, num2=40
 Locals at 0xbffffa08, Previous frame's sp is 0x0
 Saved registers:
  ebp at 0xbffffa08, eip at 0xbffffa0c
(gdb) info args
num1 = 30
num2 = 40
```

```
(gdb) info locals
result = 70
(gdb) info reg
eax              0x4670
ecx              0x00
edx              0x401548e01075136736
ebx              0x401569e41075145188
esp              0xbffffa000xbffffa00
ebp              0xbffffa080xbffffa08
esi              0x40016b641073834852
edi              0xbffffaac-1073743188
eip              0x804851b0x804851b
eflags           0x312786
cs               0x2335
ss               0x2b43
ds               0x2b43
es               0x2b43
fs               0x00
gs               0x00
fctrl            0x37f895
fstat            0x00
ftag             0xffff65535
fiseg            0x2335
fioff            0x404b42151078673941
foseg            0x2b43
fooff            0x404c69681078749544
fop              0x2e9745
(gdb) info all-reg
eax              0x4670
ecx              0x00
edx              0x401548e01075136736
ebx              0x401569e41075145188
esp              0xbffffa000xbffffa00
ebp              0xbffffa080xbffffa08
esi              0x40016b641073834852
edi              0xbffffaac-1073743188
eip              0x804851b0x804851b
eflags           0x312786
cs               0x2335
ss               0x2b43
ds               0x2b43
es               0x2b43
fs               0x00
gs               0x00
st0              0(raw 0x00000000000000000000)
st1              0(raw 0x00000000000000000000)
st2              0(raw 0x00000000000000000000)
st3              0(raw 0x00000000000000000000)
```

```
st4             0(raw 0x00000000000000000000)
st5             0(raw 0x00000000000000000000)
st6             1.147239263803680981573807073914395(raw
0x3fff92d8bc775ca99ea0)
st7             3(raw 0x4000c000000000000000)
fctrl           0x37f895
fstat           0x00
ftag            0xffff65535
fiseg           0x2335
fioff           0x404b42151078673941
foseg           0x2b43
fooff           0x404c69681078749544
fop             0x2e9745
(gdb) backtrace
#0  sum (num1=30, num2=40) at sumf.c:22
#1  0x080484ec in main () at sumf.c:14
#2  0x40048177 in __libc_start_main (main=0x8048490 <main>,
argc=1, ubp_av=0xbffffaac, init=0x8048308 <_init>,
    fini=0x8048580 <_fini>, rtld_fini=0x4000e184 <_dl_fini>,
stack_end=0xbffffa9c)
    at ../sysdeps/generic/libc-start.c:129
(gdb) info frame
Stack level 0, frame at 0xbffffa08:
 eip = 0x804851b in sum (sumf.c:22); saved eip 0x80484ec
 called by frame at 0xbffffa38
 source language c.
 Arglist at 0xbffffa08, args: num1=30, num2=40
 Locals at 0xbffffa08, Previous frame's sp is 0x0
 Saved registers:
  ebp at 0xbffffa08, eip at 0xbffffa0c
(gdb) up
#1  0x080484ec in main () at sumf.c:14
#2  0x40048177 in __libc_start_main (main=0x8048490 <main>,
argc=1, ubp_av=0xbffffaac, init=0x8048308 <_init>,
    fini=0x8048580 <_fini>, rtld_fini=0x4000e184 <_dl_fini>,
stack_end=0xbffffa9c)
    at ../sysdeps/generic/libc-start.c:129
(gdb) info frame
Stack level 0, frame at 0xbffffa08:
 eip = 0x804851b in sum (sumf.c:22); saved eip 0x80484ec
 called by frame at 0xbffffa38
 source language c.
 Arglist at 0xbffffa08, args: num1=30, num2=40
 Locals at 0xbffffa08, Previous frame's sp is 0x0
 Saved registers:
  ebp at 0xbffffa08, eip at 0xbffffa0c
(gdb) up
#1  0x080484ec in main () at sumf.c:14
```

```
14  total = sum(num1, num2);
(gdb) info frame
Stack level 1, frame at 0xbffffa38:
 eip = 0x80484ec in main (sumf.c:14); saved eip 0x40048177
 called by frame at 0xbffffa78, caller of frame at 0xbffffa08
 source language c.
 Arglist at 0xbffffa38, args:
 Locals at 0xbffffa38, Previous frame's sp is 0x0
 Saved registers:
   ebp at 0xbffffa38, eip at 0xbffffa3c
(gdb) down
#0  sum (num1=30, num2=40) at sumf.c:22
22  printf("\nCalculation complete. Returning ...\n");
(gdb) info frame
Stack level 0, frame at 0xbffffa08:
 eip = 0x804851b in sum (sumf.c:22); saved eip 0x80484ec
 called by frame at 0xbffffa38
 source language c.
 Arglist at 0xbffffa08, args: num1=30, num2=40
 Locals at 0xbffffa08, Previous frame's sp is 0x0
 Saved registers:
   ebp at 0xbffffa08, eip at 0xbffffa0c
(gdb) down
Bottom (i.e., innermost) frame selected; you cannot go down.
(gdb) n

Calculation complete. Returning ...
23  return (result);
(gdb) n
24}
(gdb) n
main () at sumf.c:15
15  printf("\nThe sum is : %d\n", total);
(gdb) n

The sum is : 70
16}
(gdb) n

Program exited with code 021.
(gdb) quit
[rr@conformix 5]$
```

• The `frame` command shows the current frame of execution for the program. In simple
  terms, you can consider a frame as a block of commands. For example, commands in
  one function are a frame. When you use the `frame` command, it displays the current
  frame starting point, the file name and current execution pointer.

- The info frame command shows more information about the current frame, including some register values. It also shows the stack pointer for the previous frame. These values are taken from the stack.
- The info args command displays arguments passed to this frame. This is also taken from the stack.
- The info locals command displays the values of local variables. These variable have a scope limited to the current frame.
- The info reg command displays values of register values.
- The info all-reg command displays register values, including math registers.
- The up command takes you one level up in the stack. This means if you are inside a function call, the up command will take you to the function that called the current function. The down command is opposite to the up command.
- You can use backtrace, up and down commands to move around in different frames. These commands are useful for looking into stack data.

A combination of all of these commands used with other execution control command can be used to display a lot of information. If you want to effectively use GNU debugger, knowledge of commands related to stack is a must.

5.5   Displaying Variables

Using the GNU debugger, you can display environment variables as well as your program variables during the program execution. You can control display of some variables so that the value of these variables is displayed with each command. Using this feature you can easily track changes taking place to these variables when you step through the program. You can also modify the program as well as environment variables. This section shows examples of how to carry out these tasks.

5.5.1   Displaying Program Variables

The following session uses the sum.c program that you already used earlier in this chapter. Go through the following gdb session and then see the discussion at the end of this session about actions taking place.

```
[rr@conformix 5]$ gdb sum
GNU gdb 5.0rh-5 Red Hat Linux 7.1
Copyright 2001 Free Software Foundation, Inc.
GDB is free software, covered by the GNU General Public
License, and you are
welcome to change it and/or distribute copies of it under
certain conditions.
Type "show copying" to see the conditions.
There is absolutely no warranty for GDB.  Type "show warranty"
for details.
```

```
This GDB was configured as "i386-redhat-linux"...
(gdb) break main
Breakpoint 1 at 0x8048496: file sum.c, line 6.
(gdb) run
Starting program: /home/rr/5/sum

Breakpoint 1, main () at sum.c:6
6   printf("Enter first number : ");
(gdb) print num2
$1 = 134518424
(gdb) print total
$2 = 134513777
(gdb) n
7   scanf("%d", &num1);
(gdb) n
Enter first number : 45
8   printf("Enter second number : ");
(gdb) n
9   scanf("%d", &num2);
(gdb) n
Enter second number : 33
11   total = num1 + num2;
(gdb) print num2
$3 = 33
(gdb) n
13   printf("\nThe sum is : %d\n", total);
(gdb) n

The sum is : 78
14}
(gdb) n

Program exited with code 021.
(gdb)
```

- First set a break point where function main starts.
- Start the program execution using the run command.
- Print values of num2 and total variables. Since these variables are not yet initialized, random numbers are present at these two locations.
- Execute the program line by line and enter values of num1 and num2 variables and then calculate the value of total.
- Print the value of num2 variable which is now exactly what you have entered.

Note that in this session, gdb does not display the values of variables automatically when a value changes. You have to use the print command again and again to display variable values. In the next section, you will see how to display these values automatically.

5.5.2   Automatic Displaying Variables with Each Command

The display command displays the value of a variable and keeps a record of the variable so that its value is displayed after each command. The following session shows how this feature works. This is an easy way to closely watch the value of variables with the execution of each line of code. It is especially useful when you are tracing through a loop where you need to know the values of some variables in each cycle.

```
[rr@conformix 5]$ gdb sum
GNU gdb 5.0rh-5 Red Hat Linux 7.1
Copyright 2001 Free Software Foundation, Inc.
GDB is free software, covered by the GNU General Public
License, and you are
welcome to change it and/or distribute copies of it under
certain conditions.
Type "show copying" to see the conditions.
There is absolutely no warranty for GDB.  Type "show warranty"
for details.
This GDB was configured as "i386-redhat-linux"...
(gdb) break main
Breakpoint 1 at 0x8048496: file sum.c, line 6.
(gdb) run
Starting program: /home/rr/5/sum

Breakpoint 1, main () at sum.c:6
6   printf("Enter first number : ");
(gdb) display num1
1: num1 = 134518424
(gdb) disp total
2: total = 134513777
(gdb) n
7   scanf("%d", &num1);
2: total = 134513777
1: num1 = 134518424
(gdb) n
Enter first number : 3
8   printf("Enter second number : ");
2: total = 134513777
1: num1 = 3
(gdb) n
9   scanf("%d", &num2);
2: total = 134513777
1: num1 = 3
(gdb) n
Enter second number : 67
11   total = num1 + num2;
2: total = 134513777
1: num1 = 3
```

```
(gdb) n
13  printf("\nThe sum is : %d\n", total);
2: total = 70
1: num1 = 3
(gdb) n

The sum is : 70
14}
2: total = 70
1: num1 = 3
(gdb) n

Program exited with code 021.
(gdb)
```

You can use the following commands to control the display of variables and get information about variables that are being displayed.

- The undisplay command removes a variable from the list of displayed items.
- The disable display command keeps the variable in the display list but disables its continuous display.
- The enable display command enables display of a variable that was previously disabled.
- The info display command displays a list of expressions or variables currently in the display list.

5.5.3 Displaying Environment Variables

Environment variables play a significant role in debugging a program. They are used to locate files and other tasks related to the file system as well as shell command execution. The following command displays the value of the PATH variable:

```
(gdb) show path
Executable and object file path: /usr/kerberos/bin:/bin:/usr/
bin:/usr/local/bin:/usr/bin/X11:/usr/X11R6/bin
```

The following command shows the current directory:

```
(gdb) pwd
Working directory /home/rr/5.
```

All environment variables can be displayed using the following command:

```
(gdb) show environment
PWD=/home/rr/5
HOSTNAME=conformix.conformix.net
PVM_RSH=/usr/bin/rsh
QTDIR=/usr/lib/qt-2.3.0
LESSOPEN=|/usr/bin/lesspipe.sh %s
```

```
XPVM_ROOT=/usr/share/pvm3/xpvm
KDEDIR=/usr
USER=rr
LS_COLORS=no=00:fi=00:di=01;34:ln=01;36:pi=40;33:so=01;35:bd=4
0;33;01:cd=40;33;01:or=01;05;37;41:mi=01;05;37;41:ex=01;32:*.c
md=01;32:*.exe=01;32:*.com=01;32:*.btm=01;32:*.bat=01;32:*.sh=
01;32:*.csh=01;32:*.tar=01;31:*.tgz=01;31:*.arj=01;31:*.taz=01
;31:*.lzh=01;31:*.zip=01;31:*.z=01;31:*.Z=01;31:*.gz=01;31:*.b
z2=01;31:*.bz=01;31:*.tz=01;31:*.rpm=01;31:*.cpio=01;31:*.jpg=
01;35:*.gif=01;35:*.bmp=01;35:*.xbm=01;35:*.xpm=01;35:*.png=01
;35:*.tif=01;35:
MACHTYPE=i386-redhat-linux-gnu
OLDPWD=/home/rr
MAIL=/var/spool/mail/rr
INPUTRC=/etc/inputrc
BASH_ENV=/home/rr/.bashrc
LANG=en_US
DISPLAY=192.168.2.115:1
LOGNAME=rr
SHLVL=1
SHELL=/bin/bash
HOSTTYPE=i386
OSTYPE=linux-gnu
HISTSIZE=1000
LAMHELPFILE=/etc/lam/lam-helpfile
PVM_ROOT=/usr/share/pvm3
TERM=xterm
HOME=/home/rr
SSH_ASKPASS=/usr/libexec/openssh/gnome-ssh-askpass
PATH=/usr/kerberos/bin:/bin:/usr/bin:/usr/local/bin:/usr/bin/
X11:/usr/X11R6/bin
_=/usr/bin/gdb
(gdb)
```

You can also use the set env command and the unset env command to modify environment variables or to create or delete variables.

5.5.4 Modifying Variables

Using the set command, you can modify any program variable during the debugging process. The following session shows an example where you entered a value 34 for program variable num1 but modified it to 11 using set command before the sum was calculated. You can see that the sum calculation process takes into account the new value.

```
Enter first number : 34
11  printf("Enter second number : ");
(gdb) n
12  scanf("%d", &num2);
```

```
(gdb) n
Enter second number : 12
14  total = sum(num1, num2);
(gdb) print num1
$1 = 34
(gdb) set num1=11
(gdb) print num1
$2 = 11
(gdb) print num2
$3 = 12
(gdb) n

Calculation complete. Returning ...
15  printf("\nThe sum is : %d\n", total);
(gdb) n

The sum is : 23
16 }
(gdb)
```

5.6 Adding Break Points

When you start debugging a program, you use the run command. This command executes the program until the end of the program or a break point is met. A break point is a place in your source code file where you temporarily want to stop execution of the program being debugged.

Break points in GNU debugger can be placed using the break command. Look at the following list of the source code file sum.c which you already have used:

```
(gdb) list
1  #include <stdio.h>
2  main ()
3  {
4    int num1, num2, total ;
5
6    printf("Enter first number : ");
7    scanf("%d", &num1);
8    printf("Enter second number : ");
9    scanf("%d", &num2);
10
(gdb)
```

To place a break point at line number 6 in file sum.c (displayed above), you can use the following command:

```
(gdb) break sum.c:6
Breakpoint 1 at 0x8048496: file sum.c, line 6.
(gdb)
```

As you can see from the above lines, when you set a break point, GNU debugger will display its information in the next line. This information contains the number of the breakpoint, memory address, file name and line number. You can also see a list of currently set break points using the following command:

```
(gdb) info break
Num Type           Disp Enb Address    What
1   breakpoint     keep y   0x08048496 in main at sum.c:6
(gdb)
```

Break points can also be set on function names. The following command sets a break point where function `main` starts:

```
(gdb) break main
Breakpoint 1 at 0x8048496: file sum.c, line 6.
(gdb)
```

Note that although the function `main()` starts at line number 2, the break point is set at line number 6. This is because the first executable instruction of the function `main` is located at this line number.

You can also set a break point at a particular line number in the currently loaded file. The following command creates a break point at line number 8:

```
(gdb) break 8
Breakpoint 2 at 0x80484ba: file sum.c, line 8.
(gdb)
```

In a multi-source file project, you set up a break point by including the file name and line number on the command line. The following command sets up a break point at line number 9 in file `sum.c`.

```
(gdb) break sum.c:9
Breakpoint 3 at 0x80484ca: file sum.c, line 9.
(gdb)
```

You can also use an offset value to set up a break point. For example if the execution pointer is on line number 6, you can set up a break point at line number 9 using the following command. Note that you can also use a minus symbol to specify an offset.

```
6   printf("Enter first number : ");
(gdb) break +3
Note: breakpoint 3 also set at pc 0x80484ca.
Breakpoint 4 at 0x80484ca: file sum.c, line 9.
(gdb)
```

All break points can be displayed using the `info` command. The following command displays three break points that we have specified:

```
(gdb) info break
Num Type           Disp Enb Address    What
```

```
1    breakpoint     keep y   0x08048496 in main at sum.c:6
2    breakpoint     keep y   0x080484ba in main at sum.c:8
3    breakpoint     keep y   0x080484ca in main at sum.c:9
(gdb)
```

If you want to disable all break points, use the `disable` command without any argument. Similarly if you want to enable all disabled break points, use the `enable` command without any argument. Normal arguments allow you to specify which break point to enable and disable.

5.6.1 Continuing from Break Point

You can continue execution of your program when you reach a break point in many ways. You can start tracing the program line by line using `next` or `step` commands. You can also use the `continue` command that will run the program from its current location until the program reaches its end or you find another break point on the way. You have already seen how to use the `step` and `next` commands. The following session creates a break point in the start of the `main` function and then uses the `continue` command to start execution from there.

```
[rr@conformix 5]$ gdb sum
GNU gdb 5.0rh-5 Red Hat Linux 7.1
Copyright 2001 Free Software Foundation, Inc.
GDB is free software, covered by the GNU General Public
License, and you are
welcome to change it and/or distribute copies of it under
certain conditions.
Type "show copying" to see the conditions.
There is absolutely no warranty for GDB.  Type "show warranty"
for details.
This GDB was configured as "i386-redhat-linux"...
(gdb) break main
Breakpoint 1 at 0x8048496: file sum.c, line 6.
(gdb) run
Starting program: /home/rr/5/sum

Breakpoint 1, main () at sum.c:6
6  printf("Enter first number : ");
(gdb) continue
Continuing.
Enter first number : 34
Enter second number : 45

The sum is : 79

Program exited with code 021.
(gdb) quit
[rr@conformix 5]$
```

5.6.2 Disabling Break Points

Break points can be disabled temporarily. You can disable a break point using the `disable` command with a number as its argument. These numbers can be displayed using the `info break` command. The following command lists currently available break points. As you can see under the `Enb` column heading, all lines contain a `y` which shows that all break points are currently enabled.

```
(gdb) info break
Num Type           Disp Enb Address    What
1   breakpoint     keep y   0x08048496 in main at sum.c:6
breakpoint already hit 1 time
2   breakpoint     keep y   0x080484ba in main at sum.c:8
3   breakpoint     keep y   0x080484ca in main at sum.c:9
6   breakpoint     keep y   0x08048496 in main at sum.c:5
```

To disable break point number 3 at line number 9 in file `sum.c` and then display the status of break points again, use the following two commands:

```
(gdb) dis 3
(gdb) info break
Num Type           Disp Enb Address    What
1   breakpoint     keep y   0x08048496 in main at sum.c:6
breakpoint already hit 1 time
2   breakpoint     keep y   0x080484ba in main at sum.c:8
3   breakpoint     keep n   0x080484ca in main at sum.c:9
6   breakpoint     keep y   0x08048496 in main at sum.c:5
(gdb)
```

Note that you can disable all break points in a single step if you don't mention any number as an argument to the `disable` command.

5.6.3 Enabling Break Points

You can enable previously disabled break points using the `enable` command. The following command shows that breakpoint at line number 9 is currently disabled because it shows an `n` under the `Enb` column.

```
(gdb) info break
Num Type           Disp Enb Address    What
1   breakpoint     keep y   0x08048496 in main at sum.c:6
    breakpoint already hit 1 time
2   breakpoint     keep y   0x080484ba in main at sum.c:8
3   breakpoint     keep n   0x080484ca in main at sum.c:9
6   breakpoint     keep y   0x08048496 in main at sum.c:5
```

The following two commands enable the break point number 3 and display the status of all break points.

```
(gdb) enab 3
(gdb) info break
Num Type            Disp Enb Address    What
1   breakpoint      keep y   0x08048496 in main at sum.c:6
breakpoint already hit 1 time
2   breakpoint      keep y   0x080484ba in main at sum.c:8
3   breakpoint      keep y   0x080484ca in main at sum.c:9
6   breakpoint      keep y   0x08048496 in main at sum.c:5
(gdb)
```

Enabling and disabling break points is useful when you want to cycle quickly through loops for a certain number of times and then start tracing once again.

5.6.4   Deleting Break Points

You can also delete break points using the `delete` command. The following session shows that you have four break points present. You delete two of these and then you can again display break points to make sure that these break points are actually deleted.

```
(gdb) info break
Num Type            Disp Enb Address    What
1   breakpoint      keep y   0x08048496 in main at sum.c:6
    breakpoint already hit 1 time
2   breakpoint      keep y   0x080484ba in main at sum.c:8
3   breakpoint      keep y   0x080484ca in main at sum.c:9
6   breakpoint      keep y   0x08048496 in main at sum.c:5
(gdb) del 1
(gdb) del 2
(gdb) info break
Num Type            Disp Enb Address    What
3   breakpoint      keep y   0x080484ca in main at sum.c:9
6   breakpoint      keep y   0x08048496 in main at sum.c:5
(gdb)
```

Note that there is a difference between deleting and disabling a break point. The disabled break point stays there although it has no impact on execution of the program being debugged. The deleted break point is gone forever and you have to create it again if needed.

5.7   Debugging Optimized Code

You can use multiple levels of optimization while building the output binaries. The generated executable code may be different for each level of optimization. If you step through the optimized code in gdb, the gdb may not step as you expected in some cases. Let us compile the sumopt.c program and see how optimization does affect. Listing below is the program source code:

```
#include <stdio.h>
main ()
{
```

```
    int num1, num2, total ;

    num1 = 4;
    num2 = 6;
    total = num1 + num2;

    printf("\nThe sum is : %d\n", total);
}
```

Now let us compile the code without optimization using the following command and then step through it.

```
gcc -g sumopt.c -o sumopt
```

Following is the gdb session to step through the code. As you can see, it is quite straight-forward. gdb executes all lines in order until it reaches end of the program.

```
[rr@conformix 5]$ gdb sumopt
GNU gdb 5.0rh-5 Red Hat Linux 7.1
Copyright 2001 Free Software Foundation, Inc.
GDB is free software, covered by the GNU General Public
License, and you are
welcome to change it and/or distribute copies of it under
certain conditions.
Type "show copying" to see the conditions.
There is absolutely no warranty for GDB.  Type "show warranty"
for details.
This GDB was configured as "i386-redhat-linux"...
(gdb) break main
Breakpoint 1 at 0x8048466: file sumopt.c, line 6.
(gdb) run
Starting program: /home/rr/5/sumopt

Breakpoint 1, main () at sumopt.c:6
6   num1 = 4;
(gdb) n
7   num2 = 6;
(gdb) n
8   total = num1 + num2;
(gdb) n
10  printf("\nThe sum is : %d\n", total);
(gdb) n

The sum is : 10
11}
(gdb) n

Program exited with code 021.
(gdb)
```

Now let us compile the program using the –O2 option for optimization. The command line for this is shown below:

```
gcc -O2 -g sumopt.c -o sumopt
```

Now let us trace through the optimized program. The gdb session for this purpose is listed below:

```
[rr@conformix 5]$ gdb sumopt
GNU gdb 5.0rh-5 Red Hat Linux 7.1
Copyright 2001 Free Software Foundation, Inc.
GDB is free software, covered by the GNU General Public
License, and you are
welcome to change it and/or distribute copies of it under
certain conditions.
Type "show copying" to see the conditions.
There is absolutely no warranty for GDB.  Type "show warranty"
for details.
This GDB was configured as "i386-redhat-linux"...
(gdb) break main
Breakpoint 1 at 0x8048466: file sumopt.c, line 10.
(gdb) run
Starting program: /home/rr/5/sumopt

Breakpoint 1, main () at sumopt.c:10
10  printf("\nThe sum is : %d\n", total);
(gdb) n

The sum is : 10
11 }
(gdb) n

Program exited with code 021.
(gdb)
```

This is quite different from what you may have expected. The first difference is in setting up the break point. We used the same command to set up the break point but now gdb set it up at line number 10 instead of line number 6 as it had done before. When we started execution of the program, it jumped to line number 10 and did not go to any line before that. This is because when we optimized code at the compile time, the compiler was smart enough to know that all values are static so there is no need to assign two static numbers to variables at the run time and then calculate their sum. All this can be done at the compile time, which results in shorter code and better execution time.

The bottom line is that if you find that gdb is not executing some lines when you debug a program, it may be due to the optimization level used when compiling a program. A fun trick might be to look at the variable values during such a debug session as well, but it's not necessary!

5.8 Files and Shared Libraries

You can find out information about the currently loaded file, its type, ELF segments, memory addresses and other things. The following command displays such information about the `sum` program.

```
(gdb) info files
Symbols from "/home/rr/5/sum".
Unix child process:
    Using the running image of child process 1860.
    While running this, GDB does not access memory from...
Local exec file:
    `/home/rr/5/sum', file type elf32-i386.
    Entry point: 0x8048390
    0x080480f4 - 0x08048107 is .interp
    0x08048108 - 0x08048128 is .note.ABI-tag
    0x08048128 - 0x08048160 is .hash
    0x08048160 - 0x080481f0 is .dynsym
    0x080481f0 - 0x0804828b is .dynstr
    0x0804828c - 0x0804829e is .gnu.version
    0x080482a0 - 0x080482d0 is .gnu.version_r
    0x080482d0 - 0x080482d8 is .rel.got
    0x080482d8 - 0x08048308 is .rel.plt
    0x08048308 - 0x08048320 is .init
    0x08048320 - 0x08048390 is .plt
    0x08048390 - 0x08048540 is .text
    0x08048540 - 0x0804855e is .fini
    0x08048560 - 0x080485aa is .rodata
    0x080495ac - 0x080495bc is .data
    0x080495bc - 0x080495c0 is .eh_frame
    0x080495c0 - 0x080495c8 is .ctors
    0x080495c8 - 0x080495d0 is .dtors
    0x080495d0 - 0x080495f8 is .got
    0x080495f8 - 0x08049698 is .dynamic
    0x08049698 - 0x080496b0 is .bss
```

You can also display information about shared libraries used by the `sum` program using the following command:

```
(gdb) info share
From         To           Syms Read    Shared Object Library
0x40047fa0   0x40140a9b   Yes          /lib/i686/libc.so.6
0x40001db0   0x4001321c   Yes          /lib/ld-linux.so.2
(gdb)
```

The command shows that the program is using `libc.so.6` and `ld-linux.so.2` during the debug session. The `ld-linux.so` is the dynamic loader, and will always be present in dynamically linked files.

5.9   Using gdb With GNU Emacs

If you use GNU Emacs to edit your programs, you can also create a debug window within Emacs using the M-x gdb command. Let us suppose that you are editing sumf.c program in GNU Emacs as shown in Figure 5-1.

Now when you use M-x gdb command, you will see that the Emacs window is split and the bottom part is used as the gdb window. The screen shot in Figure 5-2 shows this new Emacs window. You can also see that new menus appear in the menu bar at the top of the screen. You can use these menus for the usual debugging functions like creating break points, starting and stopping the debug process and so on. The Gud menu is especially of interest for program debugging.

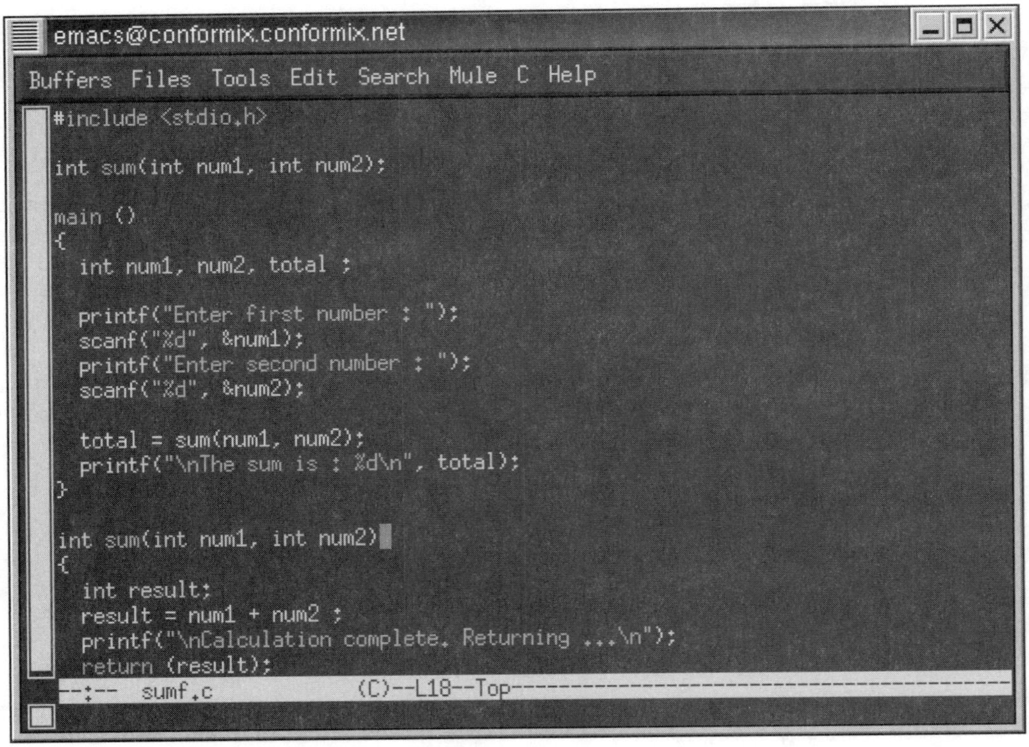

Figure 5-1 Editing sumf.c program in GNU Emacs.

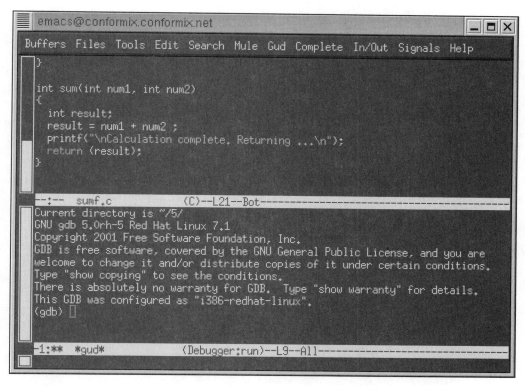

Figure 5-2 The gdb split window inside GNU Emacs.

5.10 Debugging Running Processes

In addition to stand-alone programs, running processes can also be debugged using GNU debugger. The procedure is as follows:

1. Start the process that you want to debug.
2. Use the ps command to find the process ID of the running process.
3. Start gdb.
4. Load the file containing the symbol table into gdb.
5. Use the attach command to attach to the running process to gdb.
6. Continue debugging as usual.

In this section we shall attach to a process created by executing the sumf program that we created earlier in this chapter. This program requires input of two numbers. After starting, the process waits for the user to input these two numbers. You can open a new terminal window at

this point and start gdb in the new window to attach the process. The following command starts
the process which is waiting for the user to enter the first number.

```
[rr@conformix 5]$ ./sumf
Enter first number :
```

Open a new terminal window and find out the process ID of the sumf process. This can
be easily done using the ps command as follows:

```
[rr@conformix 5]$ ps -a|grep sumf
4272 pts/4     00:00:00 sumf
[rr@conformix 5]$
```

The process ID for the running process is 4272. After getting this information, you can
start gdb and load the sumf file that contains the symbol table. This is done using the file
command. The following sequence of commands shows this process:

```
[rr@conformix 5]$ gdb
GNU gdb 5.0rh-5 Red Hat Linux 7.1
Copyright 2001 Free Software Foundation, Inc.
GDB is free software, covered by the GNU General Public
License, and you are
welcome to change it and/or distribute copies of it under
certain conditions.
Type "show copying" to see the conditions.
There is absolutely no warranty for GDB.  Type "show warranty"
for details.
This GDB was configured as "i386-redhat-linux".
(gdb) file sumf
Reading symbols from sumf...done.
(gdb)
```

Now you can attach to the program with ID 4272. Note that the program is waiting for
user input and there are many functions calls from loaded shared libraries. To come back to this
point in the main source file, you have to make a number of finish commands.

```
(gdb) attach 4272
Attaching to program: /home/rr/5/sumf, process 4272
Reading symbols from /lib/i686/libc.so.6...done.
Loaded symbols for /lib/i686/libc.so.6
Reading symbols from /lib/ld-linux.so.2...done.
Loaded symbols for /lib/ld-linux.so.2
0x40105f44 in __libc_read () from /lib/i686/libc.so.6
(gdb) n
Single stepping until exit from function __libc_read,
which has no line number information.
_IO_file_read (fp=0x401548e0, buf=0x40019000, size=1024) at
fileops.c:764
764    fileops.c: No such file or directory.
  in fileops.c
```

```
(gdb) finish
Run till exit from #0  _IO_file_read (fp=0x401548e0,
buf=0x40019000, size=1024) at fileops.c:764
0x400a68dd in _IO_new_file_underflow (fp=0x401548e0) at
fileops.c:467
467  in fileops.c
Value returned is $1 = 2
(gdb) finish
Run till exit from #0  0x400a68dd in _IO_new_file_underflow
(fp=0x401548e0) at fileops.c:467
_IO_default_uflow (fp=0x401548e0) at genops.c:389
389  genops.c: No such file or directory.
  in genops.c
Value returned is $2 = 52
(gdb) finish
Run till exit from #0  _IO_default_uflow (fp=0x401548e0) at
genops.c:389
0x400a7f52 in __uflow (fp=0x401548e0) at genops.c:345
345  in genops.c
Value returned is $3 = 52
(gdb) finish
Run till exit from #0  0x400a7f52 in __uflow (fp=0x401548e0)
at genops.c:345
0x4008bee5 in _IO_vfscanf (s=0x401548e0, format=0x80485d6
"%d", argptr=0xbffff9f4, errp=0x0)
    at vfscanf.c:610
610  vfscanf.c: No such file or directory.
  in vfscanf.c
Value returned is $4 = 52
(gdb) finish
Run till exit from #0  0x4008bee5 in _IO_vfscanf
(s=0x401548e0, format=0x80485d6 "%d",
    argptr=0xbffff9f4, errp=0x0) at vfscanf.c:610
scanf (format=0x80485d6 "%d") at scanf.c:40
40  scanf.c: No such file or directory.
  in scanf.c
Value returned is $5 = 1
(gdb) finish
Run till exit from #0  scanf (format=0x80485d6 "%d") at
scanf.c:40
0x080484b7 in main () at sumf.c:10
10    scanf("%d", &num1);
Value returned is $6 = 1
(gdb) n
11    printf("Enter second number : ");
(gdb) n
12    scanf("%d", &num2);
(gdb)
```

With every `finish` command, you can see the function that you were into and the return value of that function. When you are back in the `main` function, you can use the `next` command to start tracing the execution line by line. Note that when you trace through, the output of the process will appear in the window where you started the program. You will also enter the input values in the same window. All those functions we had to finish were just part of the standard C libraries, and you could actually step into them anytime from this program as well, but you normally wouldn't.

5.11 Installing GDB

GNU debugger is included in all Linux distributions in the development package. In certain cases, you may want to get a new copy in the source code form and build and install it manually. The compilation and building process is similar to other GNU development tools. By this time you have already built and installed the GNU compiler and the C library. With that experience, you should not find the compilation and installation of GNU debugger difficult.

5.11.1 Downloading and Building

You can download the latest version from ftp://ftp.gnu.org/gnu/gdb directory. The current version at the time of writing this book is 5.1.1. The source code is available in the compressed `tar` format. The file name is `gdb-5.1.1.tar.gz`. You have to uncompress it using the following command.

```
tar zxvf gdb-5.1.1.tar.gz
```

I have untarred this file in `/opt` directory. The `tar` program will create `/opt/gdb-5.1.1` directory and uncompress all source code tree under this directory. Move into this directory using the `cd` command. Run the `configure` script and the `make` command to build and install the debugger. This is a similar process as with all other GNU tools. The following commands will build `gdb`.

```
cd /opt/gdb-5.1.1
./configure --prefix=/opt/gcc-3.0.4
make
```

Note that `--prefix` shows the directory where the `gdb` binary and other files will be installed. Usually this is the same directory where your other development tools are installed.

5.11.2 Final Installation

The following command places the `gdb` binary and other files in the proper location. After running this command, you can start using the new debugger.

```
make install
```

5.12 Other Open Source Debuggers

In addition to gdb, there are many other debuggers available to the open source community. Many of these debuggers are built on top of the GNU debugger or they use gdb concepts. Some of these debuggers are introduced in this section. The most popular of these is the ddd debugger. xxgdb is a GUI interface to gdb and many people also use it. The kdbg comes with KDE on Linux. All of these debuggers use the same concepts as used by the gdb debugger.

5.12.1 The kdbg Debugger

KDE debugger comes with KDE desktop development utilities. It is a GUI based upon GNU debugger. You can start it using the kdbg command or from a KDE menu. Using icons in the tool bar or menus, you can open files to be debugged. Once a file is loaded in the debugger window, you can click on a line to set or remove break points. To find out the purpose of an icon, you can move your cursor over the icon on the toolbar to display a short description.

The kdbg is a simple debugger but keep in mind that you may not find it as powerful as a native GNU debugger is. The window that appears when you start the debugger is shown in Figure 5-3. In this window the pointer is on the first printf statement where we have a break point set.

You can add a variable to the watch list using the watch window. This window can be opened by selecting the "Watched Expressions" option from the View menu. The window is shown in Figure 5-4 where two variables num1 and num2 are added to the watch list. You can click on a variable and then press the "Del" button to remove a variable from the watch list.

The kdbg also has an output window that is used to display any output from the program. This output window is actually an input window as well. You can enter input for the program in this window. The output window is started when you start the kdbg debugger. The output window is shown Figure 5-5.

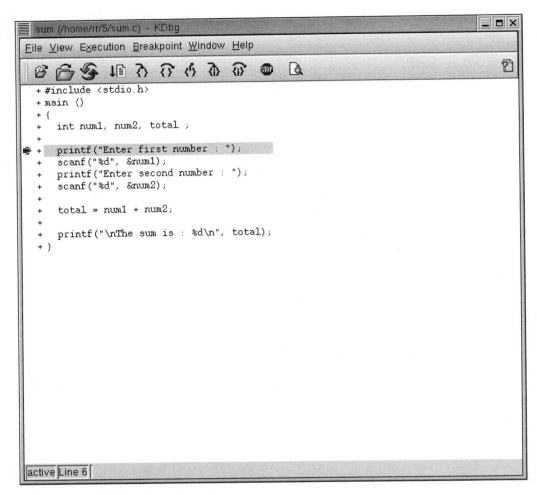

```
+ #include <stdio.h>
+ main ()
+ {
+    int num1, num2, total ;
+
+    printf("Enter first number : ");
+    scanf("%d", &num1);
+    printf("Enter second number : ");
+    scanf("%d", &num2);
+
+    total = num1 + num2;
+
+    printf("\nThe sum is : %d\n", total);
+ }
```

Figure 5-3 The kdbg window.

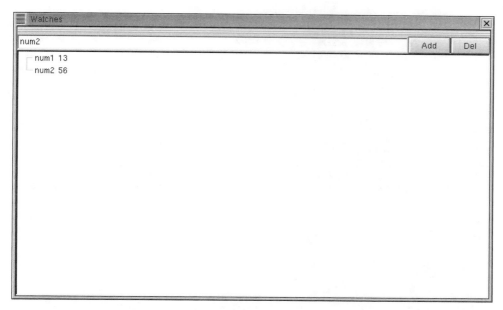

Figure 5-4 Watch window of kdbg debugger.

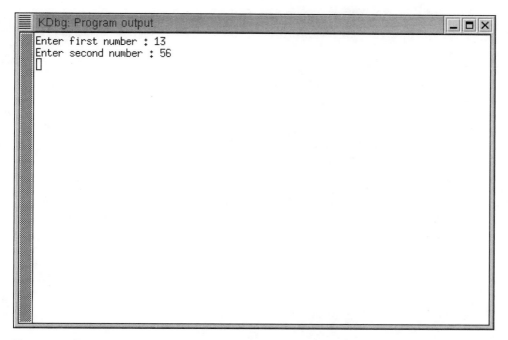

Figure 5-5 Output window for kdbg.

5.12.2 The ddd Debugger

The Data Display Debugger or ddd is a popular GUI front end to the GNU debugger. It has many additional features that are not present in native gdb. The main window of ddd debugger is shown in Figure 5-6. A complete discussion of this debugger is beyond the scope of this book.

Figure 5-6 Main window of ddd debugger.

5.12.3 The xxgdb Debugger

The xxgdb debugger is a GUI interface to the GNU debugger. You can use the command line window as well as GUI buttons with this debugger. The main screen is shown in Figure 5-7. The bottom part of the screen can be used to enter gdb commands while the top part can be used to scroll through source code and set or remove break points.

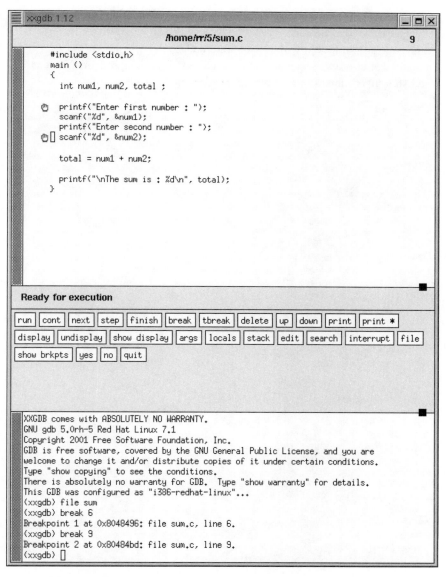

Figure 5-7 The xxgdb debugger main window.

For example, you can bring the cursor to a particular line and then press the break button to set up a break point at that line. Similarly you can use other buttons in the middle part of the window to carry out other tasks related to debugging a program.

5.13 References and Resources

1. GNU web site at http://www.gnu.org/
2. GNU debugger download web site ftp://ftp.gnu.org/gnu/gdb
3. DDD home page at http://www.gnu.org/software/ddd/
4. The gdb manual at http://www.gnu.org/manual/gdb/html_mono/gdb.html. You can find a detailed list of all commands and their explanation on this web site.

CHAPTER 6

Introduction to CVS

The Concurrent Versions System, or CVS, is a source code control application that permits developers to work in parallel on software development projects without the fear of overwriting someone else's work. In addition, it provides a complete project history that includes the ability to review previous versions of the code, and to compare old code with new code.

CVS can be used for any development project, including assembly and machine language to C and C++ and even the code and images necessary to maintain a web site.

The source code is set up in a software repository by the administrator. Each repository is identified by a unique location. A repository may be on a local machine or maintained on the network and accessed remotely. Many Open Source developers utilize anonymous CVS access in order to distribute development snapshots of the source code instead of (or in addition to) tarballs, RPM and other methods of distribution. Each repository many contain multiple projects and many versions of each project. The current version of a project may be checked out, as may older versions. Versions may also be compared to one another to determine specific changes and help to identify bugs that may have crept into a piece of software.

6.1   CVS Policies

In addition to the technical aspects of setting up CVS and granting users access to the system, there are certain operational procedures that need to be set forth prior to opening up a CVS repository for access.

One of the more important aspects deals with users checking in or committing a change into the repository.

Every time a source file is checked into the system, the version number of that file is incremented. This version is separate from the version number of the software project. The differences will be described later.

Each team or project will have to develop guidelines as to when a source file should be checked in, how long one may be checked out prior to committing it, and similar items. Checking a file out for a long period of time, making modifications and then checking it back in may result in conflicts that will have to be addressed. CVS will let you check the file in if your changes conflict with someone else's work, but someone will have to be responsible for ensuring that these conflicts are resolved.

Another policy might state that a file may not be checked back into the repository until it compiles cleanly with the rest of the project, until it has been reviewed, or until other benchmarks are met. These policies will vary from project to project, and while CVS can maintain the source code repository, it has no method of enforcing these policies. It is the role of the project owner and manager(s) to ensure that the policies are implemented and followed by the team members.

6.2   Project Management and Communication

While CVS has many tools to help you manage a software project, it has no inherent ability to manage the project on its own. There are e-mail notifications available that let individuals keep an eye on particular files for changes. There are reports available that can determine who changed which file when, as well as complete logs that describe what those changes did (or at least, were supposed to have done).

As mentioned previously, even using a version control system such as CVS will not prevent conflicts of code from arising. Communication between developers is absolutely necessary in order to ensure that projects proceed smoothly and on time.

6.3   Installing and Managing CVS

In order to install CVS, the first step is to obtain either the CVS source code or, if you are using RedHat, the RPM.

The latest source code is available at http://www.cvshome.org. As of this writing, the current CVS version is 1.11.1p1. RPM may be downloaded via RPMFind at http://rpmfind.net/linux/rpm2html/search.php?query=cvs. Follow the instructions for your preferred installation method.

6.3.1   Configuring CVS

Once CVS is installed on the server, the next step is to configure the machine properly to use CVS. The first step is to create a user and group to be the owners of the repositories. For purposes of example, assume that the user and the group are both named "cvs". This example shows how to set up CVS for local and remote "pserver" access. This method of setting up CVS is not the most secure method and does not provide a secure method for accessing the CVS repository remotely; but it is necessary if a project intends to provide remote, anonymous access to the CVS repository. For details on setting up a secure method of accessing the repository, see Section 6.7.1.

To accomplish this, as root, issue the useradd command listed below. Under RedHat Linux, this will create the cvs user and the cvs group. All of the following commands must be issued as the root user.

```
# useradd -r -c "CVS user" cvs
```

As initialized, this account will have no password and will not be able to be logged into. You can either leave it this way and, in the event that maintenance is necessary, log in as root and resolve issues, or assign a password and use that account. Leaving the account with no password is probably the most secure, but in the event that a password is necessary, simply assign one.

```
# passwd cvs
Changing password for user cvs
New UNIX password: <type cvs password>
Retype new UNIX password: <type cvs password>
passwd: all authentication tokens updated successfully
```

The next step is to create a CVS repository. For this example, assume that the CVS root is /usr/local/cvsroot. Additional repositories may be set up at this time, simply issue the CVS init command as many times as necessary; while changing the –d option to reflect the additional repositories.

```
# cvs -d /usr/local/cvsroot init
```

This will create the file structure necessary for CVS to function and will initialize all necessary files.

Once the user and repositories have been created, the ownership of the repositories needs to be changed.

```
# chmod -R cvs:cvs /usr/local/cvsroot [additional repositories here]
```

The next step is to add users to the repositories. Each repository has a password file in the $CVSROOT/CVSROOT directory. There are three fields in this file separated by colons. The first field is the user name that may or may not be the same as the user's login id. The second field is the user's encrypted password. This password is encrypted with the crypt() function. The final field is the name of the user whose request will be performed. This is the owner of the CVS repository and in our example, the owner is 'cvs'.

The easiest way to generate encrypted passwords for the password file is by using a simple perl script. An example is presented below. Simply type this script into a file using a text editor and make the file executable. Then run the program with two arguments, the username and the password.

```
#!/usr/bin/perl
#
# Simple script to take a username and password and
# return a line suitable for pasting into the CVS
# password file.
#

($u, $p)=@ARGV;
@d=(A..Z,a..z);
$s=$d[rand(52)].$d[rand(52)];
print $u.":".crypt($p, $s).":cvs\n";
```

If you have saved the file under the name 'cvspassgen' and set the permission properly, simple run the application as follows:

```
# ./cvspassgen username password
username:mU7OltQzHySmY:cvs
```

As you can see, the information is returned in the format that CVS requires. (Note: since a random salt is used to generate the password, your output will vary from what is presented here.)

You can simply cut and paste the line into the password file. Another option is to redirect the output of the script directly into the password file.

```
# ./cvspassgen username password >> $CVSROOT/CVSROOT/passwd
```

This assumes that the $CVSROOT environmental variable is set to the proper directory.

Next, the services file must be updated in order for the CVS server to respond to network requests. The following line will append to the /etc/services file. Just be sure that there are two "greater than" symbols or you will erase whatever is already in your services file.

```
# echo "cvspserver 2401/tcp" >> /etc/services
```

Next, the inetd server needs to know which service to start when requests come in. RedHat 7.x uses the xinetd server and so a file needs to be created in /etc/xinetd.d named cvspserver.

Using your favorite text editor, edit /etc/xinetd.d/cvspserver to include the following information:

```
# Description: cvspserver: version control system
service cvspserver
{
        socket_type = stream
        wait        = no
        user        = cvs
```

```
        passenv     =
        server      = /usr/bin/cvs
        server_args = --allow-root=/usr/local/cvsroot pserver
}
```

If you have installed multiple repositories, they need to be specified on the server_args line. To do this, simply insert additional −allow-root= commands. Please note that these additional arguments **must** appear on the same line.

In order for xinetd to acknowledge this change, it needs to reread its configuration files. To do this, send the server a HUP signal with the killall command.

```
# killall -HUP xinetd
```

At this point, the repository should be up and running.

To quickly review the steps for installing CVS:

1. Install the CVS application (RPM or source code)
2. Create CVS user and group
3. Create CVS repositories
4. Change the owner and group of the repositories
5. Add users to $CVSROOT/CVSROOT/passwd
6. Change file permissions on the password file(s)
7. Edit /etc/services to ensure that cvspserver is present
8. Configure /etc/xinetd.d to acknowledge CVS requests
9. Restart xinetd

6.3.2   Importing a Project into the Repository

Once you have CVS installed and configured, the next step is to import a project into the repository. This creates a directory for the project, copies the files into the repository and sets up the information that will be used to track the project as it gets modified during the development process.

Assuming that the directory /home/lcp/fuzion holds the source code and the files of the project, to import the project you need to change to that directory and issue the CVS import command.

The options for the import command include the name of the project, the vendor tag, and the release tag(s). The vendor tag is not currently used by CVS, and can contain any information that you care to put in. The release tag can be used to designate specific releases, but the source code can also be checked out by the numeric release designation. Any information that you care to put in these fields may be used, but they must be included with the import command.

```
# cd /home/lcp/fuzion
# cvs import Fuzion OSS_Software release_0_1
```

At this stage, you will be presented with your preferred editor (as defined by the environment variables $CVSEDITOR or $EDITOR). This will allow you to create a log entry that describes the project, the initial state that it is in, and anything else of importance.

When you save that file, the information, along with the imported files, will be saved in the repository.

To avoid having the editor displayed, you can include a log entry on the command line with the **–m** option. Log entries with spaces or other special characters in them should be enclosed in quotes.

```
# cvs import -m "Initialized the project" Fuzion \
OSS_Software release_0_1
```

To ensure that the files have been imported, issue the following command from the server that holds the repository:

```
# ls -l $CVSROOT/Fuzion
```

You should see a copy of each file in your project with a ', v' appended to the filename.

At this point, you should remove the original directory (after ensuring that you have a backup) and check out the project with CVS so that any modification can be committed to the repository.

```
# cd /home/lcp
# rm -rf fuzion
# cvs co Fuzion
# cd Fuzion
```

At this point you are ready to continue development on this project with CVS.

> **N O T E**   Special care must be taken if you are importing binary data into a CVS repository. This can be the case if you are importing files from a Windows platform, or if you use CVS to manage the files necessary for maintaining a web site. Graphic files and dlls will not import correctly unless special care is taken.
>
> One way to do this is with the wrapper function of CVS. To import a project and treat all files with a .jpg extension as binary data, issue the following command:
>
> ```
> cvs import -I ! -W "*.jpg -k 'b'" Pname V_tag R_tag
> ```

6.4   Using the CVS Client

There are several methods of accessing a CVS repository. The first is local access. This can be accomplished by a user logging in at the terminal or logging in remotely over the network. Either way, the developer must have a local account on the machine, a home directory, and the repository to be accessed via the local session.

Remote access can take several forms. This can be a remote connection from a user's machine to the `cvspserver` that runs on port 2401. Another method would be to have CVS connect via a remote shell (rsh) when the repository needs to be accessed.

CVS access takes place in clear text over the network with no inherent facility to prevent passwords and data from being intercepted and used by unauthorized persons to access the server. Several options later in the chapter describe a more secure method of access. One of those methods is similar to the `rsh` method, but the `CVS_RSH` environment variable is set to the `ssh` instead of the insecure `rsh` command.

6.4.1   Local Repositories

In order to work easily and efficiently with CVS, it is necessary to set up a series of environmental variables that tell CVS where your CVS repository is, which editor you prefer, etc. These variables can be set in either the system-wide or user specific files that are read when the user logs in, or each user may set or change them manually.

The first variable is `CVSROOT` and it tells CVS which repository that you wish to work with. Assuming that your CVS repository is located on the local machine, simply set the `CVS-ROOT` variable to the location of the repository.

If your repository resides at "`/usr/local/cvsroot`" and you are using sh, bash, ksh or a similar shell, simply insert the following line into your startup file (`.profile`, `.bash`, etc.)

```
export CVSROOT=/usr/local/cvsroot
```

If you are using csh or tcsh, insert the following line into your `.cshrc` or `.tcshrc` file:

```
setenv CVSROOT /usr/local/cvsroot
```

Should you wish to temporarily work with a different repository, the path to the repository can be supplied on the command line with the **-d** option, as in this example:

```
$ cvs -d /usr/local/cvsother checkout BigProject
```

Once a project has been checked out of the repository, this information is also kept in the `CVS/Root` file in the project directory, as shown below:

```
$ cat CVS/Root
/usr/local/cvsroot
```

The information in the `CVS/Root` file takes precedence over the `CVSROOT` variable in order to ensure that the files are checked back into the same repository that they were checked out from.

The `CVS/Root` file may be overridden by the -d command line option. This allows you to specifically place the file into a repository other than the one from which it was checked out.

To sum up, which checking a file back into the repository, the CVS root is determined the following order:

1. The **-d** command line option
2. The `CVS/Root` file
3. The `CVSROOT` environment variable

6.4.2 Remote Repositories

As mentioned earlier, there are several methods of accessing a remote CVS server. The first one we will discuss is the built-in functionality. This method utilizes a network connection from the developer's desktop to port 2401/tcp on the server. It requires that all of the intermediate networking equipment (routers, firewalls, etc.) permit this traffic to pass.

Accessing a repository using the `pserver` method requires additional information when compared to the local access in order to determine the name of the remote host, the user name to be used, and the remote connection method.

For example, in order to log into a remote CVS repository, you would need to specify the following:

```
# export CVSROOT=:pserver:user@hostname:/usr/local/cvsroot
```

Where user is your CVS username on the machine hostname. This may be used in the `CVSROOT` variable or on the command line with the **-d** option.

Prior to checking out, committing, importing or performing any other actions against a CVS server, the user is required to authenticate himself first by issuing a login command. With the $CVSROOT variable set as indicated, type the following:

```
# cvs login
Logging in to :pserver:user@hostname:2401/usr/local/cvsroot
CVS password:
```

Type in your CVS password, which will then be stored in a file in your home directory (`.cvspass`) for future use.

At that point you should be able to check out and commit software from the repository.

6.4.3 Checking out a Project

In order to begin work on a project contained in a CVS repository, you must first check the package out. This brings your working directory up-to-date (creating it if necessary) and creates a CVS directory in your working directory where CVS keeps information about the project locally.

To check out a project that is in the repository, simply issue the `cvs` command with the `checkout` option and the name of the project. For example, to check out the Fuzion project that was imported into the repository earlier, type:

```
# cvs checkout Fuzion
cvs server: Updating fuzion
U Fuzion/1.0.fuzion.pl
U Fuzion/em.dat
```

```
U Fuzion/fuzion.pl
U Fuzion/sk.dat
U Fuzion/tl.dat
U Fuzion/test.dat
```

CVS checks any existing copies of the project with the ones in the repository and updates all of the files on the user's machine.

The option `co` is an alias for the `checkout` option and they may be used interchangeably.

6.4.4   Finding the Status of a Project

After working on a project for a time, it may be necessary for you to determine which files in your working directory and which files in the repository have changed.

In order to accomplish this, you may use the `status` option of the CVS command. If this command is issued from the working directory without a project name, that project will be examined. If it is issued from another directory, you should include the project name to prevent CVS from trying to examine all of the subdirectories of the current directory for project information.

```
# cd fuzion
# cvs status
```

A partial example of the output is presented here:

```
===========================================================
File: 1.0.fuzion.pl      Status: Up-to-date

   Working revision:      1.1.1.1
   Repository revision: 1.1.1.1 /usr/local/cvsroot/fuzion/
1.0.fuzion.pl,v
   Sticky Tag:          (none)
   Sticky Date:         (none)
   Sticky Options:      (none)
===========================================================
File: fuzion.pl          Status: Locally Modified

   Working revision:      1.1.1.1
   Repository revision: 1.1.1.1 /usr/local/cvsroot/fuzion/
fuzion.pl,v
   Sticky Tag:          (none)
   Sticky Date:         (none)
   Sticky Options:      (none)
===========================================================
File: test.dat           Status: Needs Patch

   Working revision:      1.2
   Repository revision: 1.3      /usr/local/cvsroot/fuzion/
test.dat,v
```

```
Sticky Tag:            (none)
Sticky Date:           (none)
Sticky Options:        (none)
```

As you can see, there are two files here that are out of sync with the repository. The first one is `fuzion.pl` that has been modified, but not checked back in; and the other is `test.dat`, which someone else has modified and returned to the repository.

At this point, you can use `diff` to determine the extent of the changes and determine the appropriate course of action.

If your local copy of a file has changed, and the version in the repository has changed from the last time that you checked it out, you will receive a message indicating that the files needed to be merged.

```
File: test.dat          Status: Needs Merge

    Working revision:    1.2
    Repository revision: 1.3     /usr/local/cvsroot/fuzion/
test.dat,v
    Sticky Tag:          (none)
    Sticky Date:         (none)
    Sticky Options:      (none)
```

Again, you will want to determine the extent of the changes to the files and merge the two so that no changes will be lost when the file is checked back into the repository. Should you attempt to commit a change on a file when a newer version of the file exists on the server, CVS will complain and refuse to update the file.

```
cvs server: Up-to-date check failed for `test.dat'
cvs [server aborted]: correct above errors first!
cvs commit: saving log message in /tmp/cvsa15396
```

In the event of conflicts, you can use the `diff` option to examine the differences in the file and the `update` option to merge them. Both of these options are covered below.

6.4.5   Finding Differences

CVS can be used to determine the difference between a file in the repository and a file in the working directory. This is accomplished by using the `diff` option.

```
# cvs diff fuzion.pl
Index: fuzion.pl
===============================================================
RCS file: /usr/local/cvsroot/fuzion/fuzion.pl,v
retrieving revision 1.1.1.1
diff -r1.1.1.1 fuzion.pl
134c134
< print "=" x 40 ;
---
> print "=" x 80 ;
```

If you are familiar with the UNIX `diff` command, you will recognize the output of this command. See Section 7.3 for more information on the output of the `diff` command.

As you can see, CVS checked the repository for the latest copy of the file and compared it with the one in the working directory. This output indicates that one line has been changed at line 134 (a formatting change to the print statement).

6.4.6   Resolving Conflicts

The `update` option will merge two conflicting files into one file and insert special markers into the file that help you determine where the differences are and resolve them.

```
# cvs update test.dat
RCS file: /usr/local/cvsroot/fuzion/test.dat,v
retrieving revision 1.4
retrieving revision 1.5
Merging differences between 1.4 and 1.5 into test.dat
rcsmerge: warning: conflicts during merge
cvs server: conflicts found in test.dat
C test.dat
```

The resulting `test.dat` file is shown below, clipped for brevity;

```
# cat test.dat
aerosol
aerosolize
aerosols
aerospace
aesthetic
aesthetically
aesthetics
<<<<<<< test.dat
zebras
zenith
=======
zebras
zenith
zoological
zoologically
zoom
zooms
zoos
>>>>>>> 1.5
```

The <<<<<<< and >>>>>>> markers indicate which version of the file has had which edits made to it. The text between "<<<<<<< `test.dat`" and "=======" indicate text that was added from the time that the file was checked out until the time when the merge was done.

The text between the "=======" marker and the ">>>>>>> `1.5`" exists in version 1.5 of the file (in the repository) but not in the local working copy.

The final merged and edited file is shown below and is ready to be checked back into the repository.

```
# cat test.dat
aerosol
aerosolize
aerosols
aerospace
aesthetic
aesthetically
aesthetics
zebras
zenith
zoological
zoologically
zoom
zooms
zoos
```

6.4.7   Checking the Project Back In

Once you have made changes to a file, it is ready to be checked back into the repository. This is done with the `commit` option. The `checkin` and `ci` options are similar to the `commit` option, but instead of simply synchronizing the working file with the one in the repository, `commit` also releases the file and sets certain flags that can be used if the watch functions of CVS are being used.

```
# cvs commit -m "Added information to test.dat" test.dat
```

If there are any further conflicts, CVS will notify you that the files need to be changed.

6.4.8   Adding Files to a Project

Files may be added to a project after it has been imported. This is done by specifying the `add` option name of the file or files to be added to the project.

For example:

```
# cvs add index.html
cvs server: scheduling file `index.html' for addition
cvs server: use 'cvs commit' to add this file permanently
# cvs commit -m "new file" index.html
RCS file: /usr/local/cvsroot/fuzion/index.html,v
done
Checking in index.html;
/usr/local/cvsroot/fuzion/index.html,v  <--  index.html
initial revision: 1.1
done
```

If the file is a binary file you must specify the **–kb** option in order for it to be properly imported into the project.

```
# cvs add -kb banner.jpg
```

6.4.9   Removing Files from a Project

If you no longer wish a file to be a part of a project, you can use CVS's `remove` option to rid yourself of that file. Prior to removing the file, however, it must be deleted from the working directory.

```
# cvs remove index.html
cvs server: file `index.html' still in working directory
cvs server: 1 file exists; remove it first
# rm index.html
# cvs remove index.html
cvs server: scheduling `index.html' for removal
cvs server: use 'cvs commit' to remove this file permanently
# cvs ci -m "Removed index.html" index.html
Removing index.html;
/usr/local/cvsroot/fuzion/index.html,v  <--  index.html
new revision: delete; previous revision: 1.3
done
```

If you wish to delete a file and remove it from the project in one step, you may add the **–f** flag to the remove option.

```
# cvs remove -f index.html
cvs server: scheduling `index.html' for removal
cvs server: use 'cvs commit' to remove this file permanently
# ls index.html
/bin/ls: index.html: No such file or directory
# cvs commit -m "Removed old files"
cvs commit: Examining .
Removing index.html;
/usr/local/cvsroot/fuzion/index.html,v  <--  index.html
new revision: delete; previous revision: 1.5
done
```

Prior to committing a remove to the repository, the file may be resurrected by issuing the add command.

```
# rm index.html
# cvs remove index.html
cvs server: scheduling `index.html' for removal
cvs server: use 'cvs commit' to remove this file permanently
# cvs add index.html
U index.html
cvs server: index.html, version 1.7, resurrected
```

Additionally, if you have not yet issued the remove command, you can retrieve a copy of the file from the repository by issuing an update command.

```
# rm index.html
# cvs update index.html
U index.html
```

6.4.10 Renaming Files within a Project

There is no direct method of renaming files within the CVS repository. In order to rename a file, you must remove the old name and add in the new one. Here is an example of renaming a file from oldfile to newfile.

```
# cvs status oldfile
=============================================================
File: oldfile          Status: Up-to-date

    Working revision:    1.1
    Repository revision: 1.1    /usr/local/cvsroot/fuzion/
oldfile,v
    Sticky Tag:          (none)
    Sticky Date:         (none)
    Sticky Options:      (none)

# mv oldfile newfile
# cvs remove oldfile
cvs server: scheduling `oldfile' for removal
cvs server: use 'cvs commit' to remove this file permanently
# cvs add newfile
cvs server: scheduling file `newfile' for addition
cvs server: use 'cvs commit' to add this file permanently
# cvs commit -m "Ren oldfile newfile" oldfile newfile
Removing oldfile;
/usr/local/cvsroot/fuzion/oldfile,v  <--  oldfile
new revision: delete; previous revision: 1.1
done
RCS file: /usr/local/cvsroot/fuzion/newfile,v
done
Checking in newfile;
/usr/local/cvsroot/fuzion/newfile,v  <--  newfile
initial revision: 1.1
done
```

6.4.11 Removing your Working Copy

Once you have committed your changes to the repository, or if you wish to abandon your changes, you can release the working copy prior to deleting it. If you have any files checked out that have not been updated with the repository, CVS will inform you and give you the option of releasing the working directory.

```
# cd /home/lcp
# cvs release fuzion
A banner.jpg
M fuzion.pl
You have [2] altered files in this repository.
Are you sure you want to release directory `fuzion': Y
# rm -r fuzion
```

6.4.12 Tags and Releases

One of the strengths of CVS is its ability to create a release of a particular project. A release is a snapshot of a project at a specific point in time and is generally referred to by a numeric designation. When we refer to CVS version 1.1.11p1, we are talking about a specific release of the application that will always remain the same. If changes are made to that version of the software, the version number will change by indicating either a patch level or an increment in the major or minor version number.

This designation can be accomplished with CVS by assigning a tag to a project. Tags may be named in any fashion, symbolically with a numerical system as mentioned, or by code names, etc. It is important, however, that once a methodology for naming releases is established that it be abided by in order to prevent confusion in the future.

To apply a tag to a project, issue the following command from within the project directory:

```
# cvs tag Release_1_1 .
cvs server: Tagging .
T 1.0.fuzion.pl
T banner.jpg
T em.dat
T fuzion.pl
T index.html
T newfile
T sk.dat
T tal.dat
T test.dat
```

This does not change any information in the files; it simply places symbolic tags in the CVS repository so that when Release_1_1 of the Fuzion project is requested, these versions of the files will be retrieved from the repository.

To check a specific release back out of the repository, issue the checkout command with the −**r** option and the name of the release.

```
# cvs checkout -r Release_1_1 fuzion
```

6.5   Introduction to jCVS

For those more comfortable working with a GUI rather than a command line CVS client, there is a Java client available that uses Java that enables you to access off of the functionality of the CVS repository with a few clicks.

jCVS was written by Timothy Gerard Endres and has been released under the GNU Public License (GPL) and may be found at http://www.jcvs.org.

6.5.1   System Requirements

As previously mentioned, jCVS will run on any platform supported by Java. The current release runs on Java version 1.2 or higher. The installed application is a little over 6MB with source code, so any computer capable of running Java and X should have not problems installing and running jCVS.

6.5.2   Installation Instructions

In order to run jCVS, you must first install the Java Runtime Environment. The latest and most complete runtime libraries available from Sun are http://java.sun.com/j2se/1.4/download.html and can be found for Linux, Solaris and Windows.

Download the installer for your platform and follow the instructions provided. This generally consists of running an installer. In the example provided below, the `jre` was installed in /usr/local/jre.

Next, locate the latest jCVS tarball application archive. These are available at http://www.jcvs.org/download.html for download. For the purpose of these examples, assume that the application will be installed in /usr/local/jcvs.

```
# cd /tmp
# wget http://www.jcvs.org/download/jcvs/jcvs-522.tgz
--14:14:46--  http://www.jcvs.org/download/jcvs/jcvs-522.tgz
           => `jcvs-522.tgz'
Connecting to www.jcvs.org:80... connected!
HTTP request sent, awaiting response... 200 OK
Length: 1,976,228 [application/x-tar]
[snip]
14:14:55 (226.81 KB/s) - `jcvs-522.tgz' saved [1976228/
1976228]
# cd /usr/local
# tar xzf /tmp/jcvs-522.tgz
# ln -s  jCVS-5.2.2 jcvs
# /usr/local/jre/bin/java -jar \
/usr/local/jcvs/jars/jcvsii.jar
```

6.5.3   Using jCVS

At this point you should be faced with the main jCVS screen. (See Figure 6-1.) The tabs along the top permit you to perform various CVS commands against one or more repositories. If you have problem accessing a repository, the Test tab will allow you to check basic connectivity and access rights.

Once you have checked projects out from a repository, you may transfer them to the Work-Bench in order to have easy access to them. This is simply an area where all of your current projects can reside.

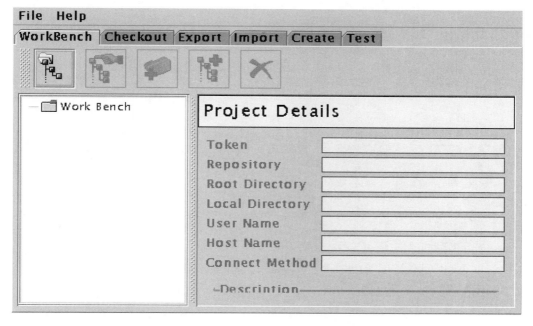

Figure 6-1 The jCVS WorkBench.

6.5.3.1   Configuring the jCVS Client

To begin, you will want to set up a few configuration options before beginning work on a project. Select **File | Edit Preferences** ... from the main menu. Select **Global | Temp Directory** in order to specify a place on the computer to store temporary files.

6.5.3.2   Checking Out a Project

To begin working with jCVS, click on the Checkout tab. The screen shown in Figure 6-2 will appear and you will be able to checkout a project from your repository.

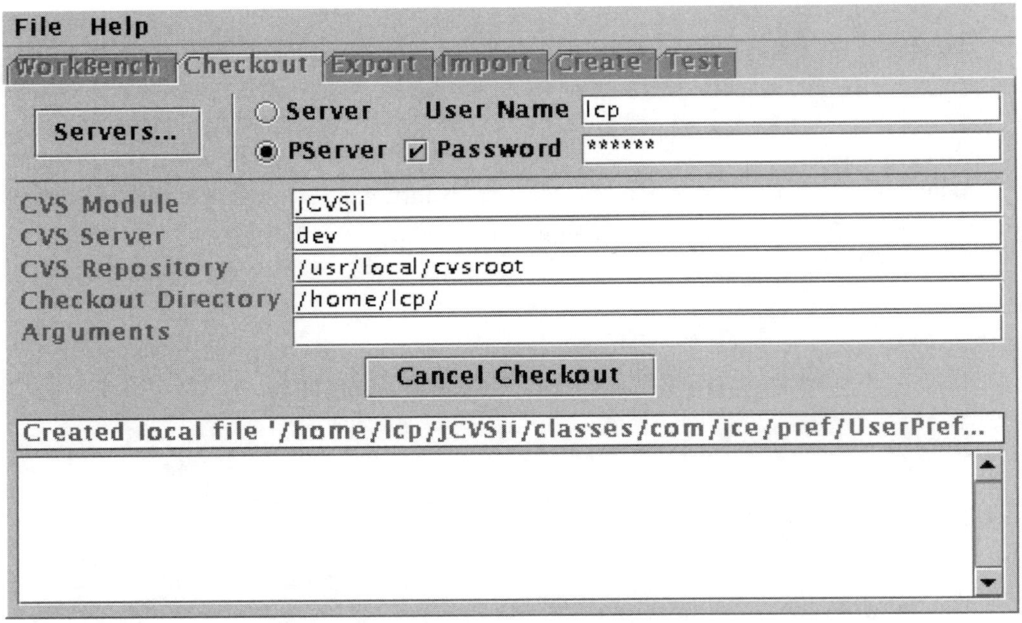

Figure 6-2 Checking out a Project from a CVS Repository.

As you can see, the fields presented map to the command line arguments that are required in order to check out a project from a repository. In the example presented, I am checking out a project entitled jCVSii from the dev server.

The Arguments field can be used to enter any command arguments or options that do not have a specific entry on the form. The entry above would be equivalent to the following commands:

```
# cd /home/lcp
# export CVSRROOT=:pserver:lcp@dev:/usr/local/cvsroot/
# cvs login
# cvs checkout jCVSii
```

When the checkout is complete, a project window will be presented displaying the file structure of the project. See Figure 6-3.

The Project Window allows you full access to the entire range of CVS commands and option. Files may be edited and committed back to the repository, the entire project may be updated, you can view the difference between the project file and the same file in the repository, view the project log, and even resurrect files as we did earlier with the remove and update commands.

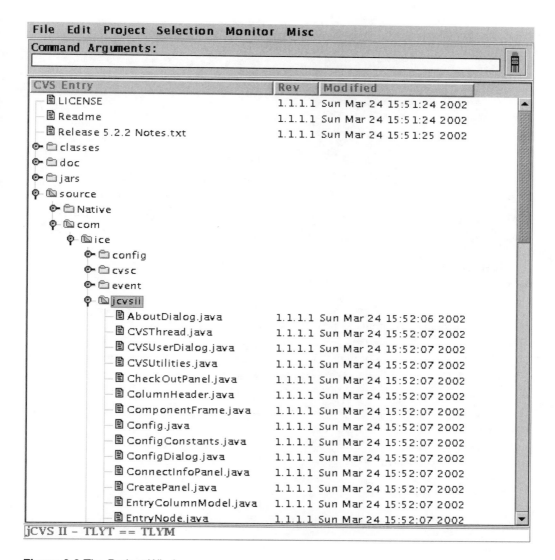

Figure 6-3 The Project Window.

6.5.3.3   Setting up the Server Definitions File

Since, in a development environment, you will be accessing one or more CVS repositories on a regular basis, you can set them up so that some of the information is retained by the system and saves you some effort if you have to switch between repositories.

To do this, create a file in your home directory entitled .jcvsdef with the following format:

```
server.myserver=true
param.myserver.method=pserver
param.myserver.name=My CVS Server
param.myserver.module=fuzion
param.myserver.host=dev.mynetwork.net
param.myserver.user=lcp
param.myserver.repos=/usr/local/cvsroot
param.myserver.desc= \
My Server Name goes here.\
As well as a description of the \
available projects.
```

In this example, you would substitute the name of your CVS repository for `myserver`. Use a short nickname, not a fully qualified domain name (FQDN). Don't use periods in this name. The entry for `param.myserver.host` should be the FQDN for the CVS repository, or the IP Address.

If you are working on multiple projects, you can leave the `param.myserver.module` blank and it will not be filled in automatically. This works for all of the fields.

6.5.3.4   Actions and Verbs

Prior to actually editing the files in the project, you must associate each file type with the application that will be used to `Open` or `Edit` the file.

From the WorkBench screen, re-open the preferences. (**File | Edit Preferences ...**) Then select **Actions | Verb Commands** from the menu on the left. This will present the screen shown in Figure 6-4.

Click on the **New** ... button. This displays a dialog button asking for a key. The key is a combination of the file extension and an action that may be used with that type of file. For example, a C Language source code file is designated by the `.c` extension and may be edited or opened. The key to edit any C source code file would be "`.c.edit`".

The key to open a .jpeg graphic file would be "`.jpeg.open`".

To create a key to edit a file with a `.java` extension, enter `.java.edit` into the field in the dialog box. Click the `OK` button.

Default actions can be defined by adding a key with the definition of '`._DEF_.verb`'. For example, to create a default editing action for all files not specifically associated with another action, use the key '`._DEF_.edit`'.

In the `Command` field, type the command line that you would use to perform the action associated with the key that you have just entered. The name of the file to be edited is substituted on the command line for the variable `$FILE`.

If, for example, you wished to use `gedit`, a simple Gnome editor, enter

/usr/bin/gedit $FILE

in the `Command` field.

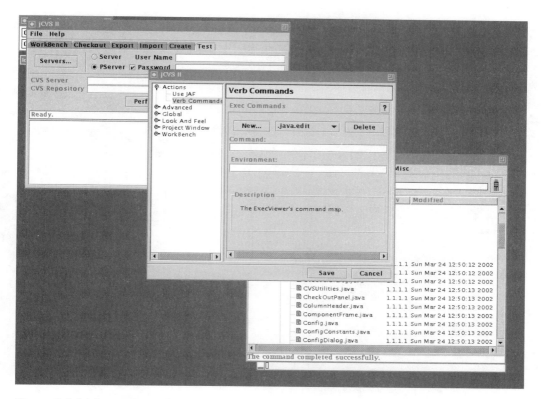

Figure 6-4 Adding verbs to jCVS.

6.5.3.5   Editing Projects

Once you have associated various file extensions with specific actions and helper applications, you are ready to begin working with your project.

By highlighting a file and right-clicking on it, you will display a menu of options for that file. If you select `Edit` from the menu that is displayed, jCVS will launch the application that you have defined for that action as shown in Figure 6-5.

The icons of files that have been modified after being checked out of the repository are shown in red for easy identification.

Running a `diff` of a file, or updating it, is as simple as selecting the appropriate option from the menu.

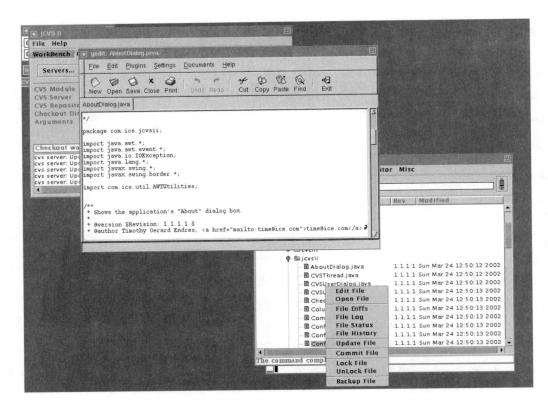

Figure 6-5 Editing source code.

6.5.3.6   Working with the WorkBench

In order to save a project to the WorkBench, you must first select a folder to save it in. You can organize your projects by adding additional folders to the WorkBench as needed. These can be divided by Vendor, Client or any other method that you choose.

When you have selected a folder for the project, in the Project Window, select **File | Add to WorkBench...** Then fill in the details of the project and press OK.

Opening a project on the WorkBench is accomplished by double-clicking on the name of the project. This opens the local copy.

To remove a project from the WorkBench, you will want to release the project from the Project screen (**Project | Release**) and then delete the project from the WorkBench.

6.6   Using Emacs with CVS

Until recently, (version 1.10) CVS has shipped with `pcl-cvs`, an interface that allowed Emacs users to integrate CVS into the Emacs environment. The latest version of `pcl-cvs` (2.9) is dated 4/15/2000 and is available at ftp://rum.cs.yale.edu/pub/monnier/pcl-cvs/pcl-cvs-2.9.9.tar.gz You will also need to retrieve the `elib` library found at ftp://ftp.lysator.liu.se/pub/emacs/elib-1.0.tar.gz.

6.6.1   Installing pcl-cvs

The `elib` library must be installed first. To do this, unpack the tarball:

```
# tar xvzf elib-1.0.tar.gz
```

Change directories into the newly created file and edit the Makefile to reflect the RedHat environment. Changes need to be made to two lines in the Makefile under RedHat 7.2. Other versions of Linux may or may not require any changes. The original lines and the correction are given below:

Original:

```
prefix = /usr/local
infodir = $(prefix)/info
```

Edited:

```
prefix = /usr
infodir = $(prefix)/share/info
```

Once these changes are made, you may compile the `elib` library by issuing the following commands as root:

```
# make
# make install
```

Once you have installed the `elib` library, you may install the `pcl-cvs` application the exact same way, by making the above changes to the Makefile and then compiling with `make`.

6.6.2   Using pcl-cvs

Complete documentation for `pcl-cvs` is available with the installed appliations in `.info` and `.tex` formats. It is also available on the World Wide Web at http://www.delorie.com/gnu/docs/cvs/pcl-cvs_toc.html.

While you will still have to check out the project from the command line, `pcl-cvs` provides you with the ability to compare files, commit changes and perform many other CVS functions from within Emacs.

If you are unfamiliar with Emacs, please refer to Chapter 2 for more detailed information about working with this editor.

As an introduction to working the CVS through Emacs, change into a CVS project directory and start Emacs. Make sure that you have the `CVSROOT` environment variable set up properly.

To begin with, let's get the status on our current project. Type in **M-x cvs-status** and press enter to accept the directory information that Emacs presents. After checking with CVS, Emacs should display something similar to Figure 6-6.

```
Buffers Files Tools Edit Search Mule CVS Help
█PCL-CVS release v2_9_9

 Repository        : :pserver:lcp@dev:/usr/local/cvsroot
 Working directory: /home/lcp/jCVSii/

 █

 In directory .:
                Up-To-Date  1.1.1.1        LICENSE
                Up-To-Date  1.1.1.1        Readme
                Up-To-Date  1.1.1.1        Release 5.2.2 Notes.txt
 In directory classes:
 In directory classes/META-INF:
                Up-To-Date  1.1.1.1        classes/META-INF/MANIFEST.MF
 In directory classes/com:
 In directory classes/com/ice:
 In directory classes/com/ice/config:
                Up-To-Date  1.1.1.1        classes/com/ice/config/ConfigureConstants\
 .class
                Up-To-Date  1.1.1.1        classes/com/ice/config/ConfigureEditor$1.\
 class
                Up-To-Date  1.1.1.1        classes/com/ice/config/ConfigureEditor$2.\
 class
                Up-To-Date  1.1.1.1        classes/com/ice/config/ConfigureEditor.cl\
 ass
                Up-To-Date  1.1.1.1        classes/com/ice/config/ConfigureEditorFac\
 tory.class
                Up-To-Date  1.1.1.1        classes/com/ice/config/ConfigurePanel$1.c\
 lass
                Up-To-Date  1.1.1.1        classes/com/ice/config/ConfigurePanel$Edi\
 torPanel.class
                Up-To-Date  1.1.1.1        classes/com/ice/config/ConfigurePanel.cla\
 ss
                Up-To-Date  1.1.1.1        classes/com/ice/config/ConfigureSpec.clas\
 s
                Up-To-Date  1.1.1.1        classes/com/ice/config/ConfigureTest.clas\
 s
                Up-To-Date  1.1.1.1        classes/com/ice/config/ConfigureTree$1.cl\
-1:%*  *cvs*                  (CVS: exit)--L6--Top-------------------------------------
█
```

Figure 6-6 CVS Project status in Emacs with `pcl-cvs`.

Files listed in the status screen may be edited by moving the cursor to the appropriate line and pressing the **o** key. This will load the file in question into another window for editing. Pressing **f** instead of **o** will result in the file being opened in the current window and replacing the status information.

When the edited file is saved with changes, the status window will be updated to reflect this and the file will be shown as being modified.

To check a file back into the repository from Emacs, you need to move the cursor to the line with the file name on it, and press the **c** key. This will open a new window in which you can type the log information that reflects the changes that you have made to the file. Press C-c twice (**C-c C-c**) to save the log information and continue checking the file in. You will be asked to confirm the action prior to the file being updated in the repository.

The **m** key will mark multiple files (indicated by an asterisk) so that they can be committed or have other actions taken on them at the same time. The **u** key can remove the mark from a file.

There are more options available within `pcl-cvs`, but this should give you enough information to begin using the application productively.

6.7 Secure remote access with CVS

The main goal of CVS is to provide a central repository for the storage of development projects and to provide access to and management tools for those projects. CVS by its nature is not a secure protocol.

Passwords, source code files and project data are transmitted across the network in clear text and available to anyone along the data path that cares to eavesdrop and analyze the data collected.

Various developers, aware of the inherent insecurity of the CVS protocol, have started using Secure Shell (ssh) to provide an additional layer of security to the development process. This chapter describes how to set up ssh on the clients and the server in order to ensure that code, data and authentication information are handled in a secure manner.

6.7.1 Secure Shell Access

When describing remote access methods to use for CVS earlier, the method for setting up rsh access to the server was intentionally omitted. The protocol used by rsh is inherently insecure in that it transmits all information across the network in plain text and encourages trust relationships to be set up between computers that can lead to system compromises.

Secure Shell (ssh) is a replacement for rsh that uses client and server authentication as well as strong cryptography. It is a little more difficult to set up ssh access to a CVS repository than to set up rsh access, but the security advantages outweigh any additional time and effort in setting up the server.

The first step is to ensure that the CVS server has ssh installed and properly configured. Ssh may be obtained from several sources. OpenSSH (http://www.openssh.org) is an open source implementation of the protocol that is widely used. This is also what ships with RedHat Linux.

Using ssh with CVS uses RSA Authentication and you need to make sure that this is turned on in the ssh configuration file. This configuration file is `/etc/ssh/sshd_config`.

Locate the RSA Authentication and configuration and make sure that it is turned on. It should read:

```
RSAAuthentication yes
```

This should complete the ssh configuration on the server.

Now log into the client machines that are going to be accessing the CVS repository. Each user that wishes to access the repository must:

1. Have a shell account on the CVS server.

2. Create a public/private key pair on the client.

3. Transfer the public portion of the key to the CVS server.

4. Set up the CVS client to use this new method.

Depending on how the CVS server is configured, it may be possible to set up ssh to bypass the requirement of typing in your password every time that you interact with the CVS repository.

> **N O T E** The key to logging in without having to type in the passphrase each time is to specify a blank password during the key generation process. While this does permit you to log into the server without supplying a passphrase, anyone who has access to your account will be able to do the same. Make sure never to leave your workstation unlocked and unattended.

Assuming that the accounts have already been set up on the CVS server, the next step is to generate the public/private key pair. This is accomplished by using the ssh-keygen program.

To generate the key pair, issue the following command (this may result in a DSA key with openssh3.):

```
# ssh-keygen -N ""
Generating public/private rsa1 key pair.
Enter file in which to save the key (/root/.ssh/identity):
<CR>
Your identification has been saved in /root/.ssh/identity.
Your public key has been saved in /root/.ssh/identity.pub.
The key fingerprint is:
32:66:ea:74:4a:7d:23:78:57:bc:90:12:a3:da:78:20 lcp@client
```

The **–N ""** option tells the program to uses a null passphrase to protect the keys.

As indicated by the program messages, this creates two files in the user's $HOME/.ssh directory. The first one, identity, is your private key. This should be kept secure and should not be shared. The second, identity.pub, as you may have guessed, is the public key. The contents of this file need to be distributed to every machine that you wish to log into and access via ssh.

To accomplish this, you can use ssh itself to copy the file between machines as follows:

```
# cd ~/.ssh
# scp identity.pub user@cvsserver:.ssh/`hostname`.pub
```

Replace user@cvsserver with your username on the CVS server. For example if your username were jon and the CVS server was named dev, you would replace this with jon@dev. You could also use the FQDN or IP Address in place of cvsserver. Also note that the punctuation marks surrounding the hostname are backticks.

Next, you need to log into the CVS server and append the newly created .pub files to a file called `authorized_keys`. The `authorized_keys` holds the authentication keys for each user/machine combination that is permitted to use RSA Authentication to log in.

```
# ssh -l username cvsserver
# cd .ssh
# cat client.pub >> authorized_keys
```

While `username` and `cvsserver` are the same as before, `client.pub` should be replaced with the name of the machine that you generated the keys on.

At this point ssh should be set up and you should be able to move ssh into the CVS repository without having to enter a password or passphrase.

The next step is to set up CVS to use this new method of connecting to the repository. This is accomplished by set two environment variables. The first you should already be familiar with; that is `CVSROOT`.

When using ssh instead of accessing the server locally or via `pserver`, the command to set up the `CVSROOT` variable should look something like this:

```
# export CVSROOT=:ext:user@hostname:/usr/local/cvsroot
```

The second environment variable that needs to be set up is `CVS_RSH`. This is used with the `:ext:` method to specify which command should be used to log into the remote server. This should be set to `ssh`. You may need to specify the full path to the ssh application if `ssh` is not in your `$PATH`.

```
# export CVS_RSH=ssh
```

At this point you should be able to use CVS via ssh.

You should be aware that each project, when it is checked out, keeps track of the method that it used to check out that project. This is kept in the CVS directory of the project in a file called `Root`. If you have any projects checked out when switching access methods, you will want to check the projects back in and release them before switching; or manually edit the files for each project to inform CVS of the change in access.

Supplying the **–d** option on the command line to change the access method would also work.

6.8   References and Resources

1. The CVS home page at http://www.cvshome.org
2. Complete CVS documentation at http://www.cvshome.org/docs/manual/
3. The jCVS home page at http://www.jcvs.org
4. The OpenSSH home at http://www.openssh.org

CHAPTER 7

Miscellaneous Tools

In addition to the standard development tools used in software development projects, many other utilities are also helpful. Most of the time these utilities are not directly related to the software development process but are used as helping aids. This chapter provides an introduction to some of these utilities that are extremely helpful in the software development process. Some of the more common uses of these utilities are presented and readers are encouraged to experiment with them. If properly utilized, they may save time and increase productivity.

The `indent` utility is helpful in implementing a common programming style scheme to all source code files in a project. The `sed` utility is useful for searching and replacing text across multiple files. The `diff` command is used to display difference between two or more files. The `cscope` and `cbrowser` are used to locate symbols in a software source code tree. The `strace` and `ltrace` utilities are useful to find out system and library calls when a program is executed. GNU binary utilities are a set of utilities that is often used for different needs. Information about GNU utilities is presented in this chapter as well.

7.1   Using indent Utility

One major objective of every software development project is that the code be well organized, structured and easy to understand for other members of the team. Proper indentation plays an important role in achieving these objectives. Most of the editors used in software development can do automatic indentation if they are configured to do so. The Emacs editor is the best example as it understands different programming languages and does indentation according to language rules and style. However you can come across code written by others that is poorly indented and you may like to re-indent it according to your own requirements or preferences. In large software development projects, you may try to enforce a particular coding style, but be assured that not everyone will follow it. The indent program is your tool to handle the situation and reformat all files in the project according to the style adopted for the project. You can do it by creating a script that goes into each directory of the project and reformats all files. In this section we shall explore some of its features and how to utilize it.

By default, the indent program uses the GNU style of coding and applies these rules to input files. It creates a backup file with original contents of the file. The reformatted file is created with the same name. The backup file ends with a tilde character ~. Note that the same scheme of creating backup files is used by the Emacs editor.

Let us see how indent works. We will take a poorly indented file and apply the indent program to it. Following is a listing of the poorly indented file hello.c.

```
 1   /**************************************
 2    * hello.c
 3    *
 4    * This file is used to demonstrate use
 5    * of indent utility
 6          **********************************/
 7   #include <stdio.h>
 8
 9   main () {
10       char string[25] ;
11      printf ("Enter a string of characters : ") ;
12        scanf ("%s", string);
13      printf ("The entered string is : %s\n ", string);
14   }
```

Line numbers are added to the listing using the "cat -n hello.c" command to explain changes. They are not part of the hello.c file. To properly indent the file hello.c, the following command is executed:

```
indent hello.c
```

The resulting hello.c file is shown below. Note how the indent program has modified the file. Lines 10 to 14 are indented to two characters (depending upon default settings).

```
1   /****************************************
2    * hello.c
3    *
4    * This file is used to demonstrate use
5    * of indent utility
6      ****************************************/
7   #include <stdio.h>
8
9   main ()
10  {
11    char string[25];
12    printf ("Enter a string of characters : ");
13    scanf ("%s", string);
14    printf ("The entered string is : %s\n ", string);
15  }
```

However line 6 is still not properly indented. By default the indent program does not modify comment lines.

To find out which version of the indent program you are using, use the following command.

```
[root@boota ftp-dir]# indent --version
GNU indent 2.2.6
[root@boota ftp-dir]#
```

7.1.1   Getting Started with Indent

The indent program may be used as a command or as a pipe. In the command mode, the program has a general format as shown below:

```
indent [options] [input filename] [-o output filename]
```

The following two lines show the simplest use of the indent program. It takes hello.c as input file and creates hello.c as output file and hello.c~ as backup file.

```
[root@boota indent]# indent hello.c
[root@boota indent]#
```

If you want to create an output file with a different name without modifying the original file, you can use the –o option with indent. When multiple input files are specified, indent reformats each file and creates a backup file for each input file. Wild card characters can also be used with indent so that you can indent all C source code files with the "indent *.c" command.

The output of another command can also be piped into the indent command. The following command does the same thing as indent hello.c but writes the output on STDOUT instead of writing it to a file.

```
cat hello.c | indent
```

This is sometimes useful if you just want to test the behavior of `indent` without modifying a file.

The most efficient use of `indent` is through a shell script that goes into each directory of the source code tree and indents each and every file in the project. You may also create a rule in the makefile of a project to indent all files in one or all directories. A typical makefile rule may look like the following:

```
indent:
    indent *.c
    indent *.cpp
    indent *.h
```

In the case of a project with multiple subdirectories, you can have a more sophisticated rule. Taking an example from Chapter 4, where we have four subdirectories, you can use the following rule to go into each directory and indent all C source code files.

```
SUBDIRS = $(COMDIR) $(FTPDIR) $(TFTPDIR) $(DNSDIR)
indent:
    for i in $(SUBDIRS) ; do    \
        ( cd $$i ; indent *.c) ;  \
        done
```

Keep in mind that after indenting all of the files, you may have to build the whole project because source code files have been modified. In big projects this process may take a while.

Indent uses a configuration file called `.indent.pro`, which should be present in the current directory or in your home directory. You can use this file to set options that you always use. If the file is present in the current directory, it is used instead of the file in the home directory of the user. By creating a different `.indent.pro` file in different directories of a project, you can apply different indentation rules in different directories. This is especially useful when a project uses multiple languages. For example, indentation rules may be different for C, C++ and assembly language files.

7.1.2   Selecting Coding Styles

Different coding styles are in use by programmers. Some common styles are defined in `indent` program and these may be invoked by a single option at the command line. The most common style of coding in the open source is the GNU style. This style can be applied using –gnu option at the command line. Options, which are used with the GNU style, are listed below:

```
-nbad

-bap

-nbc

-bbo

-bl

-bli2
```

```
-bls
-ncdb
-nce
-cp1
-cs
-di2
-ndj
-nfc1
-nfca
-hnl
-i2
-ip5
-lp
-pcs
-nprs
-psl
-saf
-sai
-saw
-nsc
-nsob
```

A list of all the options and their meanings are presented later in this chapter. You can override a particular option in a style by explicitly typing it on the command line.

The other commonly used style is Kernighan and Ritchie style, also known as K&R style. This style is applied using the -kr option at the command line and it sets the following options.

```
-nbad
-bap
-bbo
-nbc
-br
-brs
-c33
-cd33
```

```
-ncdb

-ce

-ci4

-cli0

-cp33

-cs

-d0

-di1

-nfc1

-nfca

-hnl

-i4

-ip0

-l75

-lp

-npcs

-nprs

-npsl

-saf

-sai

-saw

-nsc

-nsob

-nss
```

Again, you can override some of these options by specifying them on the command line.

The Berkley style is used by −orig option at the command line and it sets the following options.

```
-nbad

-nbap

-bbo

-bc

-br

-brs
```

```
-c33

-cd33

-cdb

-ce

-ci4

-cli0

-cp33

-di16

-fc1

-fca

-hnl

-i4

-ip4

-l75

-lp

-npcs

-nprs

-psl

-saf

-sai

-saw

-sc

-nsob

-nss

-ts8
```

7.1.3   Blank Lines and Comments

Blank lines can be used in the source code files to add clarity. The indent program allows you to add or remove blank lines from the source code files. Most commonly used options to handle blank lines are as follows:

-bad   This option adds a blank line after declarations.

-bap   This option is used to add a blank line after a procedure body. Using this option will create a blank line after each function.

-bbb   This option is used to add a blank line before a boxed comment. An example of a
          boxed comment is shown below.

```
/************************************
 * hello.c
 *
 * This file is used to demonstrate use
 * of indent utility
 ************************************/
```

-sob   This option is used to remove unnecessary blank lines from the source code.

By adding n in the start of these options, their effect may be reversed. For example, the
-nbad option will not add any blank line after declaration.

7.1.4   Formatting Braces

People have different tastes about how braces should be formatted in C language. Using
indent you can specify different ways of formatting braces. Let us consider a poorly formatted
piece of C source code and see different ways of formatting it. The input segment of source code
is shown below:

```
if (counter > 0)
{
counter-- ;
printf ("Counter value is: %d \n");
}
else
{
printf("Counter reached zero. Resetting counter\n");
counter = 100;
}
```

The default indentation of this segment of code is shown below. This is the default GNU
indentation when you use no command line switches with indent.

```
if (counter > 0)
  {
    counter--;
    printf ("Counter value is: %d \n");
  }
else
  {
    printf ("Counter reached zero. Resetting counter\n");
    counter = 100;
  }
```

Among other things, note that `indent` has placed a space after the second `printf` function call. This is the default style of putting braces in C code. Since the GNU formatting style is used with GNU `indent` by default, and it uses the –bl option, the result is as shown above. To put the starting brace on the same line, you can use the –br command line switch and the result is as follows:

```
if (counter > 0) {
  counter--;
  printf ("Counter value is: %d \n");
}
else {
  printf ("Counter reached zero. Resetting counter\n");
  counter = 100;
}
```

Other forms of `indent` can be used with different statements. See the manual pages of `indent` for a detailed list of all options.

7.1.5   Formatting Declarations

You can tell `indent` to handle the variable declarations in other ways by using different options to separate the declaration lines from other code. The most common method is to place a blank line after the declaration's end. As an example, if you use the –bad option (blank line after declarations), `indent` will place a blank line wherever it finds end of the declaration part. In the previous example of `hello.c` program, the result of using this option will be as follows:

```
1   /**************************************
2    * hello.c
3    *
4    * This file is used to demonstrate use
5    * of indent utility
6    **************************************/
7   #include <stdio.h>
8
9   main ()
10  {
11    char string[25];
12
13    printf ("Enter a string of characters : ");
14    scanf ("%s", string);
15    printf ("The entered string is : %s\n ", string);
16  }
```

Note that line number 12 is inserted into the file. You can also use the –di option with `indent` to align an identifier to a particular column. For example, using –di8 will align all identifiers to column number 8. Consider the following two lines in a C source code file.

```
int i;
char c;
long boota ;
```

After using indent with −di8 option, the output will be as follows:

```
int     i;
char    c;
long    boota;
```

You can also force creation of a new line for each identifier, using the −bc option. Consider the following code segment:

```
int i, j, k;
char c;
long boota ;
```

After using the "indent −di8 −bc" command on these three lines, the result will be as follows:

```
int     i,
        j,
        k;
char    c;
long    boota;
```

In addition to these common methods, there are other ways to arrange identifiers in declaration sections.

7.1.6   Breaking Long Lines

Long lines can be broken using indent at a defined length. The −l option controls this behavior. Consider the following line of code:

```
printf ("This is example of a long line.");
```

This line is 43 characters long. If we set the line limit to 40 characters using −l40 command line option, the line will be broken as follows:

```
printf
   ("This is example of a long line.");
```

Lines with conditional operators may be broken more intelligently. Consider the following if statement:

```
if(((counter == 100) && (color == RED)) || (string[0] == 'S'))
```

Using options "−l30 −bbo" (break before Boolean operator) will be as follows:

```
if (((counter == 100)
     && (color == RED))
    || (string[0] == 'S'))
```

Using the –nbbo option results in the following output.

```
if (((counter == 100) &&
     (color == RED)) ||
     (string[0] == 'S'))
```

The indent utility may also be used to handle new line characters in a special way using the –hnl option. You are encouraged to experiment with this option.

7.1.7 Summary of Options

Options with the indent program can be used in two ways: the long way that starts with two hyphen characters and the short way that starts with a single hyphen character. Options used with the indent command are listed below. These are taken from the manual page of the indent command. The long method also describes the meaning of an option.

```
-bc          --blank-lines-after-commas
-bad         --blank-lines-after-declarations
-bap         --blank-lines-after-procedures
-bbb         --blank-lines-before-block-comments
-bl          --braces-after-if-line
-bli         --brace-indent
-bls         --braces-after-struct-decl-line
-br          --braces-on-if-line
-brs         --braces-on-struct-decl-line
-nbbo        --break-after-boolean-operator
-bbo         --break-before-boolean-operator
-bfda        --break-function-decl-args
-clin        --case-indentation
-cbin        --case-brace-indentation
-cdb         --comment-delimiters-on-blank-lines
-cn          --comment-indentation
-cin         --continuation-indentation
-lp          --continue-at-parentheses
-cdw         --cuddle-do-while
-ce          --cuddle-else
-cdn         --declaration-comment-column
-din         --declaration-indentation
-nbfda       --dont-break-function-decl-args
-npsl        --dont-break-procedure-type
-ncdw        --dont-cuddle-do-while
-nce         --dont-cuddle-else
-nfca        --dont-format-comments
-nfc1        --dont-format-first-column-comments
-nlp         --dont-line-up-parentheses
-nss         --dont-space-special-semicolon
-nsc         --dont-star-comments
-cpn         --else-endif-column
```

```
-fca          --format-all-comments
-fc1          --format-first-column-comments
-gnu          --gnu-style
-hnl          --honour-newlines
-nhnl         --ignore-newlines
-npro         --ignore-profile
-in           --indent-level
-kr            --k-and-r-style
-nsob          --leave-optional-blank-lines
-lps           --leave-preprocessor-space
-dn            --line-comments-indentation
-ln            --line-length
-nbc           --no-blank-lines-after-commas
-nbad          --no-blank-lines-after-declarations
-nbap          --no-blank-lines-after-procedures
-nbbb          --no-blank-lines-before-block-comments
-ncdb          --no-comment-delimiters-on-blank-lines
-ncs           --no-space-after-casts
-nip           --no-parameter-indentation
-nsaf          --no-space-after-for
-npcs          --no-space-after-function-call-names
-nsai          --no-space-after-if
-nprs          --no-space-after-parentheses
-nsaw          --no-space-after-while
-nut           --no-tabs
-nv            --no-verbosity
-orig          --original
-ipn           --parameter-indentation
-pin           --paren-indentation
-pmt           --preserve-mtime
-psl           --procnames-start-lines
-cs            --space-after-cast
-saf           --space-after-for
-sai           --space-after-if
-prs           --space-after-parentheses
-pcs           --space-after-procedure-calls
-saw           --space-after-while
-ss            --space-special-semicolon
-st            --standard-output
-sc            --start-left-side-of-comments
-sbin          --struct-brace-indentation
-sob           --swallow-optional-blank-lines
-tsn           --tab-size
-ut            --use-tabs
-v             --verbose
```

7.2   Using sed Utility

The `sed` utility is a stream editor that can be used for different file editing purposes when used as a filter. The most common task for software development purposes is the use of `sed` to search and replace text in source code files. Let us take the example of the following C source code file `hello.c`.

```
#include <stdio.h>

main ()
{
  char string[25];

  printf ("Enter a line of characters : ");
  scanf ("%s", string);
  printf ("The entered string is : %s\n ", string);
}
```

In order to replace every occurrence of word *string* with the word *STRING*, you can use `sed`. The `sed` filter command and its result on this file are shown below.

```
[root@boota]# cat hello.c | sed s/string/STRING/
#include <stdio.h>

main ()
{
  char STRING[25];

  printf ("Enter a line of characters : ");
  scanf ("%s", STRING);
  printf ("The entered STRING is : %s\n ", string);
}
[root@boota indent]#
```

The `sed` command understands UNIX regular expressions. Regular expressions can be used for a higher level of stream editing. You can also use `sed` in shell scripts as well as make-files to carry out tasks in the entire source code directory tree. You can also use –f options followed by a filename. The filename contains `sed` commands. Please refer to the `sed` man pages for a complete set of options.

7.3   Using diff Utility

The `diff` utility is another useful tool that developers may need. It is used to find out the differences between two files. If you are using CVS, differences between different versions of a file in the CVS repository can be found using the `cvs` (`cvs diff`) command as well. However, if you want to find out the difference between two files that are not in the CVS repository, the `diff` utility may be quite handy. One common use may be to find out the difference between the working copy and the backup copy of a source code file. This will enable you to find out what changes have been made in the working copy of the file. The output of the `diff` utility follows similar rules to those used in the CVS `diff` command. The following command shows that files `hello.c` and `hello.c~` are different at line number 11. The line starting with the less-than symbol is taken from the first file (`hello.c`) and the line starting with the greater-than symbol is taken from the file `hello.c~`.

```
[root@boota]# diff hello.c hello.c~
11c11
<     char string[30];
---
>     char string[25];
[root@boota]#
```

The first line of the output contains the character c (changed) that shows that line 11 in the first file is changed to line 11 in the second file.

You can also use "`unified diff`" that tells you additional information about the file and displays a few lines before and after the lines that are different. See the following output of the `unified diff` command:

```
[root@boota]# diff hello.c hello.c~ -u
--- hello.cTue Jun 25 14:43:30 2002
+++ hello.c~Tue Jun 25 14:43:38 2002
@@ -8,7 +8,7 @@

 main ()
 {
-   char string[30];
+   char string[25];

    printf ("Enter a line of characters : ");
    scanf ("%s", string);
[root@boota]#
```

You can also use the –p option with the command to display the name of the function in which the modified line(s) exist.

If you add a line after line 15 in `hello.c` file and run the `diff` command once again, the result will be as follows:

```
[root@boota]# diff hello.c hello.c~
11c11
<     char string[30];
---
>     char string[25];
16d15
<     printf ("End of program\n");
[root@boota]#
```

The first part of the output is familiar. The second part shows that line 16 in the first file, which is printed next, is not present in the second file. Sometimes it is useful to display two files being compared in side-by-side format. This can be done by using the –y option. The following command shows how to use side-by-side output. The CVS rules of displaying output are used here to show modified, added or removed lines.

```
[root@boota]# diff -y --width 60 hello.c hello.c~
/************************      /************************
 * hello.c                      * hello.c
 *                             *
 * This file is used to demo     * This file is used to demo
 * of indent utility            * of indent utility
 ************************       ************************
#include <stdio.h>            #include <stdio.h>

main ()                       main ()
{                             {
  char string[30];        |     char string[25];

  printf ("Enter a string of     printf ("Enter a string of
  scanf ("%s", string);          scanf ("%s", string);
  printf ("The entered strin     printf ("The entered strin
  printf ("End of program\n" <
}                             }
[root@boota]#
```

The --width option is used to specify width of columns in the output. As you can see the | symbol is used to show a modified line and < or > symbols are used to show added or deleted lines.

The diff utility can also be used on directories. When comparing directories, diff compares files of the same name in the two directories. Directories can also be compared recursively.

Many options are used with the diff command, the most common are listed in Table 7-1. All these options start with a hyphen character.

Table 7-1 Common options used with the diff command

Option	Description
-b	Ignore changes in white spaces
-B	Ignore changes that are related to insertion of deletion of blank lines
-i	Ignore changes in case
-u	Unified output
-p	Used with –u option. Shows the function name also.

Table 7-1 Common options used with the `diff` command (Continued)

Option	Description
-c	Context output
-n	RCS style of output
-r	Compare directories recursively
-y	Use side-by-side format

7.3.1 Other Forms of diff Utility

There are two other important forms of the `diff` utility. These are `diff3` and `sdiff`. The `diff3` utility is used to compare three files and its general format is shown below.

```
diff3 [options] mine older yours
```

Suppose you and your colleague start working on a file simultaneously. The original file is the *older* file. Now you have your copy of the file (the *mine* file) and your colleague has his own copy of the file (the *yours* file). If you want to compare both of these modified copies of the file with the original *older* file, `diff3` is a useful tool. See man pages of the `diff3` command for more details.

Another important utility is `sdiff` that finds difference between two files and merges these two files into a third file. The general format of `sdiff` is as follows.

```
sdiff -o outfile [options] file1 file2
```

The `sdiff` is useful when you want to interactively merge two files. This is the case when two people have made changes to a source file and at some point you want to merge these changes into a single file. The `sdiff` utility is interactive and it displays two files being compared in side-by-side fashion. It stops on each difference with a % sign prompt. On this sign you can press different characters to make a decision. Common responses on the % prompt are shown in Table 7-2.

Table 7-2 Commands used on % prompt of `sdiff`

Command	Description
L	Use the left side of the version
R	Use the right side of the version
e l	Edit and then use the left side
e r	Edit and use the right side
Q	Quit

7.4   Using cscope and cbrowser

The cscope is a very useful utility to browse through the source code tree of a large project. It was originally written by Santa Cruz Operations and made public later on. You can download it from http://cscope.sourceforge.net. For Linux, it is available in RPM format as well.

It is a text-mode screen-oriented utility. When you start it using the cscope command, the initial screen looks like the one shown in Figure 7-1.

When invoked, cscope first creates its symbol file cscope.out in the current directory that contains a reference to symbols in source code files. This reference is generated from files with the extensions .c and .h. You can also use command line options to create this symbol file from a particular type of source code files.

The bottom part of the screen shows options that can be used to look up a symbol in the source code. The cursor is blinking at the first option and can be moved to other options using arrow keys. For example, if you want to look up symbol "msg" in all source code files, just type it in at the first line and press the Enter key. You will see a listing of files containing this symbol as shown in Figure 7-2.

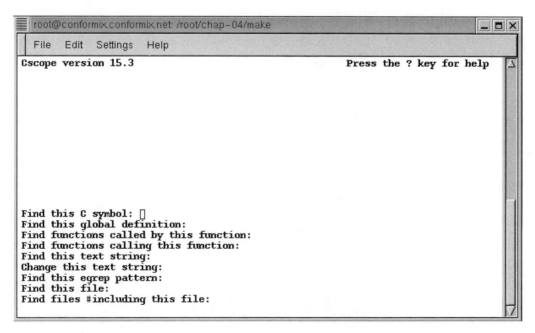

Figure 7-1 The cscope initial screen.

```
root@conformix.conformix.net: /root/chap-04/make              _ □ ×

  File    Edit    Settings    Help

 C symbol: msg

     File            Function Line
 0 common.h         <global>  9 void msg();
 1 common.c         msg       5 void msg()
 2 dnsresolver.c    main     12 msg();
 3 ftp.c            main     12 msg();
 4 tftp.c           main     12 msg();




 Find this C symbol:
 Find this global definition:
 Find functions called by this function:
 Find functions calling this function:
 Find this text string:
 Change this text string:
 Find this egrep pattern:
 Find this file:
 Find files #including this file:
```

Figure 7-2 List of files with symbol msg.

As you can see, there are five files listed in the top part of the screen that contain this symbol. This listing contains five columns as below:

1. Number of row, starting with zero.
2. File name that contains the symbol.
3. Function name where symbol is used. If the symbol is not inside a function, it is marked as global.
4. Line number where symbol is present in that file.
5. The line showing the definition or use of the symbol.

You can move the cursor to a particular line and press the Enter key to edit that file. By default the file is opened in vi editor. However, you can configure to use an editor of your choice. To move back to the bottom part of the screen to search for another symbol, you can use the Tab key. Use the Ctrl+D key combination to quit the program.

The utility is also very useful if you want to find non-utilized code in a software project. For example, if a function is present in the source code but never used anywhere in the project, it can be detected using cscope. It is also useful when you want to modify a particular symbol throughout the source code tree. Common options used with cscope are listed in Table 7-3.

Table 7-3 Options used with `cscope`

Option	Description
`-b`	Build only the cross-reference file
`-C`	Ignore case when searching
`-f reffile`	Use reffile as reference file instead of default `cscope.out` reference file. This is useful when you create a global reference file for the entire source code tree.
`-R`	Recursively search source code tree for input files

Use the manual pages of `cscope` to view a complete list of options. Its web site is also a good reference for updates and new features.

The `cbrowser` is a GUI interface to `cscope` and can be downloaded from its web site, http://cbrowser.sourceforge.net.

At the time of writing this book, version 0.8 of this utility is available. When you invoke `cbrowser`, it displays its initial window where you can select a `cscope` symbol reference file and use the same type of queries as are available on `cscope` text window. The `cbrowser` window is shown in Figure 7-3.

To use a particular `cscope` symbol file, use the "Selected Database" drop-down menu in the GUI. Click the "Symbols" button to pull down a menu of different options used with `cscope`. The box next to this button is used to type in the symbol for which you want to search. When you press the "Submit" button after typing in the symbol name, `cbrowser` displays a list of files where this symbol is used or defined as shown in Figure 7-3. An additional benefit of using `cbrowser` is that the bottom part of the window also shows the contents of the selected file. You can use cursor keys to select a different file. You can also edit these files by using options in the "File" menu. You can use syntax highlighting and other helping tools with `cbrowser` using menus.

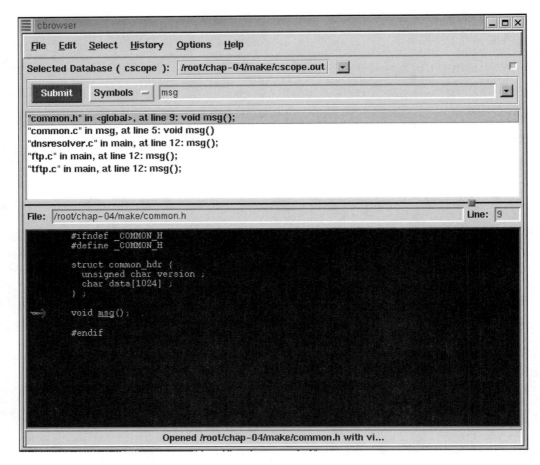

Figure 7-3 The cbrowser window.

7.5 Generating C Function Prototypes from C Source Code Using cproto

The cproto utility is used to create function prototypes from C source code files. It can also convert function definition style. The latest version can be downloaded from http://sourceforge.net/projects/cproto/.

At the time of writing this book, version 4.6 is available in source code form. You can download the file, untar it and compile it using the following sequence of commands.

```
tar zxvf cproto-4.6.tar.gz
cd cproto-4.6
./configure
make
make install
```

It can read existing C files or take its input from standard input. This utility is not exten-sively used in C software development but may be useful in some cases.

7.6   Using ltrace and strace Utilities

The `ltrace` program is a tracing utility for library function calls. It runs a program and logs all library function calls by that program. You can also use this utility to log system calls made by a program. The utility can also monitor child processes created by fork() or clone() system calls. This utility is very useful to quickly trace the failure point of an executable program. The utility may also print the time at which a particular function call or system call is executed with a reso-lution of microseconds.

Consider the simple single-line program that prints the string "Hello world" and then exits. Using `ltrace` with the executable of this program produces the following result.

```
[root@boota ltrace]# ltrace -S -tt ./a.out
22:21:48.325970 SYS_uname(0xbffff3b4)                    = 0
22:21:48.327037 SYS_brk(NULL)                            = 0x080495f8
22:21:48.327511 SYS_mmap(0xbffff104, 0xcccccccd, 0x400165f8,
4096, 640) = 0x40017000
22:21:48.328212 SYS_open("/etc/ld.so.preload", 0, 010) = -2
22:21:48.329000 SYS_open("/etc/ld.so.cache", 0, 00) = 3
22:21:48.329657 SYS_197(3, 0xbfffea64, 0, 0xbfffea64, 0) = 0
22:21:48.331719 SYS_mmap(0xbfffea34, 0, 0x400165f8, 1, 3) =
0x40018000
22:21:48.332460 SYS_close(3)                             = 0
22:21:48.332908 SYS_open("/lib/i686/libc.so.6", 0,
027777765514) = 3
22:21:48.333620 SYS_read(3, "\177ELF\001\001\001", 1024) =
1024
22:21:48.334256 SYS_197(3, 0xbfffeaa4, 3, 0xbfffeaa4, 0) = 0
22:21:48.334917 SYS_mmap(0xbfffe994, 0x0012f728, 0x400165f8,
0xbfffe9c0, 5) = 0x4002c000
22:21:48.335584 SYS_mprotect(0x40152000, 38696, 0, 0x4002c000,
0x00126000) = 0
22:21:48.336209 SYS_mmap(0xbfffe994, 24576, 0x400165f8,
0xbfffe9cc, 3) = 0x40152000
22:21:48.336953 SYS_mmap(0xbfffe994, 0xbfffe9cc, 0x400165f8,
0x40158000, 14120) = 0x40158000
22:21:48.337642 SYS_close(3)                             = 0
22:21:48.340431 SYS_munmap(0x40018000, 77871)            = 0
22:21:48.341060 SYS_getpid()                             = 32540
22:21:48.341562 __libc_start_main(0x08048460, 1, 0xbffff88c,
0x080482e4, 0x080484c0 <unfinished ...>
22:21:48.342232 __register_frame_info(0x08049508, 0x080495e0,
0xbffff828, 0x0804838e, 0x080482e4) = 0x401575e0
22:21:48.343064 printf("Hello world\n" <unfinished ...>
```

```
22:21:48.343813 SYS_197(1, 0xbfffeff0, 0x401569e4, 0x40154a60,
0x40154a60) = 0
22:21:48.344450 SYS_192(0, 4096, 3, 34, -1)          = 0x40018000
22:21:48.345154 SYS_ioctl(1, 21505, 0xbfffef20, 0xbfffef80,
1024) = 0
22:21:48.345890 SYS_write(1, "Hello world\n", 12Hello world
) = 12
22:21:48.346542 <... printf resumed> )               = 12
22:21:48.346878 __deregister_frame_info(0x08049508,
0x4000d816, 0x400171ec, 0x40017310, 7) = 0x080495e0
22:21:48.347746 SYS_munmap(0x40018000, 4096)         = 0
22:21:48.348235 SYS_exit(12)                         = <void>
22:21:48.348706 +++ exited (status 12) +++
[root@boota ltrace]#
```

The first column in each row shows the current time followed by a number that shows
microseconds. The remaining part of the line shows the system call of the library call used. By
comparing the time in two consecutive lines, you can find out the time taken by a particular system call. By looking at the output, you can also find out if a program fails during a particular
system call. This may be especially helpful when testing device drivers and reading or writing to
these drivers fails for some reason.

The most common options used with this utility are shown in Table 7-4.

Table 7-4 Common options used with the `ltrace` utility

Option	Description
-d	Debug. Displays extra information about trace.
-f	Trace child processes.
-S	Display system calls and library calls.
-r	Display time difference between successive lines.
-tt	Display time stamp with each line with a resolution to microseconds.
-o filename	Record output to a file.
-V	Display version.
-h	Display help.

The command can also read options either from its configuration file /etc/
ltrace.conf or from .ltrace.conf in the home directory of the user.

The strace utility is a more comprehensive tool and it can be used to separate different
system calls. For example, it can be used to display information about network related system

calls or for IPC related systems calls only. It displays arguments for all functions calls and their return values. A typical output from the execution of the same single line function follows:

```
[root@boota ltrace]# strace ./a.out
execve("./a.out", ["./a.out"], [/* 44 vars */]) = 0
uname({sys="Linux", node="boota.boota.net", ...}) = 0
brk(0)                                  = 0x80495f8
old_mmap(NULL, 4096, PROT_READ|PROT_WRITE,
MAP_PRIVATE|MAP_ANONYMOUS, -1, 0) = 0x40017000
open("/etc/ld.so.preload", O_RDONLY)    = -1 ENOENT (No such
file or directory)
open("/etc/ld.so.cache", O_RDONLY)      = 3
fstat64(3, {st_mode=S_IFREG|0644, st_size=77871, ...}) = 0
old_mmap(NULL, 77871, PROT_READ, MAP_PRIVATE, 3, 0) =
0x40018000
close(3)                                = 0
open("/lib/i686/libc.so.6", O_RDONLY)   = 3
read(3,
"\177ELF\1\1\1\0\0\0\0\0\0\0\0\0\3\0\3\0\1\0\0\0\200\302"...,
1024) = 1024
fstat64(3, {st_mode=S_IFREG|0755, st_size=5634864, ...}) = 0
old_mmap(NULL, 1242920, PROT_READ|PROT_EXEC, MAP_PRIVATE, 3,
0) = 0x4002c000
mprotect(0x40152000, 38696, PROT_NONE)  = 0
old_mmap(0x40152000, 24576, PROT_READ|PROT_WRITE,
MAP_PRIVATE|MAP_FIXED, 3, 0x125000) = 0x40152000
old_mmap(0x40158000, 14120, PROT_READ|PROT_WRITE,
MAP_PRIVATE|MAP_FIXED|MAP_ANONYMOUS, -1, 0) = 0x40158000
close(3)                                = 0
munmap(0x40018000, 77871)               = 0
getpid()                                = 32610
fstat64(1, {st_mode=S_IFCHR|0620, st_rdev=makedev(136, 3),
...}) = 0
mmap2(NULL, 4096, PROT_READ|PROT_WRITE,
MAP_PRIVATE|MAP_ANONYMOUS, -1, 0) = 0x40018000
ioctl(1, TCGETS, {B38400 opost isig icanon echo ...}) = 0
write(1, "Hello world\n", 12Hello world
)               = 12
munmap(0x40018000, 4096)                = 0
_exit(12)                               = ?
[root@boota ltrace]#
```

As you can see, it gives you a complete picture of what happens from the execution of a program to its end. See the manual pages of strace for a complete list of command line options. The strace utility can also be used for performance-gathering activities, and can log times spent in each function in a program. Refer to the man page for more information.

7.7   Using GNU Binary Utilities

GNU binutils is a package of many utilities that are related to manipulating library files or getting information about different types of binary files. These utilities range from finding strings in a binary file, creating library files, displaying information about binary files, assembling and disassembling files, and so on. This section contains an introduction to most commonly used binary utilities.

7.7.1   Using the ar Utility

Files can be stored into a single file using the `ar` utility. The file into which multiple files are stored is called an *archive*. The `ar` program retains file permissions, ownerships and other properties of the original files. These files can be extracted from the archive later on, if required. The program also creates an index within the archive file that is used to speed up locating a component (or *members*) of the archive.

From the development point of view, the `ar` program is used to create libraries of functions. These libraries are then used with other object files to link an executable file. The conventional name of these library files is `lib{name}.a` where *name* is any string used as a library name. For example, a library named *common* will be stored in a file called `libcommon.a`.

The `ar` program performs one of the following tasks depending upon options used on the command line.

- Delete a file from the archive (option `d`)
- Move files in the archive (option `m`)
- Print a list of files in the archive (option `p`)
- Append files to the archive (option `q`)
- Insert new files in the archive by replacing if a file already exists in the archive (option `r`)
- Displaying contents of an archive (option `t`)
- Extracting files from an archive (option `x`)

More options can be used in combination with these options to perform additional tasks. In this section we shall use some very common options to show you how the `ar` program is used in a software development environment.

We have used `ar` version 2.10.91 in this book. You can display a current version of the program on your system using –V option as shown below. The `ar` utility is usually used because of its compatibility with `ld`, the dynamic loader.

```
[root@boota ar]# ar -V
GNU ar 2.10.91
Copyright 1997, 98, 99, 2000, 2001 Free Software Foundation,
Inc.
This program is free software; you may redistribute it under
the terms of the GNU General Public License.  This program has
absolutely no warranty.
[root@boota ar]#
```

Let us create an archive of simple text files. The following command creates an archive test.a from files /etc/hosts and /etc/resolv.conf.

```
ar -r test.a /etc/resolv.conf /etc/hosts
```

This command creates a file test.a that contains the contents of the other two files. To display the contents of the file, you can use the –t option on the command line.

```
[root@boota ar]# ar -t test.a
resolv.conf
hosts
[root@boota ar]#
```

Using –x option, you can extract one or more files from the archive. The following command extracts the file hosts from the archive.

```
ar -x test.a hosts
```

Now let us create a real library file from two object files common.o and ftp.o. The following command creates a file libcommon.a from these two object files.

```
ar -r libcommon.a common.o ftp.o
```

Functions or variables in these two files can be linked to any other object file using the –l command line option with gcc compiler. The following command line creates an executable file project from this library and project.o file.

```
gcc project.o -lcommon -o project
```

Note that libcommon.a is not used with the –l option when linking functions in this library to an executable file. Instead we used common as the library name by stripping the leading lib part and .a trailing part.

Files can be inserted into the archive in a particular order. Similarly you can also use a policy when replacing existing files using different command line options. Other options that can be used with the ar command can be listed by executing the command without an argument as shown below.

```
[root@boota /root]# ar
Usage: ar [-X32_64] [-]{dmpqrstx}[abcfilNoPsSuvV] [member-
name] [count] archive-file file...
        ar -M [<mri-script]
  commands:
   d            - delete file(s) from the archive
   m[ab]        - move file(s) in the archive
   p            - print file(s) found in the archive
   q[f]         - quick append file(s) to the archive
   r[ab][f][u]  - replace existing or insert new file(s) into
the archive
   t            - display contents of archive
   x[o]         - extract file(s) from the archive
```

```
command specific modifiers:
   [a]              - put file(s) after [member-name]
   [b]              - put file(s) before [member-name]
                      (same as [i])
   [N]              - use instance [count] of name
   [f]              - truncate inserted file names
   [P]              - use full path names when matching
   [o]              - preserve original dates
   [u]              - only replace files that are newer than
                      current archive contents
generic modifiers:
   [c]              - do not warn if the library had to be
                      created
   [s]              - create an archive index (cf. ranlib)
   [S]              - do not build a symbol table
   [v]              - be verbose
   [V]              - display the version number
   [-X32_64]        - (ignored)
ar: supported targets: elf32-i386 a.out-i386-linux efi-app-
ia32 elf32-little elf32-big srec symbolsrec tekhex binary ihex
trad-core
[root@boota /root]#
```

7.7.2   Using the ranlib Utility

The `ranlib` command is used to create index entries inside an archive file. This can also be done using −s command with the `ar` command while creating or updating an archive library file. The following command creates index inside `libcommon.a` file. Note that these index entries are stored inside the archive file and no other file is created.

```
ranlib libcommon.a
```

Most of the time you don't need to run `ranlib`, as the latest version of the `ar` command creates an index by itself. Index entries can be displayed using the nm command.

7.7.3   Using the nm Utility

The nm utility is used to list symbols used in an object file. If no object file is provided on the command line, the utility assumes the `a.out` file in the current directory as the default object file and lists its symbols. A common use of the utility is listing functions defined in a library. The following command displays object file names and functions defined in the library file created with `ar` command in the previous section.

```
[root@boota]# nm -s libcommon.a

Archive index:
msg in common.o
main in ftp.o
```

```
common.o:
00000000 T msg
         U printf

ftp.o:
00000000 T main
         U msg
         U printf
[root@boota make]#
```

For each symbol, nm displays three properties of the symbol.

1. Value
2. Type
3. Name

The *value* of the symbol is displayed in hexadecimal by default. *Type* is a character, either uppercase or lowercase. The uppercase character shows that the symbol is global and the lowercase character shows that the symbol is local. The following line shows that the symbol value is 00000000, its type is T which shows that the symbol is in code section and its name is msg.

```
00000000 T msg
```

Type U in the above output of nm command shows that the symbol is undefined and no value is displayed. Note that function msg is defined in common.o but undefined in the ftp.o member of the archive. This is because of the fact that the function was defined in common.c file and it is used in ftp.c file.

Usually, the list of symbols is very long in executable files. Consider the following simple file that displays the string "Hello world".

```
#include <stdio.h>
main()
{
  printf ("Hello world\n");
}
```

Let us compile this file to create an executable a.out file. A list of symbols in the a.out executable file is shown below:

```
[root@boota]# nm -s a.out
08049540 ? _DYNAMIC
0804951c ? _GLOBAL_OFFSET_TABLE_
080484e4 R _IO_stdin_used
08049510 ? __CTOR_END__
0804950c ? __CTOR_LIST__
08049518 ? __DTOR_END__
08049514 ? __DTOR_LIST__
```

```
        08049508  ?  __EH_FRAME_BEGIN__
        08049508  ?  __FRAME_END__
        080495e0  A  __bss_start
                  w  __cxa_finalize@@GLIBC_2.1.3
        080494f8  D  __data_start
                  w  __deregister_frame_info@@GLIBC_2.0
        08048480  t  __do_global_ctors_aux
        080483b0  t  __do_global_dtors_aux
                  w  __gmon_start__
                  U  __libc_start_main@@GLIBC_2.0
                  w  __register_frame_info@@GLIBC_2.0
        080495e0  A  _edata
        080495f8  A  _end
        080484c0  ?  _fini
        080484e0  R  _fp_hw
        080482e4  ?  _init
        08048360  T  _start
        08048384  t  call_gmon_start
        08049504  d  completed.1
        080494f8  W  data_start
        08048410  t  fini_dummy
        08049508  d  force_to_data
        08049508  d  force_to_data
        08048420  t  frame_dummy
        08048384  t  gcc2_compiled.
        080483b0  t  gcc2_compiled.
        08048480  t  gcc2_compiled.
        080484c0  t  gcc2_compiled.
        08048460  t  gcc2_compiled.
        08048450  t  init_dummy
        080484b0  t  init_dummy
        08048460  T  main
        080495e0  b  object.2
        08049500  d  p.0
                  U  printf@@GLIBC_2.0
        [root@boota make]#
```

7.7.3.1   Listing Line Numbers in Source Files

Use of −1 option is very useful with this command. This option also displays filenames and line numbers where these symbols are used. The following command lists symbols in lib-common.a file in more detail. Note that it displays the path to the source code file and the line number. This information is used in the debugging process.

```
[root@boota]# nm -s libcommon.a -l

Archive index:
msg in common.o
main in ftp.o
```

```
common.o:
00000000 T msg  /root/make/common.c:6
          U printf      /root/make/common.c:7

ftp.o:
00000000 T main /root/make/ftp.c:7
          U msg  /root/make/ftp.c:12
          U printf      /root/make/ftp.c:11
[root@boota make]#
```

7.7.3.2   Listing Debug Symbols

When you compile a program with a debug option, many symbols are inserted in the files that are used for debugging purposes. Using the –a option with the nm command also shows the debug symbols.

Please see the manual pages of the nm command for a detail description of all options.

7.7.4   Using the strip Utility

The strip command is used to remove symbols from an object or library file. This is useful to reduce the size of the shipped product as these symbols are not required in enduser executable code. Using the command, you can also remove symbols partially. For example, you can remove only debug symbols, local symbols or all symbols with the help of command line options.

At least one object file must be provided at the command line. Note that the strip utility modifies the object files; it does not create new files. To get an idea of the difference in size of object file before and after using the strip command, let us take the example of a C file that prints the "Hello world" string only. The size of the executable a.out file with symbols on my computer is 13640 bytes. After using the following command, the size is reduced to 3208 bytes.

```
strip a.out
```

This is a considerable reduction in size. However, in some time-sensitive and embedded systems, stripping files may cause timing problems and code may behave differently in some cases.

7.7.5   Using the objcopy Utility

The basic function of the objcopy utility is to copy one object file to another. This functionality can be used to change the format of an object file. A common use is to create S-record or binary files from ordinary object files. S-record or binary files can be used to burn ROM in embedded systems. The following command converts the ftp file (which is a statically linked file) to an S-record file ftp.S, which may be downloaded to a ROM/PROM using the EPROM programmer.

```
objcopy -O srec ftp ftp.S
```

You can see types of both input and output files by using the file command as follows. The output file is of type S-record.

```
[root@boota]# file ftp
ftp: ELF 32-bit LSB executable, Intel 80386, version 1,
statically linked, not stripped
[root@boota]#
[root@boota make]# file ftp.S
ftp.S: Motorola S-Record; binary data in text format
[root@boota]#
```

The S-record file is in ASCII hex format and first few lines can be displayed using head command as shown below:

```
[root@boota]# head ftp.S
S00800006674702E532C
S3150804809404000000100000000100000474E5500CB
S315080480A4000000000200000002000000005000000B1
S315080480B45589E583EC08E84500000090E8DB0000F0
S30D080480C400E836610400C9C393
S315080480E031ED5E89E183E4F05054526880E2080871
S315080480F068B4800408515668E0810408E80B010056
S3150804810000F489F65589E55350E8000000005B81C0
S31508048110C3826C05008B830C00000085C07402FFC3
S31508048120D08B5DFCC9C389F69090909090909090FE
[root@boota]#
```

The following command creates a binary image of the ftp file. The binary output is a memory image of the executable and all symbols are removed.

```
objcopy -O binary ftp ftp.bin
```

Here is how you display a type of the new binary file.

```
[root@boota]# file ftp.bin
ftp.bin: X11 SNF font data, LSB first
[root@boota]#
```

It is a good idea to strip object files before converting them to S-record or binary files. Start addresses can be set using the command line options --set-start and --adjust-start.

7.7.6   Using the objdump Utility

The objdump command displays information about an object file. It can also be used to disassemble an object file. You can use different command line options to display particular information about an object file.

7.7.6.1   Displaying Header Information

The following command displays the header information of the binary file a.out.

```
[root@boota]# objdump -f a.out
```

```
a.out:      file format elf32-i386
architecture: i386, flags 0x00000112:
EXEC_P, HAS_SYMS, D_PAGED
start address 0x08048360

[root@boota]#
```

7.7.6.2   Displaying Section Headers

The following command displays information about all section headers in the a.out file.

```
[root@boota]# objdump -h a.out|more

a.out:      file format elf32-i386

Sections:
Idx Name          Size      VMA       LMA       File off  Algn
  0 .interp       00000013  080480f4  080480f4  000000f4  2**0
                  CONTENTS, ALLOC, LOAD, READONLY, DATA
  1 .note.ABI-tag 00000020  08048108  08048108  00000108  2**2
                  CONTENTS, ALLOC, LOAD, READONLY, DATA
  2 .hash         00000034  08048128  08048128  00000128  2**2
                  CONTENTS, ALLOC, LOAD, READONLY, DATA
  3 .dynsym       00000080  0804815c  0804815c  0000015c  2**2
                  CONTENTS, ALLOC, LOAD, READONLY, DATA
  4 .dynstr       00000095  080481dc  080481dc  000001dc  2**0
                  CONTENTS, ALLOC, LOAD, READONLY, DATA
  5 .gnu.version  00000010  08048272  08048272  00000272  2**1
                  CONTENTS, ALLOC, LOAD, READONLY, DATA
  6 .gnu.version_r 00000030 08048284  08048284  00000284
2**2
                  CONTENTS, ALLOC, LOAD, READONLY, DATA
  7 .rel.got      00000008  080482b4  080482b4  000002b4  2**2
                  CONTENTS, ALLOC, LOAD, READONLY, DATA
  8 .rel.plt      00000028  080482bc  080482bc  000002bc  2**2
                  CONTENTS, ALLOC, LOAD, READONLY, DATA
  9 .init         00000018  080482e4  080482e4  000002e4  2**2
                  CONTENTS, ALLOC, LOAD, READONLY, CODE
 10 .plt          00000060  080482fc  080482fc  000002fc  2**2
                  CONTENTS, ALLOC, LOAD, READONLY, CODE
 11 .text         00000160  08048360  08048360  00000360  2**4
                  CONTENTS, ALLOC, LOAD, READONLY, CODE
 12 .fini         0000001e  080484c0  080484c0  000004c0  2**2
                  CONTENTS, ALLOC, LOAD, READONLY, CODE
 13 .rodata       00000015  080484e0  080484e0  000004e0  2**2
                  CONTENTS, ALLOC, LOAD, READONLY, DATA
 14 .data         00000010  080494f8  080494f8  000004f8  2**2
                  CONTENTS, ALLOC, LOAD, DATA
 15 .eh_frame     00000004  08049508  08049508  00000508  2**2
```

```
                      CONTENTS, ALLOC, LOAD, DATA
  16 .ctors          00000008 0804950c 0804950c 0000050c 2**2
                      CONTENTS, ALLOC, LOAD, DATA
  17 .dtors          00000008 08049514 08049514 00000514 2**2
                      CONTENTS, ALLOC, LOAD, DATA
  18 .got            00000024 0804951c 0804951c 0000051c 2**2
                      CONTENTS, ALLOC, LOAD, DATA
  19 .dynamic        000000a0 08049540 08049540 00000540 2**2
                      CONTENTS, ALLOC, LOAD, DATA
  20 .sbss           00000000 080495e0 080495e0 000005e0 2**0
                      CONTENTS
  21 .bss            00000018 080495e0 080495e0 000005e0 2**2
                      ALLOC
  22 .stab           00000f9c 00000000 00000000 000005e0 2**2
                      CONTENTS, READONLY, DEBUGGING
  23 .stabstr        00002ec6 00000000 00000000 0000157c 2**0
                      CONTENTS, READONLY, DEBUGGING
  24 .comment        00000144 00000000 00000000 00004442 2**0
                      CONTENTS, READONLY
  25 .note           00000078 00000000 00000000 00004586 2**0
                      CONTENTS, READONLY
[root@boota]#
```

7.7.6.3   Disassembling a File

Perhaps the major advantage of this utility is its ability to disassemble object files. Usually the disassembly code is quite long but still you can make sense of it. The following is a segment of disassembly code from the a.out file.

```
[root@boota]# objdump -d a.out|more

a.out:      file format elf32-i386

Disassembly of section .init:

080482e4 <_init>:
 80482e4:55                         push    %ebp
 80482e5:89 e5                      mov     %esp,%ebp
 80482e7:83 ec 08                   sub     $0x8,%esp
 80482ea:e8 95 00 00 00             call    8048384 <call_gmon_start>
 80482ef:90                         nop
 80482f0:e8 2b 01 00 00             call    8048420 <frame_dummy>
 80482f5:e8 86 01 00 00             call    8048480
<__do_global_ctors_aux>
 80482fa:c9                         leave
 80482fb:c3                         ret
Disassembly of section .plt:

080482fc <.plt>:
```

```
80482fc:ff 35 20 95 04 08        pushl    0x8049520
8048302:ff 25 24 95 04 08        jmp      *0x8049524
8048308:00 00                    add      %al,(%eax)
804830a:00 00                    add      %al,(%eax)
804830c:ff 25 28 95 04 08        jmp      *0x8049528
8048312:68 00 00 00 00           push     $0x0
8048317:e9 e0 ff ff ff           jmp      80482fc <_init+0x18>
804831c:ff 25 2c 95 04 08        jmp      *0x804952c
8048322:68 08 00 00 00           push     $0x8
8048327:e9 d0 ff ff ff           jmp      80482fc <_init+0x18>
804832c:ff 25 30 95 04 08        jmp      *0x8049530
8048332:68 10 00 00 00           push     $0x10
8048337:e9 c0 ff ff ff           jmp      80482fc <_init+0x18>
804833c:ff 25 34 95 04 08        jmp      *0x8049534
8048342:68 18 00 00 00           push     $0x18
8048347:e9 b0 ff ff ff           jmp      80482fc <_init+0x18>
804834c:ff 25 38 95 04 08        jmp      *0x8049538
8048352:68 20 00 00 00           push     $0x20
8048357:e9 a0 ff ff ff           jmp      80482fc <_init+0x18>
Disassembly of section .text:

08048360 <_start>:
 8048360:31 ed                   xor      %ebp,%ebp
 8048362:5e                      pop      %esi
 8048363:89 e1                   mov      %esp,%ecx
 8048365:83 e4 f0                and      $0xfffffff0,%esp
 8048368:50                      push     %eax
 8048369:54                      push     %esp
 804836a:52                      push     %edx
 804836b:68 c0 84 04 08          push     $0x80484c0
 8048370:68 e4 82 04 08          push     $0x80482e4
 8048375:51                      push     %ecx
```

7.7.6.4   Disassembling with Source Code

The command can also be used to disassemble an object file so that the source code is also displayed along with assembly output. This is done using the −S option. Following is output of disassembly for code that is used to display string the "Hello world". You can see the assembly language instructions used for this purpose.

```
08048460 <main>:
#include <stdio.h>
main()
{
 8048460:55                      push     %ebp
 8048461:89 e5                   mov      %esp,%ebp
 8048463:83 ec 08                sub      $0x8,%esp
  printf ("Hello world\n");
 8048466:83 ec 0c                sub      $0xc,%esp
```

```
8048469:    68 e8 84 04 08        push    $0x80484e8
804846e:    e8 c9 fe ff ff        call    804833c <_init+0x58>
8048473:    83 c4 10              add     $0x10,%esp
}
```

7.7.6.5   Displaying Information about Library Files

The command can also be used to display information about library files. The following command displays information about the library file libcommon.a and shows the object file names from which this library is built.

```
[root@boota]# objdump -a libcommon.a
In archive ../../chap-04/make/libcommon.a:

common.o:     file format elf32-i386
rw-r--r-- 0/0  11668 Nov 13 19:48 2001 common.o


ftp.o:     file format elf32-i386
rw-r--r-- 0/0  11824 Nov 13 19:53 2001 ftp.o

[root@boota ltrace]#
```

Common options that are used with this command are listed in Table 7-5.

Table 7-5 Common options used with objdump command

Option	Description
-a	Display information about library files
--debugging	Show debugging information
-d	Disassemble an object file
-f	Show file headers summary
-S	Display source code with disassembly information
-t	Display symbol table entries

7.7.7   Using the size Utility

The size utility displays sizes of each section in an object file. The following command displays sizes for the object file a.out.

```
[root@boota]# size a.out
   text    data    bss     dec     hex     filename
   1015     232     24     1271     4f7     a.out
[root@boota]#
```

7.7.8   Using the strings Utility

The `strings` utility displays printable strings in an object file. By default it displays strings only in initialized and loaded sections of the object file. The object file may be a library file as well. The following command displays strings in the `a.out` file.

```
[root@boota]# strings a.out
/lib/ld-linux.so.2
__gmon_start__
libc.so.6
printf
__cxa_finalize
__deregister_frame_info
_IO_stdin_used
__libc_start_main
__register_frame_info
GLIBC_2.1.3
GLIBC_2.0
PTRh
QVh`
Hello world
[root@boota]#
```

A complete list of all strings in a file can be displayed with the –a option on the command line. Multiple filenames or wild cards can be used on the command line. Using the –f option in this case will display each filename associated with a symbol.

7.7.9   Using the addr2line Utility

The `addr2line` utility maps an address in the object file to a line in the source code file. Consider the following output section of the "`objdump  -S  a.out`" command that shows addresses and source codes.

```
08048460 <main>:
#include <stdio.h>
main()
{
 8048460:55                         push    %ebp
 8048461:89 e5                      mov     %esp,%ebp
 8048463:83 ec 08                   sub     $0x8,%esp
  printf ("Hello world\n");
 8048466:83 ec 0c                   sub     $0xc,%esp
 8048469:68 e8 84 04 08             push    $0x80484e8
 804846e:e8 c9 fe ff ff             call    804833c <_init+0x58>
 8048473:83 c4 10                   add     $0x10,%esp
}
```

The a.out file is generated from the following a.c file.

```
    1   #include <stdio.h>
```

```
2  main()
3  {
4    printf ("Hello world\n");
5  }
```

Now you can display the line number of the source code file corresponding to address 8048466 in the object file with the following command:

```
[root@boota]# addr2line -e a.out 8048466
/root/chap-07/ltrace/a.c:4
[root@boota]#
```

This is the line where the `printf` function is called in `a.c` file. The `add2line` command is useful in debuggers where you need to map addresses to a line in source code file.

7.8 Using the ldd Utility

The `ldd` utility is very useful in finding out the dependencies of an executable on shared libraries. This is necessary when you are copying executable files from one computer to another to make sure that required libraries are present on the destination computer also. The following command shows that `libc.so.6` must be present to execute `a.out` file on a computer.

```
[root@boota]# ldd a.out
  libc.so.6 => /lib/i686/libc.so.6 (0x4002c000)
  /lib/ld-linux.so.2 => /lib/ld-linux.so.2 (0x40000000)
[root@boota]#
```

So if you copy `a.out` to another computer, make sure that this library is also present on the destination computer.

7.9 References and Resources

1. GNU web site at http://www.gnu.org/
2. The `cbrowser` home page at http://cbrowser.sourceforge.net
3. The `cscope` home page at http://cscope.sourceforge.net

CHAPTER   8

Cross-Platform and Embedded Systems Development

A s you have already learned in Chapter 3, development systems consist of many tools. The discussion in Chapter 3 was about native
software development, which means that the host system on which the
software is developed and the target system on which the software runs
are the same. This chapter provides information about embedded and
cross-platform software development where the host system and the target
system are different. The issues in this type of development are slightly
different although basic programming methods and techniques remain the
same.

In this chapter I have used a single board computer from Arcom
(www.arcomcontrols.com) and a processor mezzanine card from Artesyn
(www.artesyn.com). I am thankful to both of these vendors. The Arcom
board is based upon a x86 compatible CPU and has four serial ports, an
Ethernet port and a number of other ports. The Artesyn board is PowerPC
based and it can be plugged into a Compact PCI career card. Information
about these boards can be obtained from the respective company web site.
I have listed some features at the end of this chapter.

Before reading this chapter, you should become familiar with a few concepts related to cross-platform development. The most important terms
used in this chapter are *cross* and *native*. The term cross is used for tools

that run on one type of machine but are used to carry out some service for another type of machine. For example, a cross compiler is a compiler that creates executable code for a machine which is different than the machine on which the compiler is running. Similar is the case with cross assemblers, cross debuggers and so on. On the other hand, a native tool provides a service to the same machine on which it is running. For example, a native compiler generates output code that is executable on the same machine on which the compiler runs.

8.1   Introduction to the Cross-Platform Development Process

You need a general-purpose computer for software development. This computer hosts development tools. In most cases, the computer also hosts some debugging tools. The executable code may be generated for the same computer on which you develop software or for some other machine that is not capable of running development tools (editors, compilers, assemblers, debuggers etc.). Most of the time host and target machines differ so that programs built on the host machine can't be run on the target machine. These differences may take many forms. Some common differences between host and target machines are different operating system, different system boards or a different CPU.

It's necessary to understand some basic concepts and terminology related to cross-platform development. These basic concepts are explained in the following subsections.

8.1.1   Host Machine

The host machine is the machine on which you write and compile programs. All of the development tools are installed on this machine. Most of the time this is your PC or workstation. Your compiler is built to run on this machine. When you are satisfied with your code, the executables are built and transferred to the target machine. If the host and target machines are different, the final executable can't be executed on the host machine where you built it.

8.1.2   Target Machine

A target machine may be another general-purpose computer, a special-purpose device employing a single-board computer or any other intelligent device. Usually the target machine is not able to host all the development tools. That is why a host computer is used to complete development work.

Debugging is an important issue in cross-platform development. Since you are usually not able to execute the binary files on the host machine, they must be run on the target machine. The debugger, which is running on the host machine, has to talk to the program running on the target machine. GNU debugger is capable of connecting to remote processes. Some CPUs have a JTAG or BDM connector, which can also be used to connect to processes on remote systems.

8.1.3   Native and Cross Compilers

A native compiler generates code for the same machine on which it is running. A cross compiler generates code for a machine different from the one on which it is running.

8.1.4   Cross Platform Development Cycle

The cross-platform development cycle consists of at least four stages. These stages are:

- Writing code
- Cross compilation
- Transferring binaries to the target
- Debugging

The steps may be different in some cases depending upon the type of product you are building. Figure 8-1 shows these processes and machines on which a particular process is carried out.

Let us take a closer look on these steps.

8.1.4.1   Writing Code

When you write code for cross compilation, you have to keep few things in mind. The CPU architecture of the target machine may be different from that of the host machine. This means that you have to consider word lengths, byte order and so on. For example, length of integer may be different on the target machine. Similarly, organization of memory may play an important role. As an example, the organization of bytes inside a 32-bit integer is different in Intel CPUs as compared to Motorola CPUs. This is a typical network-byte-order problem and must be considered when developing network protocols.

Some libraries' routines may be different for cross compilers than for native compilers.

8.1.4.2   Building on the Host Machine

After writing the code, you need to compile it on the host machine. In addition to a cross compiler and cross assembler that can generate code for the target machine, you need libraries that are linked to your code. These libraries are usually specific to the target machine and are cross-compiled.

If you are writing code according to some standard, your porting process is usually very quick. For example, if you have written libraries strictly using the ANSI standard, it will be relatively easy for you to port these libraries from one platform to another. In most large software development projects, it is important that you stick to some standard. This is because ultimately you may wish to port and sell the product for many platforms.

You have learned the difference between static and dynamic linking earlier in this book. Usually in cross compiling, you have to build the executable code with static linking because you may not have shared libraries available on the target system. This is especially true for embedded systems where you usually don't have a large secondary storage device.

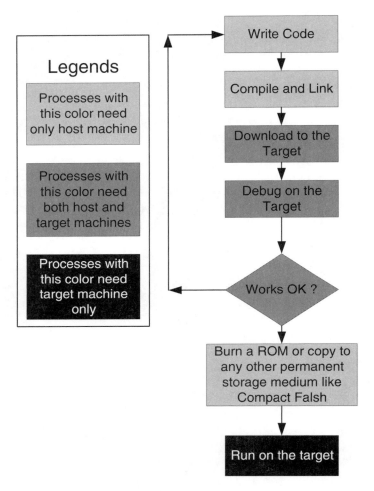

Figure 8-1 Flow chart of cross-platform development.

During the development phase, most of the time you compile code with debug information enabled. The size of the output files is usually quite large but this is acceptable. A different approach is to create multiple files, one built without debug information or stripped and at least one other file containing all symbols information. You can load the latter file into the debugger before connecting the debugger to the executable.

8.1.4.3   Transfer to the Target Machine

After building executable code for a cross-platform development project, you have to transfer it to the target machine. There are several ways to do so depending upon the target machine. If the target machine has a JTAG interface, you can use that interface to transfer the file and then use the same interface to debug it. If the target does not have a JTAG interface, you can transfer using a serial or Ethernet link. Sometimes the target machine is already running an operating system and you have to transfer an application to the target machine. In some other circumstances you may have to build and transfer a single packaged file that contains the operating system as well as applications. If the target system is already running the operating system, you can transfer you application using a network interface very easily. If you have a single packaged file, you can have a boot routine on the target machine that may download this file from a TFTP server as well.

The bottom line is that there are many methods used by developers depending upon the nature of the files to be transferred, availability of special hardware on the target machine, availability of boot routines on the target machine and the operating system used. You can select a method that best suits your needs.

8.1.4.4   Remote Debugging

In the case of cross-platform development and embedded systems, you have to debug your code remotely. There are multiple reasons for that including:

- The target machine is different from the host machine so that you can't execute the code on your host machine.
- The target system is connected to some special hardware and the software interacts with that special hardware. To debug in a real-world situation, you have to debug it remotely.
- The target system itself has some special hardware that is different from the host machine. For example, the target system may have the same CPU as the host machine but has different hardware interrupts.

There may be other reasons in addition to the ones mentioned here. In this chapter you will learn how to attach to a process running on a target machine using GNU debugger. You will use a local file that contains all of the symbol table information. Before you connect to the target machine, you will load this symbol table information into gdb and then start a debug session remotely on the target machine.

8.2   What are Embedded Systems?

There are many definitions of embedded system but all of these can be combined into a single concept. An embedded system is a special-purpose computer system that is used for a particular task. The special computer system is usually less powerful than general-purpose systems, although some exceptions do exist where embedded systems are very powerful and complicated. Usually a low power consumption CPU with a limited amount of memory is used in embedded systems. Many embedded systems use very small operating systems; most of these provide very limited operating system capabilities. However as memory and CPU power is becoming cheap, many modern operating systems are also being used in embedded systems these days. Embedded Linux products are becoming more and more popular.

Since embedded systems are used for special purpose tasks, there is usually no need to add new applications to the system once it is built. Therefore programs and operating systems are usually loaded only once into read-only memory. The read-only memory is available in many forms these days and includes some type of ROM, flash chips and flash cards. In case an upgrade is required, a new ROM chip replaces the old one.

If you look at your surroundings, you will find tiny computers everywhere. They are present even in places where you rarely notice them. Some of the most common embedded systems used in everyday life are:

- Refrigerators
- Microwave ovens
- TV, VCR, DVD players
- Cameras
- Cars (Antilock brakes, engine control, sun roof, climate control, automatic transmission and so on)
- Personal digital assistants
- Printers

Complicated and more sophisticated embedded systems include routers and switches where high performance CPUs are used.

8.2.1   Embedded Systems and Moving Parts

Most of the embedded systems are supposed to be used for a long period of time and without any maintenance. This is the very nature of embedded systems applications, to manufacture a system and then leave it to run independently for its intended life. For this reason, most embedded systems usually don't have moving components because any moving or mechanical part experiences wear and tear and needs replacement periodically. Typical examples of moving components include fans, disk drives and so on. Fans are used for cooling in power supplies and CPU heat sinks in desktop computers. Disk drives (both floppy and hard disk drives) are used as a storage medium for operating systems, applications and data.

In embedded systems, ROM is used for storage of operating system and application data to eliminate the need for disk drives. These days, flash cards are also common and you can update a system just by replacing the flash memory card. In embedded systems you have to use special types of power supplies that don't need any fan for cooling. Many different types of power supplies are available on the market that don't heat up when used continuously for long periods of time.

8.2.2 Embedded Systems and Power Consumption

Power consumption is also an important issue in embedded systems. This is also related to the moving parts issue in a sense. Components that consume more power need cooling, so some type of fan must be attached to the system. For this reason people always prefer CPUs and other components that use less power and generate less heat. It is also beneficial for systems that run on batteries to use less power. High power-consuming components drain batteries quickly.

8.2.3 Embedded Operating Systems

Since embedded systems are usually not general-purpose systems, they need not be as sophisticated as commercial general-purpose systems. These operating systems are smaller in size. Most of these operating systems also offer real-time capabilities, which are missing in general-purpose systems. Although there are hundreds of operating systems available for the embedded market, some of the most commonly used ones are:

- VxWorks
- pSOS
- Embedded Linux
- QNX
- Windows CE

When you use Linux as an embedded operating system, you can take out many parts of the kernel that are required in the general-purpose Linux systems. Which parts should be excluded from the kernel depends upon the requirements of a particular system. For example, you can take out the entire networking code if the embedded system is not going to be networked. Similarly, you can take out most of the secondary storage related drivers and file systems support. Kernel parts that are the most likely candidates for removal from the embedded Linux are:

- Disk drivers
- CD-ROM drivers
- Most of the networking code. Even if an embedded system is intended to be networked, you may not need all of the routing code and drivers for all types of network adapters.
- Sound and multimedia related drivers and components. However you may need these components if the embedded system is used as a computer game.
- Most of the file system support
- Any other thing that is not required. You can go through the kernel configuration process to determine what is not necessary.

The trimmed version of the Linux kernel will be much smaller compared to the kernels you find in most Linux distributions.

8.2.4   Software Applications for Embedded Systems

Embedded applications are tightly integrated with each other and often with the operating system as well. In many cases you will find only one big file that is loaded by the system at the time you power it up that contains all of the operating and applications data. Since resources are sparse on embedded systems, applications are usually highly optimized to take the least amount of memory and storage space. Embedded systems programmers don't have the luxury of even one extra line of code. In addition, embedded software needs to be solid because there is nobody to restart a crashed application. Watchdog timers are used to recover from any system lock.

8.3   How Development Systems Differ for Embedded Systems

Development for embedded systems is different from common practices in many ways. For new developers in the embedded systems world, there is a learning curve to understand which conventional practices are no longer valid in this new environment. To be an embedded systems developer, you need to know many things about the hardware on which your software will be executed. Often embedded systems are connected to some sort of control system (wheel rotation in an automobile anti-lock braking system, for example) and the developer also needs knowledge of that system as well. If the CPU and/or the operating system are different on the target embedded platform, you have to do cross-platform development which has its own issues. There are different testing techniques as well because in most of the embedded systems you don't have a monitor screen where you can display error messages or test results. All of these issues make embedded systems development much more complicated than writing a program on a UNIX machine and then executing it.

This section provides information on some of these issues but should not be considered comprehensive. This is just a starting point to give you an idea that you should expect new challenges when you start embedded systems programming.

8.3.1   Knowledge of Target System Hardware

The embedded system is usually different from the system on which you develop software (the host machine). For example, usually the target computer has many input and output lines, different interrupts and probably a different type of CPU. It may also have memory constraints because these systems usually have a low amount of RAM and no virtual memory because of the absence of secondary storage media. To develop software for the target, you need to know all of these things.

As mentioned earlier, most of the embedded systems are connected to some other sort of hardware. The main job of these systems is to control the connected hardware or systems using some policy. As an embedded system programmer, if you don't have knowledge of these additional system or hardware, you will not be able to program the embedded system well. Usually embedded systems have some sort of digital and analog I/O connected to this external hardware where you have to exchange data.

8.3.2   Is the Target System Real-Time?

If the target system is running a real-time operating system, you have to keep in mind many other issues as well. Usually these issues don't come into the picture when you are developing code for general-purpose machines. System scheduling is important and you need to know what type of scheduling is available on the target system. Almost all real-time systems have priority-based scheduling. However, if two processes have the same priority, then scheduling may be different depending upon the operating system. Some systems implement round-robin scheduling for equal priority tasks. On the other hand some systems run a task to completion. You need to know what happens when a process or task is scheduled on a particular real-time scheduler. Time slices for running equal priority processes on round-robin schedulers can also be changed on some real-time schedulers.

To complicate the situation, some systems also allow processes to increase or decrease their priority levels at run time.

Interrupts and their service routine are usually critical in real-time systems. If your embedded target platform is real-time, you should keep in mind limitations in this area and tolerance of critical tasks in constrained environment. You should not miss a critical event in a real-time system because that may result in disaster. If a packet is dropped in a router, it may be tolerated, but if a robot reacts to some event late, it may result in major loss. Even dropped packets aren't particularly acceptable in modern routers.

8.3.3   Testing Methodology

The testing methodology is also different in the case of embedded systems. In typical cases, an embedded system is connected to some other device or system for control purposes. These connections are not available on the host system where you are developing the software. This is true even if the operating system and CPU on the host and target systems are the same. For example, a Linux-based embedded system running an x86 family of processors may be controlling some security system. It is difficult to simulate that security system on a PC and test your software. So even if the platform is the same, you have to test and debug your programs on the target system.

In some cases testing of embedded systems may be quite complicated as you need to get results of the functionality testing sent or stored somewhere. In small embedded systems, not connected to a network or a user-friendly output device, getting these results is difficult. In such circumstances you may need to build special testing techniques or special code in your embedded system to produce test results. I would recommend a thorough knowledge of how to write testable code.

8.4   Cross Compilations

Cross compilation tools are very important for successful product development. Selection of these tools should be made based upon the embedded system itself as well as features to test and debug software remotely. Since you are developing software on a Linux platform, your cross-platform development tools should be compatible with Linux as a host machine. Depending upon CPU family used for the target system, your toolset must be capable of generating code for the target machine. In the case of GNU development tools, you need to have a number of things to work together to generate executable code for the target. For example, you must have at least the following available on your Linux machine.

- Cross compiler
- Cross assembler
- Cross linker
- Cross debugger
- Cross-compiled libraries for the target host.
- Operating system-dependent libraries and header files for the target system.

These components will enable you to compile, link and debug code for the target environment. In this section, you will learn how to develop a cross-compilation environment on your Linux machine.

You have already built a native GCC compiler in Chapter 3. Conceptually, building a cross compiler is not much different from building a native compiler. However there are additional things that you should keep in mind while building a cross compiler. The most significant of these is the command line listing of the target when running the configure script. The whole process may be slightly different depending upon targets. The best resource to find out detailed information about how to build a cross compiler is the CrossGCC FAQ and mailing list. The FAQ is found at http://www.objsw.com/CrossGCC/ and using information in this FAQ, you can subscribe to and search the CrossGCC mailing list. I would suggest getting a cross compiler from a vendor instead of building it yourself. Many companies, including RedHat (http://www.redhat.com) and Monta Vista Inc. (http://www.mvista.com), provide development tools for embedded Linux development of different CPU families.

8.4.0.1   Cross Debugging

There are multiple methods of debugging that you can use in the cross-platform development environment. Most commonly you can use emulators, JTAG, and remote debugging over serial or network links. Some of these methods are discussed in this section.

8.4.1   Software Emulators

Software emulators are software tools that can emulate a particular CPU. Using a software emulator you can debug through your code and find out CPU register values, stack pointers and other information without having a real CPU. Software emulators are useful when you don't have the real hardware available for testing and debugging and want to see how the CPU will behave when a program is run on it. Keep in mind that these are not very useful tools to simulate real hardware because there are many other hardware components that are built onto the target machine.

8.4.2   In-circuit emulators

In-circuit emulators are devices that are used to emulate a CPU. You can plug in this device in place of a CPU on your circuit board. The device has the same number of pins and the same package type as the CPU and fits into the CPU socket. The other side is connected to a PC or a workstation where a debugger is running. Using an in-circuit emulator, you can start and stop execution of a program as you wish. This is in contrast to a software emulator, where the CPU emulator is a program running on your machine, isolated from the circuit board on which you want to test your software. An in-circuit emulator provides you access to real hardware for testing purpose.

Usual arrangement of in-circuit emulator is shown in Figure 8-2. The emulator is plugged into the actual embedded system on one side and connected to your PC on the other side.

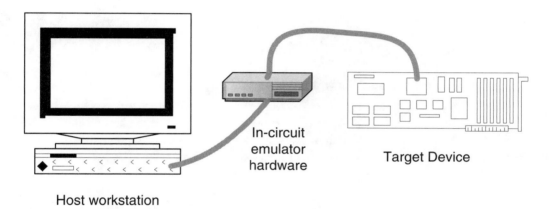

In-circuit emulator hardware

Target Device

Host workstation

Figure 8-2 In-circuit emulator connection diagram.

8.4.3   Introduction to JTAG and BDM

JTAG or Joint Test Action Group is a method of accessing memory and CPU resources without having an application running on the target. BDM or background debugging mode also achieves this objective. Many CPUs provide JTAG or BDM port/connection to connect a serial or parallel port on your host to the target CPU board using a cable. There are a few open source projects that give you information, utilities and hardware diagrams about the procedure.

Using JTAG or BDM, you don't need an in-circuit emulator and a debugger running on your host machine can connect to a target board. But keep in mind that not all CPUs provide this facility. Most Motorola controllers and PowerPC CPUs have this interface.

8.4.3.1   Building Cross Debugger

Building a cross debugger is similar to the building process of a native debugger. When you configure gdb, you need to mention the target CPU on the command line of the configure script. You also need the required libraries for the target.

8.5   Connecting to Target

Using gdb, there are two basic methods of connecting to the target machine when you debug a program. These are:

- Using gdbserver program
- Using a stub

In this section we shall discuss the gdbserver method in detail because it is the same for all platforms. The stub method differs from platform to platform and you need to create stub file(s) for your target and tailor these into your code.

8.5.1   Using gdbserver with GNU Debugger

The gdbserver utility comes with GNU debugger. I have used gdb version 5.1.1 and you can compile the gdbserver after you compile your debugger. If the host machine is different from the target machine, you must cross-compile the gdbserver program. This utility can run a program on a remote target and can communicate to gdb running on host.

When you build gdb from the source code, the gdbserver is not compiled during this process. This is what happened when I compiled gdb version 5.1.1 on my RedHat 7.1 machine. You have to compile it separately by going into the gdb/gdbserver directory. You can run the following two commands to build and install it:

```
make
make install
```

You may choose to build a static binary of the gdbserver program if you don't have dynamic libraries installed on your target board. For the purpose of this book, I used the Arcom board, which is introduced later in this chapter, and which has dynamic libraries installed. After compiling, you can strip down symbols from the binary to reduce size because embedded systems usually have small storage areas.

The gdbserver program may display some error messages when you connect to the server as it needed /etc/protocols files on the target Arcom board, which I copied manually.

The step-by-step process of using gdbserver is as follows:

- Compile a program on the host machine using the –g option.
- Transfer a stripped version of the output to the target machine. You can use a stripped version because you don't need symbols on the target.

- Run `gdbserver` on the target machine. It will control your application program. It is explained later in this section.
- Run `gdb` on the host machine.
- Connect `gdb` to the remotely running `gdbserver` process.
- Start debugging.

You can connect `gdb` on the host to the `gdbserver` running on the target over the network or using the serial port. Both of these methods are described here.

8.5.1.1   Running `gdbserver` On Target Using TCP/IP

When you have transferred the executable binary to the target, you can start the `gdbserver` process. The example below shows that the program being debugged is `/tmp/sum`, IP address of the host machine is 192.168.1.3 and we are using TCP port 2000 for connection between the host and the target machine. Note that the debugger will be running on the host machine.

In the following session, the `gdbserver` waits for connection from the debugger after starting up. When you step through the program on the debugger side, you can enter values of two numbers on the target machine. I used a Telnet session to open a window on the target. This window was used to start `gdbserver` and enter values of two numbers.

```
root@SBC-GXx /bin# gdbserver 192.168.1.3:2000 /tmp/sum
Process /tmp/sum created; pid = 154
Remote debugging using 192.168.1.3:2000
Enter first number : 5
Enter second number : 7

The sum is : 12
Killing inferior
root@SBC-GXx /bin#
```

Note that the `gdbserver` terminates when you disconnect the debugger on the host side. Source code of the program `sum.c` used in this example is as follows:

```
#include <stdio.h>
main ()
{
  int num1, num2, total ;

  printf("Enter first number : ");
  scanf("%d", &num1);
  printf("Enter second number : ");
  scanf("%d", &num2);

  total = num1 + num2;

  printf("\nThe sum is : %d\n", total);
}
```

It is the same program that was used in Chapter 5 for different examples.

8.5.1.2   Running gdb on Host Using TCP/IP

After starting gdbserver on the target, now you can start the GNU debugger on host. The host and target must be connected over a TCP/IP network for this example. In the following session on the host machine, file sum is a non-stripped version of the program that you uploaded to the target machine as it provides the symbol table to the debugger. After starting the debugger, you use the "target remote 192.168.1.10:2000" command to connect to the gdbserver running on the target machine 192.168.1.10. After that you can continue with normal debugging process.

```
[rrehman@desktop 5]$ gdb sum
GNU gdb 5.1.1
Copyright 2002 Free Software Foundation, Inc.
GDB is free software, covered by the GNU General Public
License, and you are
welcome to change it and/or distribute copies of it under
certain conditions.
Type "show copying" to see the conditions.
There is absolutely no warranty for GDB.  Type "show warranty"
for details.
This GDB was configured as "i686-pc-linux-gnu"...
(gdb) target remote 192.168.1.10:2000
Remote debugging using 192.168.1.10:2000
0x40001930 in ?? ()
(gdb) break main
Breakpoint 1 at 0x8048496: file sum.c, line 6.
(gdb) continue
Continuing.

Breakpoint 1, main () at sum.c:6
6          printf("Enter first number : ");
(gdb) n
7          scanf("%d", &num1);
(gdb) n
8          printf("Enter second number : ");
(gdb) n
9          scanf("%d", &num2);
(gdb) n
11         total = num1 + num2;
(gdb) n
13         printf("\nThe sum is : %d\n", total);
(gdb) n
14     }
(gdb) n
warning: Cannot insert breakpoint 0:
Cannot access memory at address 0x1
```

```
(gdb) quit
The program is running.  Exit anyway? (y or n) y
[rrehman@desktop 5]$
```

Note that after each scanf statement, you have to enter the input value on the target. This is because the program is actually running on the target machine. Since both host and target are connected over a network, you can open a Telnet window on the target for input and output.

8.5.1.3   Running gdbserver on Target Using Serial Port

You can also use gdbserver to connect a host and target machine over a serial port link. In the following example, you start gdbserver to communicate to the debugger over serial port /dev/ttyS1. GNU debugger uses its own serial port protocol to exchange information between host and target machines. The program being debugged is stored as /tmp/sum on the target machine. This example session is completed on an Arcom single-board computer running embedded Linux.

```
root@SBC-GXx /bin# gdbserver /dev/ttyS1 /tmp/sum
Process /tmp/sum created; pid = 180
Remote debugging using /dev/ttyS1
Enter first number : 3
Enter second number : 8

The sum is : 11
Killing inferior
root@SBC-GXx /bin#
```

Note that if you are running any other program on the serial port, it should be stopped. In most cases a getty process is running on serial ports. You can edit the /etc/inittab file to stop the getty process from using the serial port.

8.5.1.4   Running gdb on Host Using Serial Port

To connect to a target over a serial port /dev/ttyS0, you can use "target remote /dev/ttyS0" command after starting GNU debugger. A typical session to debug the sum.c program is shown below.

```
[root@desktop /root]# gdb sum
GNU gdb 5.1.1
Copyright 2002 Free Software Foundation, Inc.
GDB is free software, covered by the GNU General Public
License, and you are
welcome to change it and/or distribute copies of it under
certain conditions.
Type "show copying" to see the conditions.
There is absolutely no warranty for GDB.  Type "show warranty"
for details.
This GDB was configured as "i686-pc-linux-gnu"...
(gdb) break main
Breakpoint 1 at 0x8048496: file sum.c, line 6.
```

```
(gdb) target remote /dev/ttyS0
Remote debugging using /dev/ttyS0
0x40001930 in ?? ()
(gdb) continue
Continuing.

Breakpoint 1, main () at sum.c:6
6          printf("Enter first number : ");
(gdb) n
7          scanf("%d", &num1);
(gdb) n
8          printf("Enter second number : ");
(gdb) n
9          scanf("%d", &num2);
(gdb) n
11         total = num1 + num2;
(gdb) n
13         printf("\nThe sum is : %d\n", total);
(gdb) n
14    }
(gdb) n
warning: Cannot insert breakpoint 0:
Cannot access memory at address 0x1
 (gdb) quit
The program is running.  Exit anyway? (y or n) y
[root@desktop /root]#
```

You do not use the run command in this session because the program has already been started by the gdbserver running on the target machine.

8.5.1.5   Serial Cable

You can use a null modem cable to connect serial ports on the host and target machines. Connections for the null modem cable for a DB-9 connector are as shown in Table 8-1. However, I hope that most people can simply go out and buy a null modem cable, without worrying about pinouts.

Table 8-1 Null modem connection for DB-9 connector serial cable

DB-9 pin number (Host)	DB-9 pin number (Target)
TXD (3)	RXD (2)
RXD (2)	TXD (3)
RTS (7)	CTS (8)
CTS (8)	RTS (7)
Signal Ground (5)	Signal Ground (5)
DSR (6)	DTR (4)
DTR (4)	DSR (6)

For a DB-25 connector, the cable connections are as listed in Table 8-2.

Table 8-2 Null modem connection for DB-25 connector serial cable

DB-25 pin number (Host)	DB-25 pin number (Target)
Frame Ground (1)	Frame Ground (1)
TXD (2)	RXD (3)
RXD (3)	TXD (2)
RTS (4)	CTS (5)
CTS (5)	RTS (4)
Signal Ground (7)	Signal Ground (7)
DSR (6)	DTR (20)
DTR (20)	DSR (6)

8.5.2 Attaching to a Running Process Using `gdbserver`

Using the `gdbserver` program, you can also connect to a running process on the target. For example, the following command can be executed on the target to connect to a process with process ID equal to 375.

```
gdbserver /dev/ttyS1 375
```

You can also use the TCP/IP connection by replacing the /dev/ttyS1 with host-name:port number as you have seen earlier.

8.5.3   Using Stubs with GNU Debugger

Stubs are software routines that you can link with your program. Using a stub, you can connect the process created by the program to the GNU debugger from a remote target, eliminating the need for the `gdbserver` program.

Stubs are different for different targets. The GNU debugger contains some stubs by default in the source code tree. For example, the `i386-stub.c` file can be used for targets that use Intel CPUs. However you have to customize your stub depending on the target. Some instructions are included in the example source code files for the stub.

8.5.4   Debugging the Debug Session

If you are not successful in connecting to the target machine using GDB, you can get help from the remote debug mode of GNU debugger. After turning this mode ON, you will see a lot on information on your screen when `gdb` establishes or tries to establish connection to a remote target. This information shows packets sent and received by `gdb`. The following session shows that we set the baud rate to 9600 using the `remotebaud` command, turn the remote debug mode ON and then connect to the remote target on serial port `/dev/ttyS0`.

```
[root@desktop /root]# gdb sum
GNU gdb 5.1.1
Copyright 2002 Free Software Foundation, Inc.
GDB is free software, covered by the GNU General Public
License, and you are
welcome to change it and/or distribute copies of it under
certain conditions.
Type "show copying" to see the conditions.
There is absolutely no warranty for GDB.  Type "show warranty"
for details.
This GDB was configured as "i686-pc-linux-gnu"...
(gdb) break main
Breakpoint 1 at 0x8048496: file sum.c, line 6.
(gdb) set remotebaud 9600
(gdb) set debug remote 1
(gdb) target remote /dev/ttyS0
Remote debugging using /dev/ttyS0
Sending packet: $Hc-1#09...Ack
Packet received: OK
Sending packet: $qC#b4...Ack
Packet received:
Sending packet: $qOffsets#4b...Ack
Packet received:
Sending packet: $?#3f...Ack
Packet received: T0508:30190040;05:00000000;04:f8fdffbf;
Sending packet: $m40001930,8#62...Ack
Packet received: 54e8520000005b89
Sending packet: $m40001930,7#61...Ack
```

```
Packet received: 54e8520000005b
0x40001930 in ?? ()
Sending packet: $qSymbol::#5b...Ack
Packet received:
Packet qSymbol (symbol-lookup) is NOT supported
(gdb) continue
Continuing.
Sending packet: $Z0,8048496,1#8a...Ack
Packet received:
Packet Z0 (software-breakpoint) is NOT supported
Sending packet: $m8048496,1#41...Ack
Packet received: 83
Sending packet: $X8048496,0:#65...Ack
Packet received:
binary downloading NOT supported by target
Sending packet: $M8048496,1:cc#21...Ack
Packet received: OK
Sending packet: $m4000e060,1#89...Ack
Packet received: 8b
Sending packet: $M4000e060,1:cc#69...Ack
Packet received: OK
Sending packet: $Hc0#db...Ack
Packet received: OK
Sending packet: $c#63...Ack
Packet received: T0508:97840408;05:a8fdffbf;04:90fdffbf;
Sending packet: $Hg0#df...Ack
Packet received: OK
Sending packet: $g#67...Ack
Packet received:
f830114090840408384f1140ac40114090fdffbfa8fdffbfa0b60040fcfdff
bf97840408860200002300000 02b0000002b0000002b0000000000000000
00000000000000000000000000000000000000000000000000000000000000
00000000000000000000000000000000000000000000000000000000000000
00000000000000000000000000000000000000000000000000000000000000
00000000000000000000000000000000000000000000000000000000000000
00000000000000000000000000000000000000000000000000000000000000
00000000000000000000000000000000000000000000000000000000000000
00000000000000000000000000000000000000000000000000000000000000
00000000000000000000000000000000000000000000000000000000000000
0000000000000000000000000000000000000000000000000000000000
Sending packet: $P8=96840408#6c...Ack
Packet received:
Sending packet:
$Gf830114090840408384f1140ac40114090fdffbfa8fdffbfa0b60040fcfd
ffbf96840408860200002300000 02b0000002b0000002b00000000000000000
00000000000000000000000000000000000000000000000000000000000000
00000000000000000000000000000000000000000000000000000000000000
00000000000000000000000000000000000000000000000000000000000000
00000000000000000000000000000000000000000000000000000000000000
```

```
000000000000000000000000000000000000000000000000000000000000
000000000000000000000000000000000000000000000000000000000000
000000000000000000000000000000000000000000000000000000000000
000000000000000000000000000000000000000000000000000000000000#9
2...Ack
Packet received: OK
Sending packet: $M8048496,1:83#c6...Ack
Packet received: OK
Sending packet: $M4000e060,1:8b#3d...Ack
Packet received: OK

Breakpoint 1, main () at sum.c:6
6          printf("Enter first number : ");
(gdb)
```

All of this information is very useful to resolve problems in establishing connection between a host and a target machine.

8.6   Hardware Used for Cross-Platform and Embedded Systems Development

During development of this book, especially this chapter, I have used two single board computers. This was done to create examples and test functionality of code for cross and embedded systems development. Arcom (http://www.arcomcontrols.com) and Artesyn (http://www.artesyn.com) are the two companies that provided these systems for experimentation. Information about these two boards is provided here for reference.

8.6.1   Arcom SBC-GX1 Board

The Arcom people were very helpful in providing their SBC-GX1board development kit. This kit includes the SBC-GX1 board, cables, and adapter for supplying power to the board, documentation and software CDs. It also includes a PS/2 mouse that can be connected to the board during experimentation. Everything is enclosed in a box to carry the kit.

The CPU used on this board is an x86 compatible processor from National Semiconductor's Geode® GX1™ processor family. It is a low voltage, low power consumption CPU that can be used in application where long batter life and low power consumption are important factors. If you recall the earlier discussion in this chapter, both of these factors are very important in embedded systems applications. The CPU contains additional hardware components that are not part of x86 class CPUs. These components are:

• Integrated VGA controller, which has graphic acceleration features. Can be used to connect to CRT or TFT flat panel video devices.
• A PCI host controller.
• Additional features for graphics and audio applications.
• Integrated I/O lines.

A complete list of features can be found in the accompanying Arcom CD. The CPU on the board I received has a clock speed of 333 MHz with no fans or requirement of any other cooling method. This is a cool CPU board.

The Arcom board has the following features that make it suitable for many applications. All of this is integrated to a small sized board.

- Floppy disk controller
- Hard disk controller to which you can connect hard drives or CD/DVD drives.
- Sound Blaster
- Four serial ports
- Parallel port
- VGA connector for CRT monitors
- Interface for flat panel monitor
- PC/104 bus
- PCI bus
- 16 MB flash that can be used as a disk
- 64 MB RAM
- Ethernet controller to connect to a LAN
- PS/2 mouse and keyboard connectors
- Compact flash socket that can be used to increase storage space in case you need large applications

The board comes with Linux kernel 2.4.4 pre-installed with many features that are important for embedded systems. Arcom embedded Linux is optimized for space but has all of the commonly used applications and utilities. These include:

- A Telnet server and client
- NFS support
- FTP server and client that can be used to transfer files from host computer to the target computer
- HTTP server. You can start using the HTTP server right from the beginning. A default page is already present on the board.
- X-Windows support
- The `inetd` daemon that can be used to launch network applications on demand

In addition to these, Arcom embedded Linux has the following features that may be of interest to the developers of embedded applications.

- Kernel 2.2.4
- Journaling Flash File System (JFFS2), which is a compressed file system used on flash storage.

- Glibc 2.1.3, which allows dynamically linked programs to run on the embedded platform.
- X-Free version 4.0.2
- `Ncruses` library
- Bash shell
- Busybox which is a Swiss army knife of generally used UNIX utilities
- Networking suite and utilities
- Use management utilities
- Modules handling utilities
- Syslogd/klogd
- Terminal handling

Onboard flash memory is divided into three parts. Partition mounted on / is read-only at the boot time and contains Linux system. Two other file systems /var and /var/tmp are mounted as read-write at the boot time and can be used to store temporary files. In addition to that, you can also use the removable flash card to store files. Bundled utilities on accompanying disks can be used to re-install the operating system or add new components. In networked systems, you can also use a NFS server to add more storage space.

Arcom also provides RedHat 6.2 CD that you can use to install Linux on a PC. This PC will be used as the development system or a host machine. The Arcom embedded Linux board will act as the target system. This means that in addition to the single board computer with Embedded Linux installed on it, you also get the Linux operating system to use as a development platform.

8.6.2   Artesyn PM/PPC Mezzanine Card

The other embedded system used in the development of this book is Artesyn PM/PPC mezzanine card that can be plugged into a carrier card. Artesyn also supplied the carrier card for this purpose. It is a PowerPC 750 based card and provides the Ethernet and serial interfaces to the outside world directly from the PMC (PCI Mezzanine Card). It contains 64 Mbytes of RAM, I^2C bus, general purpose timers, real-time clock, LEDs and so on. The board also contains flash memory that can be used to store the operating system and utilities. It has a real-time clock and PLD used to setup memory map The CPU runs at 333 MHz. Boot flash is used to store the operating system. The optional JTAG connector can be used to download and debug code.

As mentioned earlier, you need a career card to power up the PMC and Artesyn provides you with a CC1000 PMC carrier card that can host up to two PMC. CC1000 can be placed into a Compact PCI chassis that allows 6U cards to be plugged in.

More information can be found on the Artesyn web site http://www.artesyncp.com or by sending an email to info@artesyncp.com.

8.7 References

1. Arcom web site at http://www.arcomcontrols.com
2. Artesyn web site at http://www.artesyncp.com
3. Embedded Linux web site at http://www.linux-embedded.org
4. Busybox for Embedded Linux at http://www.busybox.net/

## CHAPTER 9

Platform Independent Development with Java

In previous chapters most of the discussion centered around GNU development tools and programming in C and C++ languages. This chapter is devoted to Java development and describes how to use some Java tools and a Java virtual machine.

As many of the readers already know, Java is a different language compared to other compile-and-execute languages in that it needs a Java virtual machine (JVM) to execute what is called *byte code*. Each platform has its own implementation of the Java virtual machine. There are many JVMs available on Linux platform in free and open source as well as commercial domains. Some virtual machines are also available for embedded Linux platforms that are very small in size and need little memory to execute. You can select a virtual machine based upon your requirements. Java virtual machines are built on Java Language Specifications (JLS). Information about JLS and books in downloadable format can be found at http://java.sun.com/docs/books/jls/.

This chapter provides some information about how to use different development tools on Linux. The most commonly available tools are Sun SDK and GNU `gcj` compiler. Kaffe and Jboss are other very popular open source development tools on Linux and these are introduced in this chapter. However please note that this chapter is not a tutorial on Java language and if you are new to the language, you get help from many other resources on the Internet as well as in print media. Some of the most popular include Sun Java SDK, IBM Java SDK, Kaffe, and `gcj`.

9.1 How Java Applications Work

Java is a sort of interpreted language. Any program you write in Java is first compiled to generate byte code. Depending upon type of output, the byte code may be in the form of a *Java application* or a *Java applet*. In the case of Java applications, you can directly invoke the Java virtual machine to execute it. If the output type is an applet, it is usually loaded into a browser for execution.

9.1.1 Java Compiler

The Java compiler is used to build Java applications or applets from source code files. In most of the cases, the compiler is invoked as `javac` command. It also uses standard class libraries that are usually part of the Java distributions.

9.1.2 Java Virtual Machine

The purpose of the Java virtual machine is to execute Java code. In most cases, the virtual machine is available as the command `java`. To run any application, you can just invoke the `java` command with the application name as the command line argument.

9.2 Kaffe

Kaffe is one of the popular freely available implementations of the Java virtual machine. You can download it from its web site http://www.kaffee.org. At the time of writing this book, version 1.0.6 is available from the web site. I am using RedHat 7.1 for the development of this book and this version is also part of the distribution. Most of the binaries are installed in `/usr/bin` directory. The following command displays version information for Kaffe:

```
[root@desktop Java]# java -version
Kaffe Virtual Machine
Copyright (c) 1996-2000
Transvirtual Technologies, Inc.  All rights reserved
Engine: Just-in-time v3    Version: 1.0.6
Java Version: 1.1
[root@desktop Java]#
```

Note that the actual Kaffe Virtual machine is present as `/usr/bin/kaffe` and `/usr/bin/java` is simply a shell script like the following to invoke Kaffe.

```
#! /bin/sh
# Pretend Kaffe is Java
prefix=/usr
exec_prefix=/usr
exec /usr/bin/kaffe ${1+"$@"}
```

Kaffe also include class libraries associated with the Virtual machine. However, Kaffe is not official Java, which is a registered trademark of Sun Microsystems. The open source nature of Kaffe provides you with information about the internal implementation and workings of the Java virtual machine.

Basic help on using the Kaffe virtual machine is available using the `java` or `kaffe` command without any argument. The `kaffe` command produces the following output.

```
[root@desktop /root]# kaffe
usage: kaffe [-options] class
Options are:
        -help                   Print this message
        -version                Print version number
        -fullversion            Print verbose version info
        -ss <size>              Maximum native stack size
        -mx <size>              Maximum heap size
        -ms <size>              Initial heap size
        -as <size>              Heap increment
        -classpath <path>       Set classpath
        -verify *               Verify all bytecode
        -verifyremote *         Verify bytecode loaded from
                                network
        -noverify               Do not verify any bytecode
        -D<property>=<value>    Set a property
        -verbosegc              Print message during
                                garbage collection
        -noclassgc              Disable class garbage
                                collection
        -v, -verbose            Be verbose
        -verbosejit             Print message during JIT
                                code generation
        -verbosemem             Print detailed memory
                                allcation statistics
        -nodeadlock             Disable deadlock detection
        -prof                   Enable profiling of Java
                                methods
        -debug *                Trace method calls
        -noasyncgc *            Do not garbage collect
                                asynchronously
        -cs, -checksource *     Check source against class
                                files
        -oss <size> *           Maximum java stack size
        -jar                    Executable is a JAR
    * Option currently ignored.
[root@desktop /root]#
```

9.3   The Jboss Java Development System

The Jboss is probably the most popular open source Java development products suite and it provides services similar to Sun's Java 2 Enterprise Edition (J2EE). You can download it from free from http://www.jboss.org. The best thing about Jboss is that it is open source and free for use. At the time of writing this book Jboss version 2.4.4 is the stable release. Since J2EE is a big platform and this is not a programming tutorial text, you will learn only how to install the Jboss package here.

Following is a step-by-step outline how to build Jboss on Linux system.

- Download the latest version `jboss-all.tgz` from its web site.
- Unpack it using the `tar zxvf jboss-all.tgz` command
- You must have Java SDK installed to build it and JAVA_HOME variable properly set. Use the "`export JAVA_HOME=/usr/java/j2sdk1.4.0/`" command if you have SDK version 1.4 installed. If you have any other environment, use appropriate command.
- Go to `jboss-all` directory.
- Run the following command and it should display a result like the one shown.

```
[root@conformix jboss-all]# ./build/build.sh -version
Ant version 1.4 compiled on September 3 2001
[root@conformix jboss-all]#
```

- Execute the `build/build.sh init` command.
- Run the `build/build.sh` command.
- Run Jboss using the following command. It will show a list of message as it starts different processes.

```
[root@conformix jboss-all]# ./build/build.sh run-jboss
Searching for build.xml ...
Buildfile: /opt/jboss-all/build/build.xml

_buildmagic:init:

_buildmagic:init:local-properties:

_buildmagic:init:buildlog:

configure:
     [echo] groups:  default
     [echo] modules:
jmx,common,system,j2ee,naming,management,server,security,messa
ging,pool,connector,cluster,admin,jetty,varia,jboss.net,iiop

init:

run-jboss:
```

```
        [echo] Starting JBoss (redirected /opt/jboss-all/build/
run.log)

run-jboss-check-os:

_buildmagic:init:

_buildmagic:init:local-properties:

_buildmagic:init:buildlog:

configure:
        [echo] groups:  default
        [echo] modules:
jmx,common,system,j2ee,naming,management,server,security,messa
ging,pool,connector,cluster,admin,jetty,varia,jboss.net,iiop

init:

run-jboss-unix:
```

If everything goes well, the startup will be successful. You can see a log of messages in the build/run.log file. You can also run Jboss using the run.sh script.

9.4   Java 2 SDK

Java SDK is distributed by Sun Microsystems. There are two main versions of the SDK. The *Standard Edition* or J2SE is introduced in this book. The *Enterprise Edition* or J2EE is the premier product and it is comparable to Jboss discussed in this book. Please note that neither of J2SE nor J2EE are open source products. You have a limited license to use these. Please go through the license terms and conditions if you are inclined towards using Java SDK.

At the time of writing this book, Version 1.4 of the SDK is available.

9.4.1   Java 2 SDK Standard Edition

The latest version of Java SDK released by Sun Microsystems is 1.4 at the time of writing this book. There are some new features added to this version. Some important features are listed here.

9.4.1.1   Non-blocking I/O

After a long waiting period, a non-blocking I/O library is finally added to the SDK as java.nio package. Non-blocking I/O is important when you don't want to create threads for each connection in large network application. Creation of threads is very expensive compared to non-blocking I/O where you can open many I/O streams and use mechanisms similar to poll() and select() which are available with C language since long. Using this mechanism one thread may handle several connections, for example in the case of a web server.

It is interesting to note that a non-blocking I/O library was available in the open source before it is included in SDK version 1.4. You can find more information about this open source implementation at http://www.cs.berkeley.edu/~mdw/proj/java-nbio/.

9.4.1.2   Security Enhancements

Many new features have been added for security enhancements to the SDK and some existing features are refined. These features include Java Certification Path API, Cryptography, Java Authentication and Authorization Service security extensions, GSS-API with Kerberos support and so on.

9.4.1.3   Web Services

J2SE version 1.4 lays foundation for XML-based web services. Now the XML is part of the core platform which allows building interoperable web applications and services.

Different building blocks for Java platform standard edition version 1.4 are shown in Figure 9-1 taken from the Sun Microsystems web site.

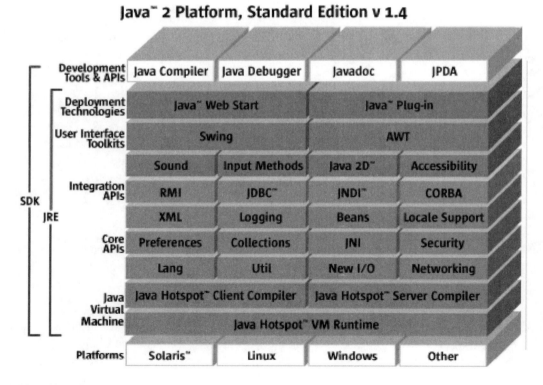

Figure 9-1 Building blocks of J2SE version 1.4.

9.4.2   Getting and Installing Java SDK from Sun

You can download the current version from http://java.sun.com. The file is available as `j2sdk-1_4_0-linux-i386-rpm.bin`. The best way is to copy this file to a temporary directory and then install it from there. I have copied this file into the `/download` directory where the first step is to make it executable using the following command:

```
chmod a+x j2sdk-1_4_0-linux-i386-rpm.bin
```

Then you can execute this file just by typing in the following command:

```
./j2sdk-1_4_0-linux-i386-rpm.bin
```

It will display the license agreement and you have to type in "yes" to agree to this license agreement. After that the self-extracting file will extract `j2sdk-1_4_0-fcs-linux-i386.rpm` file that you can install using the rpm package with the help of the following command:

```
rpm --install j2sdk-1_4_0-fcs-linux-i386.rpm
```

If you have any previous version of SDK installed on your system, you should un-install it first. To list files installed by the rpm package, you can use the following command.

```
rpm --query -l j2sdk-1.4.0-fcs|more
```

By default, files are installed under the `/usr/java/j2sdk1.4.0/` directory. The `/usr/java/j2sdk1.4.0/bin` directory contains all binary files for the SDK.

9.4.3   Creating jar Files

The `jar` utility is used to create Java-class archives. It can take multiple class files, compress these and put them into a single `.jar` file. The syntax for using the `jar` utility is similar to the `tar` program widely used on Linux and other UNIX systems. The following command creates a file `myclasses.jar` from two class file `first.class` and `second.class`.

```
jar cvf myclasses.jar first.class second.class
```

You can also add or extract classes from the existing `.jar` files. The following command adds `third.class` to `myclasses.jar` archive.

```
jar uf myclasses.jar third.class
```

The following command will extract `second.class` from the `myclasses.jar` file.

```
jar x second.class
```

You can also use wild cards with the `jar` command. If you use directory names, all files in that directory are added to the `.jar` file.

To list all files in a `.jar` file, use t command line option. The following command lists all files in `myclasses.jar` file.

```
jar tf myclasses.jar
```

9.5   Building Java Applications

A Java application is a compiled Java program that can be executed using a Java virtual machine. There are three basic steps to create a Java application. These steps are:

1. Create source code.
2. Compile it.
3. Run it using the virtual machine.

Let's see how you can go through these steps.

9.5.1   Creating Source Code File

Like any other programming language, Java source code files are created using an editor. These source code files contain Java instructions. The simplest source code file contains an instruction to print the message "Hello World", similar to your first C program. Please note that Java examples in this chapter are just to demonstrate how to use development tools.

The program that prints the "Hello World" message is shown below:

```
class HelloWorld {
    public static void main(String[] args) {
        System.out.println("Hello World!");
    }
}
```

The program must have a function main(), like C programs. The program may be saved as HelloWorld.java text file.

Note that you can use any editor to create the source code file. I would recommend using Emacs which you have already learned in Chapter 2. Emacs understands Java programming language syntax. There are other GUI editors and integrated development environment (IDE) packages that you can use to create Java source code.

9.5.2   Compiling Java Code

The Java compiler will compile the Java code into an executable. The following command creates an output file HelloWorld.class from source code file HelloWorld.java.

```
/usr/java/j2sdk1.4.0/bin/javac HelloWorld.java
```

Note that the output file name is the same as the name of the class that contains function main().

You can check the type of the output file type by using the file command. The following command shows type of the output file as compiled class data.

```
[root@desktop /root]# file HelloWorld.class
HelloWorld.class: compiled Java class data, version 46.0
[root@desktop /root]#
```

Note that in large projects, there may be many source code files, class files and other object code files to generate the output executables. In such cases, you usually don't use the Java compiler on the command line to compile individual files. The best way to carry out such tasks is to use the make utility that you have already learned previously in this book.

9.5.3 Running Java Applications

Java applications run on the top of Java virtual machine. The "Hello World" application that you created in the previous section can be executed using the Java virtual machine.

```
[root@desktop /root]# java HelloWorld
Hello World!
[root@desktop /root]#
```

Note that when you run this application, you don't use HelloWorld.class on the command line. If you do, the Java virtual machine will not be able to execute the command. I have seen many messages in mailing lists and newsgroups from people who make this mistake and then wonder why they get error messages.

9.5.4 Using gcj to Build Java Applications

The gcj compiler is part of the GCC compiler suite. It is able to compile the Java language programs. One benefit of compiling Java programs with gcj is that you can create binary executable applications instead of Java byte code. These applications can be executed on Linux without the need of Java virtual machine. The downside is that you can execute applications built this way only on the platform for which you compiled. This is in contrast to the basic Java notion of compile once, run everywhere. Detailed information about using gcj is present at its web site http://gcc.gnu.org/java/.

You can use GNU debugger for programs compiled with gcj, which is a big advantage for many programmers who are familiar with gdb. To be able to compile a program with gcj, you must have libgcj available on your system. The libgcj provides class libraries, byte code interpreter and garbage collector at the runtime. Latest version of libgcj is available from ftp://sourceware.cygnus.com/pub/java/ and method of its compilation and installation is discussed in Chapter 3. Refer to Chapter 3 for a description of how to compile programs with gcj compiler.

9.6 Building Applets

Like any Java applications, applets are also compiled using the Java compiler. The only difference is that a Java applet is not like a standard application and can be run only inside a browser. Following is a source code for the applet HelloWorld.java that is used as an example here. The applet, when compiled with the Java compiler results in HelloWorld.class file, which is Java byte code.

```
import java.applet.*;
import java.awt.*;

public class HelloWorld extends java.applet.Applet {
    public void paint (java.awt.Graphics gc) {
  gc.drawString("Hello World", 100, 90);
    }
}
```

The main thing to note here is that compiling Java applets is not different in any way from compiling Java applications. The only difference between a Java application and a Java applet is in the source code.

9.7   Testing Applets with Netscape

As mentioned earlier, a Java applet must run inside a browser. For this you have to write an HTML file. The following HTML file incorporates the applet and can be loaded to a browser like Netscape.

```
<html>
<head>
</head>
<body>
    <applet code=HelloWorld width=400 height=300>
    </applet>
</body>
</html>
```

When you load this file in the browser, the browser will execute the Java code and you can see the "Hello World" message printed in the browser window. Applets can also be viewed by applet viewers.

9.8   Jikes for Java

Jikes is an open source compiler for Java from IBM. It is fully compatible with the Java Language Specifications. You can download it from its web site at http://oss.software.ibm.com/developerworks/opensource/jikes/. Jikes version 1.15 is available right now. You have to download and install it the usual way. Typical steps are:

- Download it from its web site.
- Uncompress it using `tar -zxvf jikes-1.15.tar.gz` command.
- Go to `jikes-1.15` directory.
- Run the configure script using the `./configure` command.
- Run the `make` command.
- Run the `make install` command.

The Jikes FAQ can also be found on the above-mentioned web site. Since Jikes is a command line compiler, it can be used in Makefiles for large projects. The compiler is invoked using the jikes command. The following command lists available options with Jikes:

```
[root@conformix jikes-1.15]# jikes

Jikes Compiler
(C) Copyright IBM Corp. 1997, 2001.
- Licensed Materials - Program Property of IBM - All Rights
Reserved.

use: jikes [-bootclasspath path][-classpath path][-d dir][-
debug][-depend|-Xdepend][-deprecation][-encoding encoding][-
extdirs path][-g][-nowarn][-nowrite][-O][-sourcepath path][-
verbose][-
Xstdout][++][+B][+c][+OLDCSO][+D][+DR=filename][+E][+F][+Kname
=TypeKeyWord][+M][+P][+Td...d][+U][+Z] file.java...

-bootclasspath path prepend path to CLASSPATH
-classpath path     use path for CLASSPATH
-d dir              write class files in directory dir
-debug              no effect (recognized for
                    compatibility)
-depend | -Xdepend  recompile all used classes
-deprecation        report uses of deprecated features
-encoding encoding  use specified encoding to read source
                    files
-extdirs path       prepend all zip files in path to
                    CLASSPATH
-g                  debug (generate LocalVariableTable)
-nowarn             do not issue warning messages
-nowrite            do not write any class files
-O                  do not write LineNumberTable
-sourcepath path    also search for source files in path
-verbose            list files read and written
-Xstdout            redirect output listings to stdout
++                  compile in incremental mode
+B                  do not invoke bytecode generator
+c                  do not discard comments from lexer
                    output
+OLDCSO             perform original Jikes classpath order
                    for compatibility
+D                  report errors immediately in emacs-form
                    without buffering
+DR=filename        generate dependence report in filename
+E                  list errors in emacs-form
+F                  do full dependence check except for Zip
                    and Jar files
```

```
+Kname=TypeKeyWord   map name to type keyword
+M                   generate makefile dependencies
+P                   pedantic compilation - issues lots of
                     warnings
+Td...d              set value of tab d...d spaces; each d
                     is a decimal digit
+U                   do full dependence check including Zip
                     and Jar files
+Z                   treat cautions as errors

Version 1.15 - 26 Sept 2001
Originally written by Philippe Charles and David Shields
of IBM Research, Jikes is now maintained and refined by the
Jikes Project at:
http://ibm.com/developerworks/opensource/jikes
Please consult this URL for more information and to learn
how to report problems.
[root@conformix jikes-1.15]#
```

The following command will compile the hello.java program to create the hello.class output.

```
jikes hello.java -classpath /usr/java/j2sdk1.4.0/jre/lib/
rt.jar
```

Note that you must have core classes installed on you system to use the compiler. In the above example, the classpath is mentioned on the command line.

9.9 Miscellaneous

This section contains a brief summary of information and links to some other fields related to Java. With major industry players like Sun and IBM behind Java technologies, it is being pushed in many different areas.

9.9.1 Embedded Java

Sun has introduced Java Embedded Server, which enables developers to build embedded applications based upon the Java platform. In addition to other things, it includes a Java implementation of SSL. Information about Embedded Java is available at http://java.sun.com/products/embeddedjava/.

9.9.2 Real Time Java

Efforts are being made to implement a real-time Java virtual machine. Specifications for real-time Java can be found at http://www.rtj.org/. The specifications include information about how to manage memory, interrupts, scheduling, garbage collection and so on.

9.9.3   Wireless Applications

Java 2 Micro Edition or J2ME from Sun Microsystems introduces Wireless Java Technology. Information about using Java technology in wireless applications can be found at http://java.sun.com/products/embeddedjava/ .

9.10 References

1. Kaffe is available from its web site http://www.kaffe.org
2. Most of the Sun Java information is available from http://java.sun.com
3. Non-blocking library at http://www.cs.berkeley.edu/~mdw/proj/java-nbio/
4. The Jboss at its web site http://www.jboss.org/
5. The Jboss information at sourceforge.net http://sourceforge.net/projects/jboss/
6. Java Language Specifications at http://java.sun.com/docs/books/jls/
7. The Jikes compiler at http://oss.software.ibm.com/developerworks/opensource/jikes/
8. Information about gcj compiler at http://gcc.gnu.org/java/
9. The libgcj library from ftp://sourceware.cygnus.com/pub/java/
10. Real-time Java specifications at http://www.rtj.org/
11. Embedded Java at http://java.sun.com/products/embeddedjava/

APPENDIX A

Typical Hardware Requirements for a Linux Development Workstation

There are many factors that go into selecting an appropriate hardware specification for any given task; and the final specification will vary greatly depending on a particular environment, budget and time available to accomplish the task. In general, however, the things that need to be considered are: the speed of the processor, the amount of memory, size of the local hard drives, network connectivity, the video card and the display. Depending on the development projects to be undertaken, additional devices such as modems, sounds cards and the like will also need to be considered.

The three situations that we will consider are a single developer working on a project alone, a distributed environment in which multiple developers are accessing a single machine via remote log-on (telnet, ssh or X-Windows), and a distributed environment utilizing a software repository.

A.1 Parts of a Workstation

Computers consist of many parts working in conjunction with each other to turn fluctuations in current into meaningful output on the display screen. Much of the work of the computer takes place using the motherboard, the processor(s) and the computer's memory. These components provide the "horsepower" that largely determines how fast the computer runs.

Working in conjunction with these parts are things like the hard disk drive that provides the internal long-term storage. There is also the video card that is used to convert the information in the computer into something that is readily usable to us mere mortals and the modem or network interface card that permit computers to communicate with one another.

Externally there are things such as the keyboard and the mouse that permit the user to enter data into the system, and the monitor which enables the computer to present information in a way that the operator can easily understand.

When evaluating a new computer system, remember that the motherboard, the processor and the memory determine *how fast* your computer will be able to perform the tasks required of it.

The hard disk drives, the network and video cards, etc. determine *what and how much* your computer will be able to do. However, speed of hard drive is also a major factor in overall speed of compilation in case your computer is low on memory.

Lastly, the input and output devices determine *how much style* your computer will have while it goes about doing whatever it was told to do.

While there is some overlap in function, these definitions provide a general outline of the parts of the computer and can give us a basis for determining a base-line system.

A.2 Section 1—The Processor and Memory

Systems are available with one or multiple processors. Random Access Memory (RAM) is presently cheap and easy to find. Processor speed seems to double every eighteen months and almost as soon as a new system is purchased, it becomes obsolete.

The speed and the number of processors will determine the sheer raw power that a computer has. Speed is measured in megahertz (MHz) and more is always better.

The memory that a system has installed will also effect the overall speed of the computer. If the system runs out of physical memory, it will, if the space has been set aside for it, start paging memory to disk. This is the process of writing a portion of memory that has not been used recently (in computer terms that could mean milliseconds) to the disk in order to free the memory up for more immediate usage. When the information on the disk is required again, the computer frees up physical memory and reads the data from the disk into that area.

As the hard disk drive is several orders of magnitude slower than simply reading the information from memory, this slows down the entire computer as it waits for the information to be written and read from the drive. If your computer sits idle while there are large amounts of access to the disks, it is possible that the computer is low on memory and swapping to the disk. Adding more memory to the system should speed it up.

A.3 Section 2—The Disk Drive

At present, there are two main types of drives available on the market for personal computers: IDE and SCSI (pronounced "scuzzy"). The first and most common is the IDE drive. This is the type sold with most off-the-shelf workstations. A standard computer will be able to support up to four IDE drives at a time. These drives may be hard drives, CD-ROMs, DVD drives or even tape drives. Once the maximum of four devices has been installed into the computer, no more may be added until one is removed. This and the fact that IDE drives have traditionally been slower than

SCSI drives are the main limitations in using this type of device. They are however, cheaper and somewhat easier to install than SCSI drives.

SCSI devices may also be used for mass storage, CD-ROM and DVD drives, but SCSI devices can also include scanners, printers and other devices as well.

Up to seven devices may be attached to a single SCSI interface card inside the computer and a computer may have more than one interface card. The total number of SCSI devices installed on one computer is limited to the number of available interface slots on the motherboard, times seven. On most modern workstations and servers this will allow a total number of SCSI devices ranging from seven to over thirty. New SCSI standards allow more devices to be connected to a single SCSI adapter.

SCSI drives are often configured in a Redundant Array of Inexpensive Disks (RAID) that can be used to increase the reliability or the speed of the system. The trade-off in this configuration is a loss of available drive space. The decrease in available space may be anywhere from negligible to 50% of the total space on the drives depending on the RAID level used.

A.4 Sizing the Task

When developing requirements for any computer system, it is important to understand exactly what the system will be used for and how it will be used. Once the purpose of the computer is understood, potential bottlenecks can be located and the potential for these to cause problems can be minimized or eliminated.

A.5 Stand Alone Development Workstation

In this configuration a workstation will be used to develop applications locally. The source code will be kept on the local hard drive and the editing and compiling will take place on the same machine.

The main concern with this configuration would be in the area of processor and memory, and in having a backup system in place to ensure that data is not lost in the even of a hardware failure.

A typical developer's machine will have a processor in the 800+ MHz range and, depending on the scope of the application being developed, may have more than one processor. The available memory will again depend on the type of application be written with typical machines having in excess of 256 MB of memory and, in the event that large amounts of data have to be manipulated, more than a gigabyte of memory.

The Linux OS, with development tools, can be installed utilizing approximately 1 gigabyte (GB) of disk space. The source code for the OS, which represents a decade of work from people all over the globe, can be installed in less than 50 megabytes of space. A single developer working full-time would have to be very productive in order to fill up most drives available today as these typically come in 60GB sizes. Hard drive space is more often used for development libraries and tools, separate runtime environments, etc.

Again, disk size may have to be increased if large volumes of data are being used in the testing of the application.

These estimates for simply generic in nature and would be a good starting place for new equipment purchases. It is entirely possible for productive development to take place on older, used equipment in the sub 300 MHz range. It depends entirely upon the application being developed and the time available to accomplish the task.

However, with the cost of equipment constantly falling, it is often well worth the investment in newer equipment in order to reduce the compile time of the application.

A.6 Distributed Development—Remote Access

This example supposes that multiple developers will be accessing a remote server and developing on that platform. The source code will reside on the server and the server will be used to compile the programs.

In this instance, the requirements for the workstations will be modest compared to the previous example, but the need for central server is added. This server will need to be far more powerful than the previously specified workstation.

The server should be as fast as the budget and circumstances permit, and the number of simultaneous developers using the platform should be considered. You will almost certainly want a server with several processors.

It will require more disk space, preferably with RAID enabled and the most utilized file systems spread out over several physical disks. A complete backup strategy should be in place and tested on a regular basis in order to ensure that the data is secure and can be restored in the event that any problems should arise.

This server will require a large amount of memory as well. Several gigabytes is not unreasonable for a small number of developers. Several developers trying to compile at once can quickly drain the system's resources.

If the remote access strategy includes using a secure shell (ssh) to connect to the server, additional processing power will be required due to the encryption overhead.

On the other hand, the actual workstation in this example would be comparatively modest. Most workstations capable of handling word processing and e-mail tasks should be up to handling this type of load with little difficulty. All of the storage, access and intensive processor use will take place on the server.

A.7 Distributed Development—Source Code Repository

This last example is a combination of the other two designs, and has probably supported more Open Source developers than any other model. In this design, a relatively small-scale server is used as a software repository and individual workstations similar to the one in the first example are used to provide the actual processing power.

The main requirement for the server is a large disk storage space and a modest amount of memory. CVS, the source code control application used in this book, as well as others, can use quite a bit of memory while comparing old and new versions of files with one another. As a result, the server should have at least 256 MB of memory and potentially much more if you expect to use large source code files.

The server will not be responsible for compiling the application, so a fast processor is not necessary.

What would be helpful, however, would be to ensure that the server has a well-tuned networking subsystem, and possibly some redundancy in that area as well. Additionally, if required by a particularly active source code repository, multiple NICs (Network Interface Cards) may be set up on different subnets to help reduce any network congestion that might arise.

As previously mentioned, individual workstations will resemble the ones listed in the first example in this section—the stand-alone developer workstation.

A.8 Summing Up

While there is no way to accurately give minimal and optimal recommendations for any and all software development projects, these guidelines should give you an understanding of some of the issues that arise in selecting the servers and workstations necessary to provide development support.

INDEX

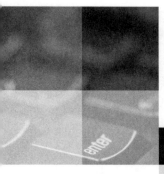